THE
LONGEST JOURNEY

The Inside Story of Sussex's Championship Triumph

PAUL WEAVER AND BRUCE TALBOT

Foreword by John Barclay

SUTTON PUBLISHING

First published in 2004 by
Sutton Publishing Limited · Phoenix Mill
Thrupp · Stroud · Gloucestershire · GL5 2BU

British Library Cataloguing in Publication Data
A catalogue record for this book is available from the British Library.

ISBN 0-7509-3829-3

Typeset in 10.5/14 pt Sabon.
Typesetting and origination by
Sutton Publishing Limited.
Printed and bound in England by
J.H. Haynes & Co. Ltd, Sparkford.

CONTENTS

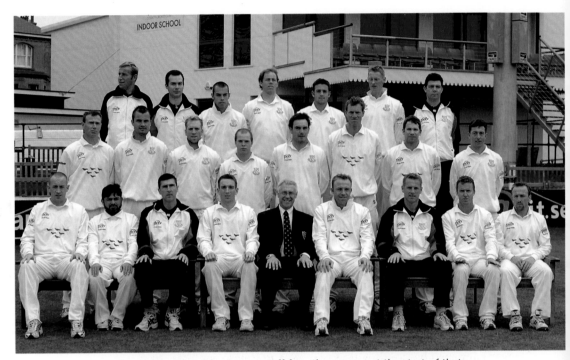

Ready for action. The Sussex staff face the camera at the start of their
Championship-winning season. Back row, from left: Stuart Osborne (physio),
James Carmichael (physio), Carl Hopkinson, Billy Taylor, Shaun Rashid, Paul Hutchison,
Keith Greenfield (academy director). Middle row: Mark Davis, Bas Zuiderent, Matt Prior,
Tim Ambrose, Michael Yardy, Robin Martin-Jenkins, Richard Montgomerie, Kevin Innes.
Front row: Jason Lewry, Mushtaq Ahmed, Mark Robinson (coach), James Kirtley,
Hugh Griffiths (chief executive), Chris Adams, Peter Moores (director of cricket),
Murray Goodwin, Tony Cottey. *(Simon Dack/Brighton Argus)*

FOREWORD

by John Barclay

'Sussex will win the Championship some day', I wrote at the end of my book about our campaign in 1981. 'And the joy will be great when the time comes.' Little did I know when I wrote those words only two years ago that we would all be sharing in the joy of finally reaching the summit and preparing to relive the strong emotions through the words and pictures of a new book, in which fresh characters come into our lives and steer us to the greatest landmark yet in Sussex's impressive cricketing history.

Perhaps it was the waiting that made the moment such a treasured one. I remember well how each year successive chairmen would wish us all luck before the start of each new season. 'Now this is our year for the County Championship', they would say with a cheery optimism reserved for pre-season. You see, they all really wanted to win the Championship with a passion. It had never happened before. It was the dream and it has now come true.

Perhaps in the past Sussex cricketers played more with style than as cut-throat winners. It is not for me to speak of the great heroes of yesterday as, of course, I never saw them play, but I can't believe that Ranji, his nephew Duleep and Fry did not play with the distinctive fluency that perhaps only David Gower has emulated in recent years. For my part, I started my relationship with Sussex with David Sheppard on a glorious August day in 1961 when I travelled with my family from Horsham to watch Sussex play cricket at Hove for the first time. It was the then traditional bank holiday match against Middlesex, and we sat on the splintery wooden benches in the south-west corner of the ground. Hove was full, or so it seemed, and this impressionable little seven-year-old watched Sheppard make a hundred amidst sunshine and picnic and much happiness. I was captivated by the magical strokeplay, by the majesty and elegance of both class and style. I was hooked and from then on all I wanted to do was to play cricket and to try to imitate those golden moments of childhood.

The melodic Mozart-like strains of Sheppard gave way quickly to the Wagnerian thunder of Dexter. Here was the ultimate hero, someone you would travel far and wide to watch. No other man that I have seen had greater presence at the crease than Dexter. It was even worth coming along just to watch him walking in to bat – upright, arrogant, purposeful and very menacing. In 1964 I squeezed into the County Ground next to the old Cowshed at the sea end and watched Dexter and Parks in full cry in the Gillette Cup semi-final against Surrey. How good it was to beat our arch rivals on that day, and thrilling, too, to sweep past them again 39 years later in the County Championship, which they had all but won in early August.

Sussex in the sixties under Dexter mastered the new one-day game, but still the ultimate prize, the Championship, proved elusive. The trouble was that Sussex cricket had always been inconsistent – brilliant one moment and oh so watchable, but then despairing the next. All my heroes tended to be batsmen; yet we all know that it's the bowlers who really win matches. You usually need to take about 20 wickets to win a match. You may remember that it so nearly happened as recently as 1981. Then it was the furious pace of Imran Khan and Garth le Roux that took the country by storm, and by taking more than 150 wickets between them, they brought Sussex within a whisker of clinching the title for the first time.

And how extraordinary and, in some ways, ironic that it should have been a spin bowler in 2003 who finally did the trick. Ironic, I feel, because Sussex in their history have never fully understood the nature of spin bowling, and certainly have not used it very often or very effectively. Spin has usually been employed more as an afterthought, as a last resort, when all else has failed and frequently when batsmen are well set, rather than as a front-line method of attack. So it has been used sparingly and not with any sense of conviction. One reason for this might be that Sussex cricket has throughout its history been dominated by the weather. Sea frets, high tides and moisture have contributed to the well-grassed pitches at Hastings, Eastbourne and, of course, Hove, on which Maurice Tate and later Ian Thomson, with swing and seam, proved so deadly. They were not the only ones either. But in 2003, all of a sudden the strategy changed and Sussex grabbed at the opportunity to recruit a magical leg-spinner from Pakistan called Mushtaq Ahmed. Although he was already well known to cricket-lovers the world over, no one could have foreseen the impact he was to have upon an already promising Sussex team. I am told that it was his googly that caused the most trouble; that is the devilish ball that pretends to be a leg-break but is in fact an off-break, as if batting isn't hard enough without that.

This book tells the story of how Sussex finally pulled it off in 2003 and for the first time won the County Championship. How thrilling it was to get there after all these years, and what's more, I have a feeling that it will not be so very long before the next triumph. What fun it will be to read all about it when the time comes.

INTRODUCTION AND ACKNOWLEDGEMENTS

This is not a history of Sussex County Cricket Club. That has already been well and comprehensively written by Sir Home Gordon, Arthur Gilligan, John Marshall and Christopher Lee. Nor is it a straightforward chronicle of the season of all seasons for Sussex, the oldest of the county clubs, although a match-by-match breakdown does appear in Chapter 8. Instead, we have attempted to piece together how it all happened, going back to that dramatic evening in the Empress Ballroom of Brighton's Grand Hotel seven years ago. We have talked to the players, on and off the field, who made that joyous, sunlit afternoon on 18 September 2003 possible.

Because cricket, perhaps more than any other game, is shaped by its history and traditions, we have also tried to place this special achievement in context by looking at other high summers and talking to former Sussex players about their reaction to the county's long-awaited success.

We would like to thank everyone at Sussex County Cricket Club for their cooperation, in particular David Green, Hugh Griffiths, Simon Dyke, Francesca Watson and Neil Lenham. On the cricket side, Peter Moores, Chris Adams and the players, in particular Matt Prior, Mushtaq Ahmed and Jason Lewry, were unfailingly helpful. So were David Gilbert and Tony Pigott in building the background to our second chapter. We would also like to express our gratitude to the club librarian, Rob Boddie, for supplying many historical pictures and fine-tooth-combing through the text, to Jim Pegg, who cast his expert eye over the text, and to Norman Epps and David Llewellyn for statistical input.

We would like to thank our employers, the *Guardian* and the Brighton *Argus*, for their forbearance, in particular Richard Taylor, Simon Dack, Cara Minns and Jim Holden at the *Argus* for their help with pictures.

Special mention must go to our agent, David Luxton, and our editor, Sarah Bryce, for their unflagging enthusiasm and encouragement, to John Barclay for providing the foreword and to Matthew Engel for his discreet wisdom.

Finally, a special thanks to those countless authors and historians whose works we have plundered. In addition to those mentioned above we found volumes by the following authors invaluable: John Wallace (too many to mention but in particular his *Sussex 100 Greats*), Nicholas Sharp (*Sussex – Seven Times the Bridesmaid*), David Frith (*By His Own Hand*), Alan Hill (*The Family Fortune*), Christopher Martin-Jenkins (*World Cricketers*), Dermot Reeve (*Winning Ways*), *Barclays World of Cricket*, Chris Westcott (*Cricket at the Saffrons*). And, of course, we have consulted more *Wisden*s than you could shake a stump at.

Paul Weaver and Bruce Talbot, Brighton, April 2004

After 113 years of waiting, Sussex supporters can finally celebrate their side's first Championship. *(Jim Holden/Brighton Argus)*

1

MAKING HISTORY

Sussex supporters, rather like Lewis Carroll's father William, have developed the rather idiosyncratic habit of standing on their heads; the Championship table usually reads better that way. Far away from the drumbeats and bugles of glory, Sussex County Cricket Club, despite the most exotic of histories, have often conducted their business to an altogether different accompaniment – the dull rattle of wooden spoons.

Ten times they have finished bottom of the table. They came last in 1890, the very first year the Championship was formally recognised – having been bottom on many less official occasions before then – and propped up the rest twice more before the century closed. Six times since 1968, including as recently as 1987, 1990, 1997 and 2000, they have traipsed in last, wheezing and red-faced like the cross-country duffer we all remember from school.

Then, at 1.43pm on Thursday 18 September 2003, something remarkable happened. The oldest of the county clubs, having been formed 164 years before, finally won the domestic game's greatest prize. Murray Goodwin, on his way to a more personal epiphany, pulled a short delivery from Leicestershire's Phil DeFreitas to the midwicket boundary; life at a small green patch in Hove, at the venerable Eaton Road ground, would never be the same again.

Play was suspended for seven minutes in that fourth over after lunch. 'Sussex by the Sea', the First World War quick-march song, blared over the Tannoy. Spectators, like history itself, cleared their throats and raised the song sheets that had been distributed in advance. Some who did not know the words might have struggled, for some sheets trembled with the emotion of it all. Children cavorted, aware of the frisson of celebration but not of the texture of its meaning. Some even played cricket, of all things. At the north of the ground, in the blue-and-white deck chairs, elderly members, some with ready-made trembles, clutched the paper with hands blotched by *anno Domini*. Some stood, knocking over Thermoses as their knee-rugs fell about their ankles, sticks forgotten as if by some miraculous healing process. They knew the meaning of this all right. So did the merely middle-aged.

At Hove the ground tilts sharply towards the sea like the deck of a stricken liner and the club had foundered on many occasions over more than a century and a half. Now, it seemed, the *Titanic* had been raised.

Out in the middle Goodwin and his partner embraced. Fittingly, that partner was the Sussex captain, Chris Adams, who had jumped in the air three times when the runs were scored. He would go on to score another century. Champagne was delivered to the middle on a silver salver. Soon the entire playing staff, including some young men who had seen about as much of the limelight as bashful bats, galloped onto the turf for an emotional lap of honour.

Whatever did the umpires, Mervyn Kitchen and Trevor Jesty, make of it all? This brief, ecstatic break had been prearranged by Jim Parks, the Sussex president and one of its finest players, who beamed ruddy-faced beneficence from the committee room balcony. There were tears and alcohol spillages everywhere. The motorised 'Blotter' machine that soaks up moisture, the supporters' club's latest gift, had hardly been used in this hot and glorious summer, but it was needed now. The moment felt almost astronomical in its significance; it was like a flypast by a famous comet that only pops in every 164 years. In some ways it felt eerily unreal, like an eclipse, though the sun had never shone as brightly in Hove as it did on 18 September 2003. Was it Peter Moores or Patrick Moore who had orchestrated this?

Kipling's 'Sussex by the Sea' was still going strong and the Tannoy was in full voice as the umpires, the party poopers, tried to get on with something called cricket.

Just 17 months earlier the atmosphere here had been very different. In fact, the ground had never been so deeply melancholic. Then, the black-arm-banded cricketers of Sussex and Surrey, united by a terrible grief, formed a silent, head-bowed semi-circle as they paid tribute to the brief lives of Umer Rashid and Ben Hollioake. The minute's silence was broken only by the screaming of the seagulls and the rustle of the nearby apple blossom that shivered in the chill sea breeze. A cricketer's death is particularly sad in the springtime of the year, Neville Cardus once observed. But he could never have imagined anything as poignant as this. It was almost unbearably sad. Rashid, a gifted Sussex all-rounder, had died on the first day of that month of April, aged 26, drowned as he vainly attempted to rescue his younger brother Burhan at Concord Falls, a beauty spot in Grenada where the county's players had been enjoying a pre-season tour. The accident happened just a week after the funeral of Ben Hollioake, the Surrey and England all-rounder, who died in a car crash in Perth, Australia.

Now, a little more than a year later, Hove BN3 3AN was witnessing its most joyous moment, its greatest, hand-pumping, champagne-spilling, jigging, jolly, shouting, is-this-a-dream, whoopee time in its long, hoary history. It was most appropriate, therefore, that the club dedicated the winning of their historic Championship to the memory of Umer and his brother.

There were some who suggested, a little unkindly, that Sussex's triumph was the biggest piece of larceny since the Brinks Mat heist. But the wonderful thing about their success was that it was fully deserved. On paper, both Surrey and Lancashire, their main rivals, had stronger squads. But by winning four more matches than anyone, and by finishing 34 points clear of the field, Sussex, driven by their captain and coach, were the outstanding team of the season.

Some time afterwards, Adams would receive a letter from Adam Hollioake, in which the Surrey captain said: 'In the coming weeks you'll have so many people coming up and telling you why you won it, giving you excuses and reasons and all sorts of different versions why Sussex won the league this year. There's only one reason why Sussex won it and that was because they were the better team.'

Some said that Sussex would not have won it without Mushtaq; others argued that it was a team effort. And both observations were perfectly valid. Mushtaq, the bearded alchemist, was, of course, the biggest single factor. Here was not only a bowler in search of a hundred wickets but also a man looking for a more personal resurrection. If Harbhajan Singh had joined the club, as Adams and coach Moores dearly wanted, Sussex would not have won the title. Instead, Harbhajan was lured to Manchester, where injury and frustration awaited. By taking 103 wickets in the Championship, Mushtaq ensured that Sussex would win, or go damn close – even if he did arrive for that last match of the season against Leicestershire on Wednesday morning having left his whites in his Brighton kitchen. A fast driver was immediately dispatched.

There are many admirable traditions associated with Sussex cricket – exciting play, dashing batsmen, a proud lineage of fast and fast-medium bowlers, terrific fielding over several epochs – but spinners? Over the years Sussex have not had their fair share. Now one had helped conjure the grandest moment of them all. The Asian link has always been there. The late Alan Ross, a writer who would have revelled in the success of his beloved county, once associated the County Ground with 'an odour of Empire, of curry powder and whisky, retired colonels and actresses, the ailing old and the robust young'.

After the genius of Mushtaq, the biggest single factor was the ambience created by the drive and enthusiasm that flowed from Adams and Moores. But the positive mood was seized upon by everyone else; all the established members of the side played at least one crucial part in the taking of the title. And, as we shall see, the seeds of victory were sown long before last summer. This was more than just a romantic triumph. By winning the Championship, Sussex also gave a valuable pointer to the way the county game should be played. Of the 18 first-class counties, they had the smallest staff, just 18 players, and they used only 15 of them. There was much those ball-wreckers

100 up. Leicestershire's Brad Hodge is bowled and Mushtaq Ahmed has his 100th wicket of the season. *(Simon Dack/Brighton Argus)*

Mark Davis holds the trophy aloft on the players' balcony. *(Jim Holden/Brighton Argus)*

Tears from Chris Adams and Mark Davis as the immensity of their achievement begins to sink in. Richard Montgomerie is on the right. *(Liz Finlayson/Brighton Argus)*

Magic man Mushtaq Ahmed acknowledges the cheers of the Sussex crowd. *(Jim Holden/Brighton Argus)*

of county cricket, otherwise known as the Cricket Reform Group, could have learned here. Attempting to cure the ills of the game without a feeling for its values and traditions is a little like attempting to solve the Northern Ireland problem without an O-level in history. On that hot and heady afternoon in Hove excited young boys could be seen picking up bat and ball and searching out a space where they could replicate the deeds of the day.

The tightness of the Sussex squad encouraged an already healthy team spirit and allowed the county to pay them well for their success. And, as the players frolicked round the boundary in celebration, it was easy to see how they had all contributed. Murray Goodwin finished the season with his bat ablaze and with almost 1,500 Championship runs. Richard Montgomerie recovered from a poor start to consolidate the top order and Tony Cottey, who had already won a Championship with Glamorgan, was the best batsman in the side in the early part of the season. Adams, always determined, ambitious and aggressive, brought the best out of his players as captain and though his own form was poor for the first half of the season, he scored four centuries in the second. Tim Ambrose and Matt Prior were once again two of the best wicketkeeper-batsmen in the country, and the latter's batting flourished when he gave up the gloves. Robin Martin-Jenkins, one of the leading all-rounders on the circuit and now approaching his prime, contributed more with the bat this time, while Mark Davis atoned for an otherwise disappointing season with a match-winning innings of 168 against Middlesex. James Kirtley missed five Championship matches because of England and injury but still took 49 wickets with skiddy pace, while Jason Lewry was among the best swing bowlers in the country when conditions permitted. The back-up came from Billy Taylor, Kevin Innes, Paul Hutchison and Michael Yardy. And behind them all was the coach, or director of cricket to give him his proper title, Peter Moores, whose latest technical gizmos failed to disguise the fact that his greatest asset was his pure passion, his heart-on-sleeve eagerness to work with cricketers.

Sussex had gone into that final game needing just six points to confirm the Championship. They had missed their chance at Old Trafford, where a draw would have been enough, and where Mushtaq failed to take the single wicket he needed to reach 100. It was a blessing. Hove was where both county and player would find their apogee before a more appreciative crowd.

It seemed that only an unscheduled visit from Hurricane Isabel, who was on a world tour, could deny Sussex on that bright Wednesday morning. On a flat pitch Sussex had wanted to bat first. But when Leicestershire chose to bat they were bowled out for 179 in just 69.5 overs. Sussex had three bowling points and just three more were needed. Mushtaq, who had played league cricket for Little Stoke in Staffordshire the previous season, took his 100th wicket of the season in the last over before lunch when Brad Hodge played half-forward to a leg-break and heard his off-stump knocked backwards. The ball would be mounted and presented to the bowler. The Championship became clearly visible in the afternoon session when Leicestershire lost four wickets in four overs while scoring a single run.

When Sussex batted they knew that whatever happened at Trent Bridge, where Lancashire were playing Nottinghamshire, they only needed to score 300 and take three batting points to win the elusive prize. At the close, playing with some restraint, they had reached 137–1 and need 163 more to make history.

What happened, a short time after lunch on that second day, has already been described. But Sussex did not stop there. By the time they declared, at 614–4, they led Leicestershire by 435. Goodwin, Sussex's other overseas player, was 335 not out, not only a personal best but also the highest individual score in the club's history, eclipsing Duleepsinhji's 333 on the same ground in 1930.

On the third morning the side were led out not by Adams, who missed the first session with tennis elbow, but by vice-captain Kirtley, a nice touch. Kirtley was not playing in the match because of shin splints. But he had played a salient part in the story, regularly skimming the cream off the top of the opposition's batting.

The victory on Friday, their tenth to equal Surrey's first-division record, was delayed. Perhaps it was the absence of the injured Mushtaq. Perhaps it was the long and liquid celebrations that had gone on in the Sussex Cricketer pub the evening before. Perhaps those celebrations were the reason why some miserable members complained that the match should have been wrapped up earlier. Some people are never satisfied. And some members, after all, are more familiar with whingeing than winning because they've served a full apprenticeship.

For the Adams family to win by an innings and 55 runs after tea on the third day, following a 5–6 burst from Lewry, was still a reasonably good effort, all things considered. There was a reprise of 'Sussex by the Sea' and then Queen's 'We Are The Champions'. In a remarkable balcony scene Adams was awarded the Frizzell County Championship trophy. Fireworks fizzed and screeched and more bottles popped.

A nice moment came when John Carr, Director of Cricket Operations at the England and Wales Cricket Board, said: 'Congratulations to Surrey for winning the County Championship.' Cackling laughs and mock boos all round. Some habits are difficult to break.

Some celebrated afresh. Others, with small red eyes like holly berries, looked as though they didn't have much left over from the night before.

Historically, it had been a long vigil for Sussex supporters, a little over a century and a half. From now on, though, nothing will be quite the same again. And anything that happened to Sussex County Cricket Club prior to 2003 will be known as Sussex BC, before Championship. Best of all, it's no longer necessary to stand on one's head.

2

REVOLUTION!

Sussex finally won their first Championship on 18 September 2003, a day never to be forgotten by those privileged to witness it. The greatest day in the club's long history? Certainly. The most dramatic? Perhaps not. How about the extraordinary events of 19 March 1997 in the Empress Ballroom of Brighton's seafront Grand Hotel? It was the night democracy in its rawest form totally changed the direction of the oldest first-class county. It swept away a regime that was perceived to be totally out of touch by the seething majority of what was, after all, a members' club. The management of the time had overseen one of the blackest periods in Sussex's history, culminating in the departure of the captain and five capped players in the winter of 1996. What was worse, they seemed utterly powerless to prevent it happening.

In a little over an hour the membership, roused from their deckchairs by the thought that for once they could actually make a difference, swept away the old guard. Jim May, who played a big part in what became known as the Sussex revolution and eventually took his place on the new committee, likened it to Eastern Europe before and after the Iron Curtain came down. No one has come up with a better comparison.

Older members might have been reminded of the events of March 1950, when an acrimonious meeting of members at the Royal Pavilion in Brighton reached a climax when the president, the Duke of Norfolk, resigned and stormed out, followed by the committee, after a vote of no confidence. The unrest followed the decision to replace the captain, Hugh Bartlett, with joint captains, R.G. Hunt and G.H.G. Doggart. The secretary, Billy Griffith, also resigned. In the end James Langridge was appointed captain, a new committee was elected and the Duke of Norfolk remained as president.

Sussex, as a credible force in English county cricket, was re-born that night 47 years later. But the problems that had threatened to engulf the club in that incredible winter of 1996/7 began on a late summer's day over four years earlier.

❖ ❖ ❖

On NatWest Final day, 4 September 1993, Lord's was packed. It was the showpiece finale to the domestic season, although probably the game the neutrals didn't want. Sussex had beaten Glamorgan in a gripping semi-final at Hove, thus denying the great Viv Richards the chance to end his illustrious career at headquarters against Somerset, the county who had sacked him seven years earlier. Somerset had already been soundly beaten on their own patch by an emerging Warwickshire.

No one could deny that Sussex's 2003 Championship-winners were a fine team, but player for player the side that met Warwickshire were arguably as good, if not better. We'll never know what would have happened had Sussex won that day. They certainly should have. Everyone from the county who was in the full-house crowd of nearly 26,000, and thousands back in Sussex, watching spellbound on television as the drama unfolded, still remember the match with uncomfortable clarity more than ten years later.

Inspired by a brilliant 124 from opener David Smith and audacious cameos by Martin Speight and Neil Lenham, Sussex piled up a Lord's one-day record of 321-6 from their 60 overs – and still lost. In what is still regarded as the greatest limited-overs final ever played, Warwickshire squeezed home by five wickets, winning off the last ball. Even today, those who played in it and those who watched it wonder how Sussex threw away the chance to collect their first major honour since 1986. Peter Moores, who kept wicket, still shudders when he recalls the events of that day. He is convinced Sussex would have established themselves as a genuine force in the county game had they won: 'We had a very talented team, there's no doubt about it. You had international-class performers like Alan Wells, Franklyn Stephenson, David Smith, Bill Athey and some guys who were just emerging as quality players like Ed Giddins and Ian Salisbury. We threatened to be a very good side, but for whatever reason we lacked consistency. Beating Warwickshire should have been a launching pad but things just started to go downhill.'

Player for player everyone agreed that Sussex were a better side than Warwickshire. But captain Dermot Reeve, a former Sussex player himself, and coach Bob Woolmer were putting innovative coaching ideas into practice at Edgbaston. The following year they won three trophies, including the Championship, and dominated domestic cricket during the mid-nineties. Sussex, in contrast, never got anywhere near to fulfilling their potential. Instead, they started to go into steady decline.

In 1994 they improved by two places to finish eighth in the Championship, but their one-day form was disastrous. They lost in the first round of the NatWest Trophy and the Benson and Hedges Cup and won only five Sunday League games. The batting, in particular, was poor, with no one scoring 1,000 runs. There was no discernible improvement in 1995 despite the form of skipper Alan Wells, who belatedly won his solitary England cap. They finished 15th in the Championship and made little impact in the one-day competitions. By mid-July cricket manager Norman Gifford had resigned after seven seasons, prompting a fundamental overhaul of the club's coaching structure. Gifford's replacement was confirmed a month after the season's end when former West Indies opener Desmond Haynes was charged with the task of reviving the county's fortunes and, in particular, getting the balance right between experienced campaigners and players, like James Kirtley, who were emerging from a youth system regarded at the time as one of the best in the country. The new year, 1996, started with renewed optimism. It ended with the club in turmoil and the team threatening to disintegrate. The intervening months offered little solace for the county's supporters, although a fine win over Yorkshire at Eastbourne, inspired by the batting of Moores and Vasbert Drakes, should have given the side the impetus to finish in the top six. Instead they lost five out of the last six games and came 12th. Ed Giddins took 6–47 at the Saffrons – his best figures for the county in what turned out to be the fast bowler's last game for Sussex.

At the end of May Giddins had failed a random drugs test during the match against Kent at Tunbridge Wells. Two months later the Test and County Cricket Board (now the ECB) found him guilty of using a prohibited substance, rejecting his assertion that the drug (cocaine) had been ingested inadvertently. Giddins was sacked by the county two days later and an appeal in November was dismissed. Giddins was banned for 18 months by the authorities and sacked by Sussex, but by then his fate was looking like the least of Sussex's worries.

Having underachieved for so long, it was inevitable that there would be rumblings of discontent, both from within the dressing room and outside, about Wells' style of leadership. Dave Gilbert, who was to join Sussex in 1998 as cricket manager, was coaching Surrey at the time. He says his players always looked forward to their meetings with Sussex because invariably they would win quickly and earn themselves an extra day off. 'The Sussex side at the time was very experienced, with guys like David Smith, Ian Salisbury and Peter Moores, and emerging players like Jason Lewry,' he recalled. 'But we always felt they were captained by someone out of touch with his team. We knew that if we put them under any sort of pressure they would buckle simply because they didn't want to do it for Alan Wells.'

At the end of the season, Wells left a meeting with chairman Alan Caffyn convinced he would be reappointed. But half an hour after returning from a benefit tour to Barbados in early October he was phoned by Caffyn's deputy, Alan Wadey, and told he was being replaced by Moores, one of his closest friends as well as his vice-captain. At a hastily-arranged press conference in the garden of his local pub at Berwick, Wells came out fighting: 'People have just not been straight with me. It's not so much that I've lost the captaincy but the way it has been handled.'

Caffyn later claimed that Haynes had advocated a change of captaincy as early as May 1996 and was convinced the decision to replace Wells would be popular in the dressing room. In February 1997, in a rare interview which was to be his last as chairman, Caffyn told the Brighton *Argus*: 'When we eventually replaced Alan Wells with Peter Moores all the players, almost to a man, said, "Thank goodness he's gone." They admired him as a player but didn't like his captaincy at all.' Moores suddenly found himself in the top job. 'I remember sitting in the corridor outside Alan Caffyn's office in Eastbourne when he asked me to captain the side and wondering if it really was what he and the club wanted,' he recalled. 'I felt some sympathy for Alan Caffyn. He was a great supporter of Sussex cricket and still is to this day, and he just wanted to get it right. But things had been building for a while and you knew at some stage that it would blow up.' Moores tried to persuade Wells to play under him, but he left with two years of his contract remaining and signed for Kent before retiring in 2002.

With Giddins also gone and opening batsman Jamie Hall released against his will, the new captain knew he would start the 1997 season without three capped players. Within weeks that number had doubled. Ian Salisbury's relationship with Wells had been strained for some time after the former captain had criticised his leg spinner in his account of the 1994 season, *A Captain's Year*. But when Salisbury rejected Sussex's offer of a five-year contract to sign a three-year deal with Surrey in November, he insisted that Wells wasn't an issue. 'Both the county and I need a change of direction,' he said. How prophetic those words turned out to be.

A few weeks later all-rounder Danny Law left to join Essex, much to the disappointment of Haynes, who had taken a special interest in the development of a player who never went on to fulfil his undeniable potential. The departure of Martin Speight to Durham, the sixth capped player to leave Sussex in a little over three months, was always likely once the appointment of Moores blocked his ambitions to keep wicket in both forms of the game. Nevertheless, the loss of another senior pro was a further blow to the new captain and the club.

While all this was happening, Haynes was finishing off his playing career in South Africa. Whether his presence at Hove during Sussex's own winter of discontent might have helped prevent the exodus of players will never be known, but Moores certainly needed all the assistance he could muster as he began the task of rebuilding his ravaged squad.

When an Old Harrovian with three initials joined Sussex in 1976 there was always a chance that he might end up running the club. But no one could have foreseen that A.C.S. Pigott would be the man to lead the bloodless revolution that was to transform the county. Probably not even Pigott himself.

There can't have been many cricketers in the history of the game with stronger affinities to a county than 'Lester'. Although he was born in Fulham, Tony Pigott always regarded himself as a son of Sussex. His family relocated to the county when he was two months old, and as an 11-year-old he even persuaded his father not to move 200 yards across the county border into Kent. A product of the Sussex Young Cricketers, he made a sensational start to his career when his first three wickets in first-class cricket were a hat-trick – Intikhab Alam, Arnold Long, who went on to captain Sussex, and Robin Jackman – in only his second match, against Surrey in 1975. Pounding in on the fast side of fast-medium, he went on to take nearly 700 wickets for the county. In 1981 a surgeon told him his career was over after he was diagnosed with a double stress fracture of the vertebrae, but he recovered. Three years later he won his only Test cap when he was called into England's depleted ranks on Bob Willis's tour of New Zealand while playing state cricket for Wellington. On an awful wicket at Lancaster Park in Christchurch he removed Bruce Edgar with his seventh ball in Test cricket and also took the wicket of Jeremy Coney, although England, who failed to reach 100 in either innings for the only time in the century, lost heavily. Pigott had postponed his wedding to play, but he was eventually married in a friend's garden in Wellington a few weeks later.

Pigott's wholehearted approach to his craft attracted other counties and when he returned from New Zealand several of them expressed an interest in signing him. He'd asked permission to speak to other clubs when Sussex refused to pay their annual £300 bonus to capped players. Somerset captain Ian Botham wanted him to form a new-ball partnership with the great West Indian Joel Garner and everything was agreed. But on the eve of his departure to Taunton for a medical, a deputation of teammates, led by captain John Barclay, persuaded him to stay at Hove. 'I couldn't bowl for Somerset like I bowl for Sussex,' he said after his change of heart, 'even though Sussex were getting nowhere management-wise.'

By 1996 it seemed little had changed. Pigott had been released by the county the day after playing in the infamous 1993 NatWest final and promptly signed a two-year contract with Surrey. He saw out his playing days there before becoming second XI coach under Dave Gilbert, who had been recruited from the Australian Cricket Academy to become Surrey's cricket manager. Pigott developed his business acumen by working in the commercial department at The Oval, while Graham Thorpe and Alec Stewart were the first high-profile clients in a cricket-management group he had helped to set up. But he kept in touch with events at Hove and, as autumn turned to winter in 1996, had become increasingly alarmed as he watched Sussex do their utmost to self-destruct. The catalyst for Pigott came on 16 January 1997 when he spoke at a meeting of the Sussex Cricket Society.

Sussex had already lost five capped players and another – Martin Speight – was about to go and you could tell how upset people were about it that night. They were very critical of the chairman and the committee, which surprised me a bit. Sussex supporters weren't supposed to be fiery and passionate, but they were that night. There was a lot of discontent in that room.

Afterwards I joined a few of the people who were there for a drink and among them was Jim May, who had decided to put himself up for election to the committee and try and change things from within. Jim felt the same way as me. But he knew that I would have more of a chance of doing something because I was an ex-player who was still very close to the club and had a bit of a profile. So I went away, had a think and decided I would do something.

Pigott consulted a solicitor who told him that, under the club's rules, it only needed the signatures of 50 members to call for an extraordinary general meeting, where Pigott could put forward a motion of no confidence in the committee and call for their resignation *en bloc*.

I actually knew people who wanted to buy the club, but the solicitor wrote back to me and told me the best way to change things was by calling this EGM, getting rid of the committee and becoming chairman myself. Within a couple of days or so I had 66 signatures. I already knew a lot of people who were happy to sign, I even went into the Sussex Cricketer [the famous pub at the entrance to the County Ground] and got some people in there to sign as well. I then walked down to the club offices one morning in early February and handed in the letter with the signatures.

The club called the EGM for 8 April. Meanwhile, Pigott employed a public relations firm to give his campaign for change a bit more profile. Events now began to move at a bewildering speed. Alan Wells, with support of the Professional Cricketers' Association, hit back, contradicting Caffyn's newspaper comments about his sacking as captain. On 4 March Richard Barrow resigned from the committee and would later join Pigott's 'rebels'. Two days later the club confirmed that Caffyn had resigned after seven years with immediate effect – he had been widely criticised, most vocally by Pigott, for his newspaper criticism of Wells. It was confirmed that he would be giving up his seat on the committee as well. Ken Hopkins, a committee member for 13 years, was appointed as Caffyn's successor, but with the club in turmoil, Pigott gathered his forces and seized the moment.

The days of the 'old Sussex' were effectively numbered once the results of the annual committee elections had been announced a few days later. Three new members were elected with hefty support, ahead of their six rivals for the vacancies. They were Jim May, a former local councillor, retired bank manager Dick Holste, who had been treasurer of Pigott's benefit in 1991, and, most interestingly of all, a former Sussex captain, Robin Marlar. May and Marlar, incensed by the departure of so many capped players, had hatched their plans to change things from within while watching the Varsity rugby match at Twickenham in December 1996, a month before Pigott got involved. Marlar then headed off to New Zealand to cover the England cricket tour for *The Sunday Times* and returned to find all hell had been let loose.

Like Pigott, Marlar was steeped in the traditions of Sussex cricket. Born in Eastbourne, he played 223 times for the county between 1951 and 1968, including five seasons as captain in the late 1950s, taking 740 wickets with his off-breaks. He hardly looked like a revolutionary, but Marlar enjoyed living up to his reputation as something of a maverick and wasn't afraid of upsetting people in his newspaper columns. He condemned the appointment of Haynes and Moores, and now, just a few hours after returning from New Zealand, he met Pigott and his supporters at Gatwick, two days before the AGM. An irresistible pincer movement, which would sweep away the old guard, was in place. They even had a name, Sussex 2000, and an impressive manifesto for change. In Pigott's corner were the three new committee men plus Barrow. The remaining committee members were Hopkins, vice-chairman Wadey, club surgeon Frank Horan and former captain John Barclay, who was thought to hold the balance of power.

Two days later, on 19 March, came the regular annual general meeting. Peter Moores had been to a few in his time as a player, and normally they were attended by no more than 200 members who would get through the business on a nod of the head. This was different. 'I arrived and Tony's supporters were outside the Grand with Sussex 2000 leaflets. You could see they had planned things well,' recalled Moores. 'There were quite a few people in the ballroom and the club had hired a room upstairs so we could draw up our battle plans. I came back downstairs about 20 minutes later and the place was jammed. The room was absolutely buzzing. I had never known an atmosphere like it. You just knew something momentous was going to happen.'

Pigott had done countless television and radio interviews that day to outline his plans, but the one he still vividly remembers was for BBC Breakfast News.

'I was in London and Ken Hopkins was in Southampton and he was being so blasé about the whole thing. He thought we would have the AGM and then the EGM and everything would be sorted out. But it was a lot more serious than that. There was definitely a momentum building.'

The tone was set even before the serious business of the AGM got under way when Wadey told the meeting that secretary Nigel Bett would not be in attendance because of illness. The previous day, under the headline 'Cheeky pic leaves Nigel blushing', the Brighton *Argus* had reproduced a picture, taken by Bett's wife Barbara, which had appeared in *British Naturism* magazine, showing her husband on a nudist beach in the Canary Islands with just a strategically placed black-and-white scarf protecting his modesty. It was a total irrelevance of course, but highly embarrassing to the club all the same. When ironic laughter filled the hall after Wadey's announcement, the vice-chairman must have sensed the mood of the meeting.

The EGM should have been the last item on the agenda, but May surprised the committee by proposing an unprecedented rejection of the annual report for 1996. He was loudly applauded as he labelled the management style of the committee 'aloof, autocratic and arrogant'. It quickly became apparent that the EGM would not be needed. Wadey told members: 'There's no doubt whatsoever that we as a committee are going to have to go and that is accepted by all of us.' It was too much for Horan. Just before Wadey stood up to deliver the committee's resignation speech, he walked off the top table, condemning the assembled members as 'rabble rousers', and stormed out of the room to a mixture of jeering and laughter. In less than an hour the old guard had been swept away, although Hopkins remained on the committee temporarily to help ensure a smooth transition.

'That's democracy,' shouted a voice from the back of the hall as the members began to take in what they had helped to achieve. The old committee had been staggered by the tidal wave of opinion that had changed so much in such a short space of time. Now their replacements – all three of them – convened in a lounge at the Grand as the members filed out.

There was no way Pigott could return to his job with Surrey. He had gone too far and achieved too much. 'I'd met with Robin Marlar for the first time at Gatwick and explained what I wanted to do. He told me he had a different idea, which for a second or two was a bit worrying, but he thought that if we took over the club I should become part of the admin side with him as chairman. I'd never considered that before. To be honest I was quite happy to be pushed where people wanted me to go.' Pigott was duly made director of

The morning after the night before. Tony Pigott (left) and Robin Marlar get ready for business, having ousted Sussex's discredited management at a momentous AGM in March 1997. *(Brighton Argus)*

cricket and acting chief executive while Bett returned only to clear his desk. 'People were telling me that I should be rewarded for being the architect of change but I didn't feel like that,' said Pigott.

As president of his own well-respected head-hunting company, the new chairman was ideally qualified to help establish a new management structure at Hove. 'The thing's got to be run as an executive body,' Marlar said shortly after taking on the top job. 'There must be someone to look after the cricket, in the same way as a production manager operates in a factory. The same applies in marketing, which is absolutely crucial, and administration. It's classic organisation really.'

The Sussex 2000 manifesto was an impressive start. Attacking the previous regime for 'ineffective management, lack of success, loss of capped players and wasting a successful youth policy', they pledged to develop Hove into a ground capable of staging international cricket and to implement policies that would improve communication, finances and development as well as bringing playing success.

The vacancies for the six remaining committee places were soon filled by Pigott supporters, including two former Sussex players, John Spencer and John Snow, along with Richard Barrow, Roger Dakin, who had chaired Alan Wells' benefit committee, sports book publisher Charles Frewin and Don Trangmar, a long-standing supporter of youth cricket in the county with considerable business acumen developed during 15 years as a board director of Marks & Spencer. Trangmar would play an increasingly active role in the club's affairs over the next few months.

Inevitably there were casualties. Surprisingly, the first was the club's venerable librarian, 'Ossie' Osborne, and the circumstances of his departure summed up the muddled thinking that had pervaded Sussex cricket for so long. The affable Osborne resigned when Pigott decided to move the cricket office into the building where the club's collection of books and artefacts were housed. 'The library was the best office in the ground,' recalled Marlar. 'The cricket office was in a Portakabin behind a sightscreen without windows and facing the flats at the sea end. What's the club for? For playing cricket! So Tony said he wanted to move it and I said go for it.'

No sooner had the dust settled than the new season began. The county fielded three debutants – batsman Neil Taylor, seamer Mark Robinson and left-arm spinner Amer Khan – in their opening Championship game against Northamptonshire, and controlled the game until rain wrecked the final two days. Indeed, when they quickly earned a bowling point on the first day Marlar bounded up the steps of the pressbox crying 'We're top of the table!' to bemused journalists. He was actually wrong, but he was given plenty of encouragement by Sussex's performances in those early weeks before the season soon went into a predictable nosedive. By July the county were anchored to the bottom of the Championship after a succession of heavy defeats and Marlar decided to give Pigott more input in team selection. Coach Desmond Haynes, halfway through a three-year contract, saw that as a threat to his own position, although his public pronouncements on the situation were carefully worded. 'I don't know if it compromises my position, that's something you would have to ask the chairman,' he remarked. But Haynes knew what was coming. Within a month he had gone, the remaining 12 months of his contract paid up. He even missed the highlight of the season – a run to the semi-final of the NatWest Trophy, which included incredible wins over Lancashire and Derbyshire before the wheels came off in the semi-final against Sussex's old nemesis, Warwickshire.

Off the field, Pigott was determined to fulfil his pledge to bring an 'atmosphere of change', although it was hard work to start with. 'The club was an absolute shambles. It was being run like an amateur cottage industry,' he remembered. 'The staff didn't even have job descriptions and weren't assessed regularly. There were so many things wrong. But the first job was to stop the downward spiral and stabilise the club because it was in a terrible state.'

Pushed forward by Pigott's enthusiasm, things started to improve. The county, so long regarded as a cricketing backwater, began to embrace all manner of ideas designed to raise their profile and get more customers through the gates. The start times of certain Championship matches were put back to encourage people to watch cricket after work, while arguably Pigott's most successful initiative was to bring floodlit cricket to the County Ground.

Surrey had been due to stage the first one-day league game under lights in June 1997, but the match was washed out. In the event, the honour fell to Warwickshire, who attracted a remarkable crowd of 15,174 for their game with Somerset in July. The cranes on which the huge floodlight towers were mounted then rumbled into Hove for the game with Surrey on 27 August. The weather – damp and dreary – was unappealing, but a crowd of more than 4,000, double what would have been expected on a normal Sunday afternoon, turned up. Sussex even added the sobriquet 'Tigers' to their name for the evening, but these particular tigers proved toothless and lost easily. Nevertheless, the county were delighted with the public response and began exploring the possibility of installing permanent floodlights.

Pigott also had to get used to the ways of Marlar:

Robin was a bit of a loose cannon and dealing with him was one of the most difficult things I had to contend with. I remember an incident after I'd become a selector. Robin and I both agreed that we needed James Kirtley to play in a Championship game, but James wasn't quite fit and felt he needed another match in the second team and Peter Moores agreed. On the day of the match, Robin turned up about 20 minutes after play started, found out James wasn't playing, stormed into my office and went ballistic. Quite how I managed it I don't know, but I told him to listen to the reasons before exploding and never to speak like that to me again. He got up, apologised profusely and walked out. That was what Robin was like. There was never a dull moment.

The biggest coup Pigott made that season was the recruitment of Dave Gilbert, who was to follow a well-worn path between The Oval and Hove, trodden by countless players in years gone by. He had monitored events at Hove with interest.

I first had dealings with Tony at Surrey, where we appointed him second XI player-coach in 1996. At the end of the year the Surrey cricket committee didn't want to renew his contract. I said it would be unfair to flip him having given him the job knowing that he had no coaching experience. I felt that morally it was the wrong thing to do. The cricket committee reluctantly agreed with me and we gave him another year.

That winter he told me he was going to stand for the Sussex committee. I reminded him that it was an unpaid job and that he should be careful about giving up on a thirty-grand job at The Oval. Then, in March, he left. No one at Surrey could believe it when Robin [Marlar] made him chief executive.

In two years, Gilbert had coached Surrey to two one-day trophies, but he saw his long-term future in cricket adminstration. The deal was concluded when the sides met in the Championship the day after the inaugural floodlit match, but the initial overtures had been made much earlier.

Within a month of taking over Tony was on the phone asking me to come to Hove. Something similar to what happened at Sussex had gone on at Surrey 18 months earlier and we were now starting to reap the rewards. We won a couple of one-day trophies and were putting together a top quality squad. Sussex had lost all those players and were struggling, so it wasn't very appealing cricket-wise. But I'd been coaching for five years and wanted to move on into the administration side of the game. I told Tony that if such a position became available I would consider it and he eventually came back to me.

In October 1997 Gilbert was appointed deputy chief executive and director of cricket on a two-year contract with a wide-ranging remit that would involve work in the coaching, financial and commercial operations of the club. It soon became apparent that there was still a lot to do six months after Pigott had begun the Sussex revolution. 'I was genuinely shocked when I first started,' Gilbert remembered.

Basically a structure didn't exist. Tony was effectively serving two masters in Robin Marlar and Don Trangmar, who was playing a bigger role as vice-chairman, and a lot of the time it was a case of the tail wagging the dog. I remember going to a staff meeting just prior to my commencement, which was held in the staff room at Marks & Spencer in Worthing of all places, and being shocked at just how much people who were performing minor roles in the operation had to say about everything to do with the club. To be fair, Tony inherited an absolute mess. I was brought in to help him bring some structure to the place.

The club made a loss of £83,000 in 1997 but within a year the deficit had more than doubled to £193,000. Around £40,000 of that loss was spent on a disastrous committee-approved local TV advertising campaign that only attracted a handful of new members. Adam Tarrant proved an ill-judged appointment as commercial manager, as Pigott readily admitted when Tarrant was dismissed after just six months and replaced by a former Sussex player, Neil Lenham. The rebranding of the old squash club at the County Ground into 'Willows', a restaurant/bar, also cost the county a considerable amount of money when a year went by without any rent being collected. That episode was to have long-term ramifications for the relationship between Pigott and his new number two, Gilbert.

Marlar soon handed over the chairmanship to Trangmar, a man of relatively few words but whose business brain and enthusiasm for Sussex cricket earned him considerable respect, particularly from Peter Moores. By now Moores had been replaced as captain by Chris Adams, the county's first high-profile playing recruit, so he could concentrate on his role as full-time first-team coach.

Tony Pigott welcomes Dave Gilbert to Sussex in September 1997. Their relationship turned sour and Pigott left the county three years later. *(Jim Holden/Brighton Argus)*

Gilbert recalled his first meeting with Trangmar when Surrey played Sussex at Hove in August 1997: 'I remember speaking to him and being very impressed. Of all the people in management I worked with at the club I think I got on best with Don. He loved Sussex cricket and wanted it to be successful, but he was nobody's fool.'

But by 1998 the club's financial bleeding was becoming an increasing source of anxiety to Gilbert, who had reduced his involvement with the cricket side of operations after his appointment as general manager. Pigott was asked to turn his attention to external matters and inevitably their relationship began to suffer. 'You can't help but like Tony, he's a lovable rogue,' said Gilbert. 'But his spending was irrational and largely unaccountable and I was getting increasingly fed up clearing up the wreckage. It was very unfair on Tony to give him a job for which he was entirely unsuited. He was always popular with the members and the committee because he always wore his heart on his sleeve as a player, giving absolutely everything, and then he was the catalyst for change when the club changed direction. But I felt he was simply not up to the job.'

Dave Gilbert and Don Trangmar formed a close working relationship once Trangmar had succeeded Robin Marlar as chairman in 1998. *(Simon Dack/Brighton Argus)*

Sussex continued to be both innovative and intuitive, despite tensions behind the scenes. In 1998 they staged two more successful day-night games (although a third was cancelled due to lack of sponsorship) and the club duly became the first in the country to erect permanent floodlights in 1999. That didn't stop Trangmar and Pigott bringing the possibility of a move away from Hove to the top of the agenda. In May 1999, 6,216 spectators had shoehorned themselves into the County Ground for the World Cup match between India and South Africa. Hundreds more watched from vantage points in surrounding streets, but Hove's inadequacy for staging international matches had been hopelessly exposed.

The county also made an audacious bid to sign Shane Warne. As well as being a proven match-winner, the mercurial Australian leg-spinner would have been a surefire public attraction and Sussex's interest prompted a lot of publicity. Warne did meet Pigott in Southampton, but Gilbert was never confident he would end up at Hove: 'Warney was big mates with Robin Smith and I think he was always destined to join Hampshire. I remember leaving five messages on his answerphone at home when he was supposed to be making a decision, but he never returned any of them. That told me enough.'

Sussex finally had some tangible reward for their hefty investment in new players in 1999, when they won the second division of the National League, small beer compared with what followed four years later, of course, but a sign of progress on the field none the less. However, a couple of weeks after champagne celebrations on the pavilion balcony at Derby, where the title had been won, the club was rocked by a new crisis, and one that no one on the outside looking in had seen coming. On 23 September it was announced that Pigott was leaving the club for 'personal reasons'.

The committee, and chairman Trangmar in particular, had wanted Gilbert to have a bigger role in the day-to-day running of the club for several months, fearing that he would leave when his contract expired in October. Changing his job title had failed to end confusion over areas of responsibility in a top-heavy administration. There was no suggestion that Gilbert had held a gun to the committee's head, but it had been clear to him for a while that either he or Pigott would have to make way, and he told Trangmar so.

I had confided in Don two or three months earlier that I was planning to see the season out, then move on. Whether watching the team at home or away, as soon as I met up with the opposition club's hierarchy, someone would buttonhole me and ask exactly what was the difference between Tony's and my roles at Sussex. It was all a bit embarrassing. The club's financial position was still pretty precarious. We just seemed to be on a course that had no strategy. I genuinely feared that, because of the spending, the club would go bankrupt and I was never going to be part of that. My credibility and reputation are very important to me.

In those last few weeks before he left, Tony and I hardly spoke. Our relationship had deteriorated quite badly. That was a shame because we had been good friends and he was, after all, the person who created the position and brought me to the club.

Pigott had talked Gilbert out of resigning four months earlier. But long before his own departure, he felt that Gilbert had been undermining his own position.

When Don took over as chairman and then David came, I felt a lot easier because I knew that if I was to be run over by a bus the future of the club was in the hands of two people who shared the same vision as me. From the moment I appointed him, David told me he didn't want the job of chief executive, but as time wore on I felt he was undermining me. I remember attending a meeting before the World Cup game. The Indian team manager couldn't believe I was chief executive. He thought David was because in their dealings he hadn't told him otherwise.

I assessed David as his boss in May 1999 and I just said that we had to work together for the good of Sussex cricket. A week later he offered to resign if we paid up the rest of his contract, but I refused.

At least the latest bout of Sussex blood-letting was over quickly, and for Pigott there were no regrets.

When I first started I told people I would not do the job for ever. I had no experience of running a club when I took over. A couple of years earlier I'd still been a player. I was always going to make mistakes, but I think we achieved a lot while I was there as well. I don't regret anything that happened. If you asked me today would I still have appointed Adam Tarrant, I would say yes. Would I have not tried to talk Dave Gilbert out of resigning? No, because I believed at the time it was the right thing for Sussex cricket.

Even now, five years later, there is little hope of a reconciliation between two people who were once colleagues and friends. 'I think Dave felt guilty about what happened. Every time I came to the ground after that he would run a mile,' claims Pigott. 'Everything I did was for the good of Sussex cricket, but I'm not sure everything David did was.' Gilbert, naturally, refutes this.

Don Trangmar always preferred the company of players. Here he discusses tactics with Michael Bevan at Arundel in July 2000. *(Simon Dack/Brighton Argus)*

Trangmar and Gilbert settled down to form an effective leadership of the club as the new millennium dawned. Trangmar supervised the ECB's working party, which successfully introduced central contracts for England players, while, closer to home, he worked with Gilbert to make sure costs were more strictly controlled. In 2000 the county were able to announce a small profit, two years after losses of nearly £300,000.

Trangmar grew into the job. He would happily wander around the ground all day, watching the cricket and listening to bouquets and brickbats from members, which came in equal numbers. He loved talking to players and preferred the atmosphere of the dressing room to the committee room. He made sure they were well looked after and was happy to reward good performances. It appeared he was in for the long haul. In August 1999 he told the Brighton *Argus*: 'Any chairman will tell you that you need five or six years in a job like this, with good support around you, to actually achieve something. I find the challenge quite stimulating and I didn't take the job to fail.' When he disclosed that the club would not be leaving their home because of a lack of alternative sites there was further rejoicing among the membership, who appreciated Trangmar's accessibility and his obvious passion for Sussex cricket.

Moores and Adams were grateful for his backing too at the end of the 2000 season, which finished with Sussex bottom of the pile in the first season after the 18 counties had been split into two divisions. Six weeks earlier they had topped the table, but four defeats in the last five games sent them tumbling down. There were calls for change in the club's cricket management, but Trangmar recognised that more upheaval was the last thing Sussex needed. It wasn't long, however, before another crisis loomed.

At the end of July 2001, Gilbert confirmed that he would be leaving Sussex after the season closed to take up the job of chief executive of the New South Wales Cricket Association. For a Sydneysider, who had played for his state as well as his country, it was the dream job and there was never any doubt once it had been offered to him that he would take it.

The job was advertised in May of that year and I was invited to apply, which was an encouraging sign. But if I'd missed out then that would have been it, I would have stayed in England with Sussex. As a family we'd had something like nine moves in ten years and I knew this would probably be the last move for me. But it was a big wrench. I like to feel I contributed towards Sussex progressing as a county during my four years and I loved every minute of it. Of course I had a few run-ins, but that happens everywhere. The happy memories definitely outweigh the bad ones.

Gilbert's combination of administrative acumen and cricketing knowledge was always going to be hard to replace. The job was advertised at the end of the 2001 season and in the meantime Trangmar took a more hands-on role in the day-to-day running of the club's affairs. Eventually, eight months after Gilbert's departure, Sussex announced that his replacement would be Sussex supporter Nigel Russell, a former Army major who had become a bursar at a private school in Surrey. 'It's my dream job,' he said when he was appointed in May 2002. 'But there's no sentimentality involved, even though I have a love for Hove, a love for cricket and a love for Sussex.' He lasted just three months.

In the meantime, and once again to the surprise of everyone outside the committee room, there was another round of Sussex blood-letting when Trangmar resigned as chairman the day before the first home match of the 2002 season. It should have been a day of celebration as Hove hosted Division One cricket for the first time. The official line on this occasion was 'personal reasons', but there were worrying echoes of events five years earlier. Trangmar's detractors on the committee felt he had railroaded them into the appointment of Russell. Some were said to find his methods too autocratic. When Trangmar sensed the mood, he offered his resignation and it was accepted with hardly a murmur. He returned to the ground the following day, clearly upset by this sudden turn of events, to say his goodbyes: 'If you haven't got the full support of everyone what's the point of carrying on. It was their decision to make the change but I was disappointed. They said I resigned for personal reasons which was nice, but it wasn't true.'

It came as no surprise to Pigott, who worked under him, and Marlar, an equally combustible character. 'That was always going to be the way Don went,' said Pigott. 'That's the nature of the beast. I had felt more unsettled when Don was chairman because he wanted to make more decisions himself.'

Since that day Trangmar has maintained a dignified silence over his sudden departure. He resigned from the committee shortly afterwards and the only disappointment for his successor, David Green, during the Championship-winning celebrations 19 months later was that only two of the four men who had done so much to make it possible, despite the personal conflicts, weren't there to witness history being made. Dave Gilbert was settling into his new job on the other side of the world while keeping a close eye on events through the internet as Sussex closed in on the title, but Trangmar simply stayed away. At least Tony Pigott, who, it should not be forgotten, appointed both Moores and Adams, and Robin Marlar were there, no doubt reflecting proudly on the part they played in the success during the most eventful six years in Sussex's long history.

The last word is perhaps best left to Peter Moores, who had seen both top jobs – chairman and chief executive – change hands four times since he took over the captaincy in 1997: 'There were times of stress and I had run-ins with all of them – Tony, Dave, Robin and Don – at one stage or another, but what you could never deny was that they all wanted success for Sussex cricket. They all played their part in laying the foundations for the Championship win.'

3

THE MERRY GHOSTS

'Sussex may not win a match,' Neville Cardus, one of the greatest of cricket writers, once said, 'but I have never watched Sussex with my eyes on the scoreboard, calculating results. I have watched with the eyes and affection of a lover of the game who knows a Sussex cricketer at sight, a cricketer who plays the game with all his heart to his heart's content.' Cardus, by the way, didn't come from Haywards Heath or Chichester; he was a Lancastrian.

Sussex may not have won the Championship until 2003, but their players have given more pleasure than most over the years. Because of this, and the fact that cricket is the most nostalgic of all games, in writing this book we decided to talk to a number of the county's former players. Many had come close to winning the Championship themselves. So what did it feel like, looking on from the boundary as others finally grasped the elusive prize?

We could not, of course, talk to the great players of the early 1900s and sadly, all those who played in the fine side three decades later have also passed on, but we spoke to a number who experienced the frustration of coming second. Most of the 1953 team are still around, though elderly, while the players of 1981 have now reached their forties, at the least. This is how they responded to the greatest day in the club's history.

CHARLES OAKES (1935–54)

Born: Horsham, 10 August 1912

The oldest surviving capped Sussex cricketer will be 92 in the summer of 2004. He lives in a residential care home in traffic-jammed Southborough, near Tunbridge Wells in Kent. It is a bitterly cold January afternoon. Outside, pedestrians, cocooned in coats and mufflers, scurry along on their urgent mission to find a warmer place. Nearby, at the Royal Victoria Hall Theatre, *Cinderella* is advertised. Inside Charles Oakes' room it feels cosier. The room is small and perhaps a little too warm. But, essentially, it's comfortable.

Around his neck are the headphones for his latest audio-book and on a table beside his chair is a cup of milky tea; he feels round the edge of the blue china to locate the handle. His sightless eyes are closed now and his hearing has been damaged by time. His mind, too, is a worry at first. He wants to know if his father, 'Joker' Oakes, the old Horsham groundsman, is still alive. He also asks about his brother, Jack, who died in 1997. He is normally better than this, says the nurse. A cold has troubled him more than it should have and the discomfort appears to have loosened his orientation. After a while, and a sip or two of tea, lucidity is recovered.

Charlie Oakes, the oldest living Sussex cricketer who celebrated his 91st birthday in August 2003. He is pictured here in 1939, four years after joining the county. (Sussex CCC)

'There are times when he's fine and times when he loses it a bit,' says his only son, Stephen, a hydrologist with the Environment Agency. 'But basically he's in pretty good shape for almost 92. He only moved into the home in October, and then it was at his own request. He wanted 24-hour care and my mother, Pip, died in 1996. He was getting increasingly frail and wobbly and was afraid that if he tripped over the dog, there might not be anyone there to pick him up.'

Stephen did not follow the family's rich cricketing traditions: 'Everyone expected me to be good at cricket because I was an Oakes and I rebelled against it. I remember, at school, meeting a couple of equally disaffected members of the Edrich family. The headmaster put us in the team because of our names and we were all pretty hopeless. I might have been able to play the game but basically I didn't give myself the chance. I didn't have Dad's killer instinct.'

Charlie Oakes was a fine cricketer and but for the Second World War, which wrenched the heart out of his career, his contribution would have been even more substantial. He was born in a white cottage beside the Horsham ground. He joined the county in 1935 and established himself as an all-rounder in 1937, when he scored more than 600 runs and took 37 wickets. He was an aggressive right-hand batsman and a wrist-spinner who bowled more top-spinners and googlies than leg-breaks.

His game was still maturing at the outbreak of hostilities. He played his best cricket after the war, in which he served in the RAF, but he was 34 when play eventually resumed after six lost summers. In each of the five seasons from 1946 to 1950 he scored more than 1,000 runs, and 1950 represented the high-water mark of his career when he scored 1,543 runs and took 72 wickets. By then his England chances had slipped by, though he had been close to selection for the 1948/9 tour to South Africa. He was so relaxed that he would often fall asleep while waiting to bat, only to be awoken by mischievous cries of 'Charlie, you're in now!' when, in fact, no wicket had fallen.

After his retirement he became, for a few years, the Horsham groundsman, like his father. He was then a popular coach at Stowe School for 20 years.

I heard the news about the Championship on the wireless and was absolutely delighted. We never thought about things like that in my time, although we did go close once. To be honest I never thought it would happen. I'm afraid I can't remember when I last went to Hove, because my memory is not what it was, but it was a long time ago.

I loved playing at Hove, and of course Horsham, because of the family connections there. My brother Jack hit the ball very hard, harder than me, though I don't think he did himself justice really. He didn't get the runs he should have.

We had a pretty tough upbringing. My father wasn't very pleased if I didn't do well. My mother used to stop me at the door whenever I got home and ask how I'd done. And if I hadn't done very well my father didn't take it very well. So I was delighted to hit a six into the family garden on my way to a hundred against Surrey before the war.

I preferred batting to bowling, though I can't remember very much, even about my centuries. My career really covered two epochs. When I first got involved with the club, the likes of Maurice Tate, Duleep, Ted Bowley and Jim Parks senior were the players everyone at Hove

Charlie Oakes hits out against Middlesex at Lord's in 1950. *(Sussex CCC)*

was talking about. By the time my career came to an end I was playing with up-and-coming cricketers like young Jim Parks, Ken Suttle and Ian Thomson.

Because I'm old and blind I don't get down to Hove now. Not being able to see gets me down a bit. I do get a bit browned off. And every time I feel a pain I think, 'Well, this is it.' I suppose we don't live to much more than 90, do we? I've had my fair share. I do hear from Alan Oakman from time to time. He will phone or send me a card.

But you can say that I enjoyed my cricket and I played at a good time for the game. I'm afraid I don't think much of England these days. They have no one outstanding. No one like Denis Compton, who was my favourite cricketer.

I get by with other things these days, enjoying the wireless and my books, although by the time I get halfway through a book I've forgotten what it's about and have to go back to the beginning!

RUPERT WEBB (1948–60)

Born: Harrow, Middlesex, 11 July 1922

There are not many male models in their eighties. But for Rupert Webb, who also played a small role in the film *Four Weddings and a Funeral*, life became

more exotic after his retirement from the cricket field in 1960. Encouraged by his actress wife, Barbara Whatley, Webb became a middle-aged model and he's still going. He has recently advertised banks, building societies and First Direct, and was even seen promoting hot tubs in Hastings.

Webb was at Lord's as a youngster but moved to Sussex on a special registration and first played for the county in 1948. He was the regular Sussex wicketkeeper between 1950 and 1956. The following season he shared the gloves with David Mantell, but in 1958, when he was injured, Jim Parks did a turn behind the stumps. That injury was a costly one for Webb. Parks became England's premier wicketkeeper-batsman and Webb retired after his benefit season in 1960. He then worked in the oil industry before, in 1980, he started preparing for photo shoots.

Rupert Webb was an accomplished wicketkeeper who, after retirement, successfully turned his hand to modelling. He even made a cameo appearance in *Four Weddings and a Funeral. (Sussex CCC)*

I got down to Hove a number of times last season [2003], though not, unfortunately, for the Leicestershire game at the end. But I have some difficulty with this Championship. It was a terrific effort but is it the first time we have won the Championship in 164 years, or the first time we've won it in the four or five years that we've had two divisions?

When we were second in 1953 we played all the teams. Last season Sussex played only half of them. And one overseas player took all the wickets while another scored most of the runs. I think we were much more of a team when I played. And we had a truly outstanding captain in David Sheppard, who led from the front in the same way that Len Hutton did for England.

I remember playing Hampshire and David said, 'If we let Derek Shackleton bowl at us, we'll be bowled out for 250 or less.' So for the first three overs he jumped down the wicket to him and hit him out of the attack. It was marvellous batting but also great leadership.

I remember another time we were playing Leicestershire at Grace Road and David thought they should have declared. The new ball was due and David decided to take it but told everyone to keep it in its wrapper, a little waxy envelope that we used in those days.

David adjusted the field a few times while the bowler had one or two practice run-ups. Then the Leicestershire captain came running down the pavilion steps and declared. David said with a big grin, 'I knew they couldn't afford another new ball.' The other remarkable thing about David is that I never remember him dropping a catch.

But it's like comparing melons with oranges, looking at the game then and now. Those were the days of uncovered wickets and great spinners like Laker and Lock. Poor Tony Lock would turn in his grave if he saw Ashley Giles bowling for England today.

But some things have improved. I remember, in the fifties, having a Sussex committee of 36 – 36 amateurs! One year they gave John Langridge and Harry Parks, two great Sussex servants, a joint benefit.

TED JAMES (1948–60)

Born: Newton Longville, Buckinghamshire, 7 August 1924

Ted James, the man who didn't recognise Len Hutton while the great batsman scored an unbeaten 176 off his bowling, was, until the arrival of Ian Thomson, the mainstay of the Sussex attack in the early fifties.

A village green cricketer and the village baker in rural Buckinghamshire, he became one of the stalwarts of postwar county cricket and in 1955 took 111 Championship wickets at 21.31.

In that year he took nine Yorkshire wickets for 60 runs at Hove with his medium-pace leg-cutters, although his figures of 7–12 against Hampshire four years earlier are, perhaps, even more memorable.

Although he batted near the bottom, his technique was good enough to open the Sussex innings on occasions and he scored an unbeaten 63 against Nottinghamshire at Trent Bridge in 1950, the year he won his county cap.

Ted James, who had 12 seasons with the county after joining in 1948, was a typical, hardworking county pro. He took 50 wickets in all but three of those years. (*Sussex CCC*)

What a great thing, winning the Championship! And I was particularly pleased for James Kirtley, who I know very well because I also live in Eastbourne. I did pop along to Hove last season, along with many other senior citizens from the fifties.

It's a different Championship these days. We played 28 games in my time, when Surrey were very much the team to beat. The best team I played in was the one led, for one season, by David Sheppard. He led by example, a little like Chris Adams today, and was very tough.

I was an off-spinner when I came out of the Royal Air Force in 1948. That was when Sussex offered me a trial and then a contract. Then Jim Wood pulled a shoulder and the captain, Hugh Bartlett, chucked the ball to me and asked me to open. I hadn't even bowled medium-pace in the nets until then.

I remember, at the start of my career, playing against Yorkshire at Bramall Lane in Sheffield and taking four wickets with my spinners. Then this bloke came in and made 176 not out. 'Who's he?' I asked when we got back to the pavilion. There was laughter all round. Then someone told me that it was Len Hutton.

I still do some coaching at Eastbourne College. I've got two artificial hips now and that makes golf, which I loved, very difficult.

KEN SUTTLE (1949–71)

Born: London, 25 August 1928

He is white-whiskered now, but the eyes still dance with mischief and fun. Even in middle-age Ken Suttle was an eager, vital cricketer whose enthusiasm and consistency made him a most popular player for many years at Hove. One of the fittest of county players, he is still involved in the game, coaching and umpiring at Christ's Hospital School in Horsham.

A reliable left-handed batsman, either opening or in the middle order, he stands alongside such great players as Len Hutton, Denis Compton, Maurice Leyland and Viv Richards, having scored 1,000 runs in a season on 17 occasions. He was also a slow left-arm bowler and an outstanding outfielder.

Between August 1954 and July 1969 he played in 423 consecutive Championship matches. He was a natural ball player who played football for Chelsea 'when we got £9 a week, though Tommy Lawton got £11', before transferring to Brighton and Hove Albion. His football career ended with a spell as player-manager of Sussex League club Arundel. He finished his cricket career with 30,225 first-class runs. Among Sussex players only C.B. Fry, Jim Parks, and John and James Langridge made more. His best season was in 1962, when he scored 2,326 runs at an average of 39.42.

Ken Suttle scores runs off Australia's Richie Benaud in the 1961 tour match at Hove. Suttle made a remarkable 423 consecutive Championship appearances for Sussex between 1954 and 1969. *(Sussex CCC)*

I wasn't at Hove on the day we won it but I had attended that game, against Leicestershire, a little earlier, along with a number of other former players and we all knew they were going to do it. It was a great feeling.

I keep thinking how I would like to be young again and still playing, but I would miss the crowds. When I played in the fifties the spectators often had to get there by 9.30 in the morning for the big matches, or be locked out. The bank holiday Middlesex matches were sell-outs.

We also had a lot of fun. I remember talking to a very young Tony Greig when we were batting together against Yorkshire and I was looking up towards the sky because he was more than a foot taller than me. Then Fred Trueman came along and lifted me up and held me there for about half a minute, with Greigy and I nose to nose, until we had finished our conversation. You don't get so much of that these days.

We went close to the Championship in 1953 and then, at the end of the season, I was chosen to tour the West Indies under Len Hutton. It wasn't an easy England team to break into, with Sir Len and Watson followed by the likes of Compton, May, Graveney, Evans, Bailey, Laker, Lock, Trueman and Statham. There was a batting vacancy for the Bridgetown Test and I had been the top scorer in both innings in the warm-up game against Barbados with 96 and 62. But they ignored me and chose the manager, Charlie Palmer, who was an amateur, instead. That's what cricket was like then.

My biggest disappointment at Sussex was the way it all ended in 1971. I scored three centuries in the middle of the summer and the cricket chairman, Eddie Harrison, told me: 'You're embarrassing us, Ken, because we're not offering you a new contract next year.'

I really wanted to play in 1972 because Jim Parks and I had a joint testimonial that year. Then, when Essex offered me a two-year contract, Sussex threatened to cancel my testimonial. That wouldn't happen today either. The club is much friendlier and better run these days.'

IAN THOMSON (1952–72)

Born: Walsall, Staffordshire, 23 January 1929

Ian Thomson, 75 in 2004, describes himself as 'the oldest supply teacher in the country'. He turned to teaching after an unhappy spell in the car trade in London. Thomson played his final match for Sussex in 1972, at the age of 43, after coming out of retirement to help out in a few John Player League matches in the previous season. He was the finest bowler of medium-pace produced by Sussex since Maurice Tate. He first played for the club in 1952 and the following season topped the county's bowling averages with 101 wickets at 20.06 each. He took 1,597 wickets in his first-class career at an average of 20.57 and collected 100 in a season on a dozen occasions, just two fewer than Tate.

After an ugly-duckling approach to the wicket, he bowled in-dippers and leg-cutters – so Alec Bedser was clearly a big influence – and he used his cutters on wet pitches. But such fine medium-pacers as Tom Cartwright and Derek Shackleton were among his contemporaries and as a result he played just five Test matches.

His best performance in Championship cricket came at Worthing in 1964 when he took all ten Warwickshire wickets in the first innings and followed up with five in the second for match figures of 15–75. Talking about the 2003 triumph, he said:

I was in the garden when I heard the news. I was absolutely delighted. My only disappointment is that so many of the players, about seven or eight, don't come from Sussex. There are so many overseas and EU players around now that the county game has become more like football. Then there are the players, including the captain, who came from another county. I couldn't imagine Maurice Tate leaving Sussex and going off to play for someone else. Having said that it was a magnificent effort. And I do know that if we had had Mushtaq Ahmed in 1953 we would have won the title.

We had a good side that year and were runners-up. We had to beat Surrey at Hove near the end of the season to have a good chance of winning but could only draw. We still did well to get that close. It was early on in Surrey's great run of titles and they had bowlers like Alec Bedser, Peter Loader, Jim Laker and Tony Lock.

Our bowling was made up of Ted James, Jim Wood, Robin Marlar, Alan Oakman and myself, so I suppose we did well to get that close. David Sheppard was an excellent captain and apart from young players like Jim

Jim Parks (left) and Ian Thomson at Hove before the start of the 1962 season. Thomson took more then 1,500 wickets for the county between 1952 and 1972, including all ten against Warwickshire at Worthing in 1964. *(Sussex CCC)*

Parks, Kenny Suttle and myself we had plenty of experienced players like John and James Langridge and Charles Oakes. We went down the pan after '53. Robin [Marlar] was never such an effective bowler once he became captain.

My Sussex highlight as a player was winning the Gillette Cup in 1964. We beat Warwickshire in the final and I was Man of the Match after picking up four wickets. Mike Smith was the Warwickshire captain and he was chosen to skipper England in South Africa that winter. He picked me for the trip because of how I'd bowled against Warwickshire.

DAVID SHEPPARD (1947–62)

Born: Reigate, Surrey, 6 March 1929

Cricket was just one part of this remarkable man's career. The first ordained priest to play Test cricket, he was an outstanding county captain for all too brief a period, and also led his country before becoming Bishop of Liverpool and a member of the House of Lords. For an outstanding cricketer Sheppard was not among the most naturally gifted of players. But a powerful will was enough to make the most of his considerable talent and he played many great innings, for both Sussex and England.

He was a tall right-hander and particularly powerful on the off-side. He was also an exceptional close fielder and among the most inspirational of captains. He announced himself early, first as a schoolboy at Sherborne and then at Cambridge University. He showed his remarkable powers of concentration by sharing first-wicket partnerships with John Dewes of 343 against the West Indies at Fenner's and 349 against Sussex at Hove in 1950. After another successful season with Cambridge in 1951 he was appointed captain the following summer. In 1952 he led the national averages with 2,262 runs at an average of 62.62, including a career-best 239 not out at Worcester.

He was appointed Sussex captain the following year and the players of that era are generally agreed that he was the finest they ever played under. He lifted the side from 13th the previous year to second place, and at one time it seemed possible that they would displace the mighty Surrey as Champions.

By now he was already an England player. He won his first Test cap against the West Indies in 1950, toured Australia in 1950/1, scored 119 against India in 1952 and captained the side, in Len Hutton's absence, against Pakistan in 1954. At Old Trafford in 1956, a match best remembered for Jim Laker's heroics, he scored a memorable 113. His appearances for both county and country became fewer, but he toured Australia again in 1962/3, scoring 113 at

Melbourne. But after he dropped one or two catches in the slips, Fred Trueman remarked: 'It's a pity Reverend don't put his hands together more often in t'field.'

I was delighted to follow their fortunes every day in 2003. What was important to me was that this was not only a highly successful Sussex side but also one that enjoyed their game.

I talked to Chris Adams and he told me how much fun the experience had been. I think it's great that the first-class cricketers of today can play to win and still have a lot of fun along the way. I have sent them my congratulations. Winning the Championship was a great achievement.

We were top of the table in July back in 1953. Our batting was strong. We had five players who scored over 1,000 runs, including John Langridge, who played for the club before I was born. But we had a lot of drawn matches in August. We had some good bowlers but not a real fast bowler who could roll over the tail after we had made our usual inroads.

ALAN OAKMAN (1947–68)

Born: Hastings, 20 April 1930

Outside Sussex, Alan Oakman is best remembered as the tall, gangling figure in Jim Laker's leg-trap, grasping a succession of catches to help the bowler take 19 wickets in the Old Trafford Test of 1956.

Sussex members nurture more substantial memories. He first played for the club in 1947 and retired 21 years later. He was a better-than-average batsman, best remembered for his immense reach and fluent driving, but he was also an outstanding close fielder and, until the arrival of Robin Marlar, the leading off-spinner in the side. His best season with the bat was 1961, when he scored 2,307 runs and made his highest score of 229 not out against Nottinghamshire at Worksop. He never took 100 first-class wickets but went close in 1954 with 99 at 20.97. He played two Tests.

He became an umpire and after a spell as head coach with Warwickshire he joined the Edgbaston club's administrative side, where he still works part-time.

I thought we did well in '53 to come second to Surrey and finish ahead of a good Yorkshire side, but this beats everything. No longer can people say that Sussex did well in the Gillette Cup but they never managed to win the Championship. I still love my trips to Hove and got there last season.

I was a batsman, mostly, but I bowled a lot early in my career and one of the most memorable moments in my time with Sussex was when I turned one of my off-breaks through the gate to bowl the great Denis Compton in

Alan Oakman plays another typically stylish stroke. Oakman scored more then 20,000 runs in a Sussex career spanning 21 years. His under-rated off-breaks also brought him more than 700 wickets for the county. *(Sussex CCC)*

front of a packed bank holiday crowd. But not everyone shared my joy. The umpire groaned, 'Oh, Denis.' And Charlie Oakes walked up to me and said, 'You prat – I love watching him bat.' But that wicket won me a lot of respect in the Army when I did my National Service.

The best captain in my time was Lord Sheppard. The Lord was our Sheppard, you might say. But he hadn't done the job for long when he saw the light and joined the Church.

At the end of that wonderful '53 season David wrote me a personal letter thanking me for everything I'd done. That's most unusual.

In my time it was virtually all Championship cricket. We'd play 28 games and, apart from Oxford and Cambridge and the touring sides, that was it, with the odd benefit game at the weekend. We didn't have all the one-day competitions and the hectic fielding which, I think, knocks about five years off today's players.

We played hard but we enjoyed it and tried to convey that enjoyment to the crowd. There were none of today's clenched fists. I played in the Gillette Cup but retired the year before the Sunday League arrived. One of my last matches for Sussex was against Warwickshire. I didn't know I'd be moving to Edgbaston as head coach the following season.

ROBIN MARLAR (1951–68)

Born: Eastbourne, 2 January 1931

An intelligent and singular man, Robin Marlar's independence of thought was evident on the cricket field and, much later, in the pages of *The Sunday Times*, where his views – whether you agreed with them or not – were required reading.

He first played for Sussex in 1951, when he was still at Cambridge University. The following year he took 108 wickets. Throughout the fifties he was one of the best off-spinners in the country. He was unfortunate to play at a time when England had a number of quality off-break bowlers, most notably Jim Laker.

His first full season with Sussex was in 1954, when he played under Hubert Doggart. When Doggart returned to teaching, Marlar was appointed captain for the 1955 season and led the county to fourth position in the Championship. He kept the job until the end of the 1959 season, when he handed over to Ted Dexter. He was not highly regarded as a batsman, although he did score 64 against the 1956 Australians, including five sixes and six fours. Even more memorably, when he was once asked to bat as nightwatchman he was out, stumped, second ball for six!

Robin Marlar led Sussex to fourth place in his first year as captain in 1955. He became club chairman in 1997 after the revolution led by Tony Pigott overthrew the old regime at Hove. *(Sussex CCC)*

More recently, as the county chairman for a year after the revolution of 1997, he showed his maverick qualities by making Tony Pigott his chief executive. Many considered it a bizarre appointment, but Pigott, in turn, was the man who brought Chris Adams to the club and appointed Peter Moores as coach.

When they asked me how I felt [about winning the 2003 Championship] I referred them to Lewis Carroll, because he said it all. "Twas brillig' and as for Thursday and Friday, when the Jabberwock, the demon who stood between Sussex and victory, had been slain, 'Oh frabjous day! Callooh! Callay! We chortled in our joy.' We were champions at long, long last.

JIM PARKS (1949–72)

Born: Haywards Heath, 21 October 1931

Jim Parks might represent the epitome of a Sussex cricketer. The most illustrious member of a famous family, his berry-brown face was regularly creased with a smile and there were smiling strokes to match, most memorably his square and cover drives. He appeared to enjoy his cricket and he conveyed that sense of fun to the crowd. As Alan Ross observed, he may not have hit the ball as hard as Ted Dexter but 'he made the game look easier and he scored just as fast.'

A brilliant strokemaker and fielder, he played for England as a batsman, in 1954, before making a second career for himself as the country's premier wicketkeeper-batsman in the sixties. He first played for Sussex in 1949 and did not keep wicket until 1958 when the regular 'keeper, Rupert Webb, was injured. He made the position his own with both Sussex and England, although, in the latter case, Middlesex's John Murray occasionally displaced him and Kent's Alan Knott ultimately succeeded him.

He was rarely seen at his best as a batsman in his 46 Tests but, as a late addition to the tour party, he scored a match-saving 101 not out in Port of Spain in 1960. He captained Sussex in 1967 and 1968. He is now the Sussex president.

I don't agree with those who say that the Championship means less because we played only half the teams. We played the teams in the better half, and we played them twice. The title was thoroughly deserved and what really pleased me is that we played well as a team, just as we did when we went close 51 years ago, and that we have enough good players here to challenge for trophies for the next few years.

It was good timing for me. Not only am I serving as club president but it is 80 years ago that a Parks, my Dad, first played for Sussex. The win took me back to the season 50 years before, when we went so close and actually beat Surrey, the champions that year, before drawing with them at Hove. It was very much David Sheppard's year. He was the best skipper I ever played under and I was fortunate to play my first Test under his captaincy, too, against Pakistan in 1954.

My career with Sussex ended, rather sadly, at the end of the 1972 season. I was working for Whitbread's at the time and they had been very supportive of my cricket. I agreed with them that I would play for one more year before giving up cricket to concentrate on the other job. I approached the county, who were dealing with players' contracts at the time, only to be told that I would be offered appearance money, if fit, in 1973. I felt insulted by this because I had never broken down in 24 years with the club. I had scored over 1,000 runs in '72 and averaged over 40 in the Championship.

I signed for Somerset, where I had a most enjoyable end to my career. I told Sussex that they were losing two players for the price of one because my son Bobby, who went on to play for Hampshire, was making a name for himself at the time.

But I'm delighted to say that I never fell out with Sussex – just Eddie Harrison who was chairman of the cricket committee – and I was delighted to return as the club's marketing manager.

DON BATES (1950–71)

Born: Hove, 10 May 1933

With his grey hair and glasses, there was a professorial aspect to Don Bates at the end of his career, which his probing and thoughtful bowling did nothing to dispel. His career, spread over more than 20 years, was a long one for a medium-fast bowler. He joined the staff in 1949, first played in 1950 but did not win his cap until 1957, when he took 82 wickets. He was at his best in the late fifties and early sixties and in 1961 he took 113 wickets at 22.65.

A pupil of Jim Langridge's wise coaching, he pitched the ball up to allow it to swing and, when he hit the seam, often achieved surprising bounce for a bowler of such unremarkable height and pace. He was a consistent performer in the county's one-day successes in the sixties. He was also a professional footballer, playing right-half in the Brighton side that won promotion to the Second Division in 1957/8. He lives in the Brighton area and is a regular spectator at Eaton Road.

I was there when the Championship was won and to celebrate a team that did something we were never able to achieve. They might have struggled without Mushtaq, who is the main reason why they won it, but you have to be consistent to win the Championship and that's what they were. James Kirtley was a big factor too.

Don Bates was a true sporting all-rounder. Born a mile from the County Ground, he played football for Brighton and Hove Albion and took more than 900 wickets for the county. He is pictured just after joining the staff in 1950. *(Sussex CCC)*

We went close in 1953, but to be honest it was an ordinary side which David Sheppard, a terrific captain, made the absolute most of. He was a truly inspiring leader.

All we won in my time was the Gillette Cup in 1963 and 1964, the first two years of the competition. Ted Dexter, our captain then, worked out the tactics before anyone else, which basically was to operate with fielders pushed back on the boundary to save runs.

The biggest regret of my career was going to Germany to do my National Service in the RAF between 1951 and 1953. I envied Jim Parks and Alan Oakman, who did their National Service in England and whose cricket was not disrupted in the same way. In Germany, when I did play, I usually bowled leg-spin instead of my usual medium-fast. It was a crucial period of my development and when I returned to Sussex my action was no longer a natural thing. I suffered a lot of injuries and there was some back trouble in particular.

TED DEXTER (1957–72)

Born: Milan, Italy, 15 May 1935

He flew private planes, rode motor-bikes, played scratch golf, followed the horses and stood (unsuccessfully) for Parliament. It is a pity that Ted Dexter, or Lord Edward, then Lord Ted, as he became known, didn't devote more time to cricket, because he was one of the great draw-cards of the 1960s and, with the exception of Peter May, possibly the finest batsman produced by England since the war

He certainly played enough to show what an exceptional cricketer he was before his retirement in 1965, when he was at his peak but suffered a broken leg. When he was called out of retirement to play for England against Australia in 1968 he decided to have a net with Sussex and in his first innings for three years hit 203 against Kent, scoring his second hundred in 103 minutes. He was also a useful medium-pace bowler.

Although his career was relatively short, he scored 4,502 runs from his 62 Tests at 47.89 and Garry Sobers had no hesitation in calling him a great player, 'because he always looked to dominate the bowling and never looked in any trouble'.

He hit the ball extremely hard, with driving his special glory. He first played for Sussex in 1957 though he did not play a full season until 1959. He was made captain the following summer, a post he held for five years. At Sussex, he is best remembered for leading the county to victory in both of the first two Gillette Cup competitions, county cricket's first taste of the one-day game, in 1963 and 1964. He ran his own PR company, a strange choice for an essentially shy man, but was not lost to cricket. He became chairman of England selectors and then president of the MCC.

I'm delighted to say that I managed to get to Hove [during the 2003] season and see for myself how well they were playing. We had one of our old boys' reunions during the Middlesex match and they played fantastically well, digging themselves out of a big hole to eventually win the game.

Ted Dexter captained both Sussex and England. The county finished fourth on two occasions in the Championship, but excelled in the early years of one-day cricket under his leadership. He later became chairman of England's selectors. *(Sussex CCC)*

I was lucky enough to win the Gillette Cup a couple of times with Sussex in the sixties and when it happened I said, 'At long last Sussex has won something.' But the ultimate goal is still the Championship.

I think they've got a good all-round side and someone always manages to chip in when the big names fail. But little Mushy has made a huge difference.

LES LENHAM (1956–70)

Born: Lancing, 24 May 1936

A studious opening batsman, Les Lenham had the mind-set that would help him become one of the country's outstanding coaches in later life. Early on, it seemed that he might become an outstanding player. He never quite achieved that, but in the late fifties and early sixties he was a dependable performer, and in 1961 he scored 2,016 runs, including a hundred before lunch in the Middlesex match at Hove. He scored 1,334 runs in both the following two seasons and on the second occasion this included an unbeaten 191 against Warwickshire, his highest score.

On his retirement he became the county's coach before becoming the National Cricket Association's chief regional coach in 1974. He still works with the players, assisting the coaching staff in a consultative capacity.

I first became involved with Sussex cricket in 1952, although I had to wait a few years before I made my debut because of National Service. So by the end of last season [2003] I had completed an association with the club of 52 years. That's why I was celebrating on the players' balcony when the Championship was finally won.

My favourite memories were batting throughout an innings against Surrey's Laker, Lock, Bedser and Loader, and also of scoring an unbeaten 20 out of an all-out total of 40. And of course there were the Gillette Cup wins.

The biggest difference from my day is the fielding, particularly the outfielding. If I got a green mark on my flannels I thought: 'Oh dear, that will cost me two-and-six in the cleaners.' That's not quite the attitude today. And throwing from the boundary is so much better because many counties, like Sussex, have employed a throwing coach, in our case one with a baseball background. But I'm not sure the close fielding is as good. I played in the era of uncovered wickets, when finger-spinners were far more prominent, and there were such outstanding close catchers as Peter Walker and Tony Lock.

I don't like the modern trend of playing with the bat behind the pad and pretending to the umpire that a shot is being played. It's something I discourage when I work with the batsmen. And I do find some of the seam bowling ordinary these days. Jack Bannister used to say that Tom Cartwright bowled at the leg side of the off-stump – that's how accurate he was. The bowler's aim was to restrict the batsman to two strokes, the forward defensive and the drive, and the drives would usually be cut off. And if you couldn't bowl line and length you were out the door.

But there are more pressures on today's players. When I played, the season was over by the end of May if you were out of the running for the Championship, and if you finished tenth that was okay. Today there is greater pressure, and in many more competitions. The club, the media and the sponsors all expect success.

JOHN SNOW (1961–77)

Born: Peopleton, Worcestershire, 13 October 1941

Even lolling in the outfield, with arms akimbo and a poet's nose thrown high as if to scent a passing sonnet, there was something about John Snow. The smooth menace of his fast bowling made him England's finest since Fred

John Snow feels the cold at a pre-season press day in the late 1960s. Snow was an enigmatic character, but he was one of the finest English postwar bowlers. These days he serves on Sussex's committee. *(Sussex CCC)*

Trueman and Brian Statham, and he was also the best produced by Sussex, if Maurice Tate, like Ian Thomson, is counted as medium pace.

He had a straight and simple approach to the wicket and bowled on the run, without the classical side-on delivery. He was capable of genuine pace, a nasty, skiddy bouncer and he seamed the ball all over the place. He generally slanted the ball into the batsman before moving it away off the pitch. There could also be an aggression, even a meanness, about his bowling. By 1970, the time of his Ashes-winning tour of Australia, he was the world's champion fast bowler, though Dennis Lillee and a number of West Indians would soon challenge his supremacy.

This vicar's son first came to the attention of Sussex as a batsman. But by the early sixties he was established in the side as one of the best fast-bowling prospects in the country. He first played for England in 1965, was outstanding in the West Indies in 1967/8 and reached his peak, which he held for a couple of years, with the competitive series against the Rest of the World in 1970. He last played for England in 1976.

His relationship with Sussex was not always the easiest and in the latter half of his career most of his best performances were reserved for England. In 1971 the county even dropped him for a lack of effort. He left Sussex in 1977, played a few Sunday League matches for Warwickshire in 1980 and then went into the travel business and is now vice-chairman of the club.

> My biggest disappointment about Sussex winning the Championship, and it's difficult to think of one, is the fact that I wasn't there to celebrate it. I was driving through France on a holiday which had been delayed on a number of occasions, but which simply couldn't be delayed any longer. So I missed out on all the celebrations, which were fully deserved.
>
> As a club I think we have a history of under-performing, so it was great to win this time, particularly as we should have won in 1981 when we had a very good attack.
>
> In my time we never got that close to winning it. Beating the West Indies stands out, and winning those Gillette Cups under Ted [Dexter]. The committees were very badly organised in those days.

GEOFF ARNOLD (1978–82)

Born: Earlsfield, Surrey, 9 September 1944

Geoff Arnold was known to his teammates as ''Orse' because his initials are G.G., although the sobriquet could just as easily have been a reference to his work-rate when conditions were in his favour.

When he played for England, between 1967 and 1975, he was overshadowed first by John Snow and then by Bob Willis. But for a long time he was the most

Geoff Arnold made his mark as a bowler, but he could play a few shots as well. Here he takes on the Kent attack at Hove in 1980. *(Sussex CCC)*

skilful fast-medium bowler in the country. He employed swing and cut to take 1,130 first-class wickets, though he was usually less effective overseas.

He was, essentially, a Surrey player, first appearing for that county in 1963 and winning his cap four years later, when he made his debut for England. He moved to Sussex in 1978 and the pitches at Hove encouraged his style, allowing him to make a successful conclusion to his career. But he was more than just a highly skilled bowler. His tactical awareness was often employed by the captain, John Barclay, and he organised the side's training sessions throughout their near-miss year in 1981. He bowled exceptionally well against Surrey in the Benson and Hedges Cup that year, greatly impressing the umpire, the infamous Shakoor Rana, who halfway through the spell remarked: 'It is a great honour for me to stand here while John Snow is bowling so well.'

Arnold, who has established a reputation as one of the shrewdest of bowling coaches, often working with the England team, returned to his true home – The Oval – for the 2004 season.

Surrey was my main county. I only played for Sussex for a few seasons but they were very memorable. We won the Gillette Cup in 1978, my first season, and the Sunday League in 1982, my last, before a foot injury forced me to finish. And in 1981 we should have won the Championship.

We were the best side that year, when the fast bowling was led by Imran Khan and Garth le Roux, with plenty of seamers to back them up. In the end Notts won it, but were lucky to do so. Imran had Mike Bore lbw when we played them at Trent Bridge, but the umpire didn't give it and it proved to be a costly decision because they clung on for a draw.

We were a very good one-day side then, packed with all-rounders, and we had a captain in John Barclay who seemed to bring the best out of everyone.

They deserved this Championship, if only because they should have won it 22 years earlier.

MIKE BUSS (1961–78)

Born: Brightling, 24 January 1944

The younger brother of opening bowler Tony Buss, Michael's rather modest career figures betray him. As an all-rounder he was capable of match-winning performances, particularly in one-day cricket, with his dashing, left-handed batting at the top of the order and his parsimonious medium-pace.

He was called up for the England under-25 tour of Pakistan in 1966/7, though his performances were a disappointment. He was never close to the England Test team but in the modern era his one-day talents would have been closely inspected by the selectors.

He was originally a left-arm spinner but moved up a gear in 1967. In 1971 he struck 121 against Nottinghamshire at Worksop, including 15 fours and three sixes, and put on 165 with Ted Dexter at eight runs an over. He was at his best in the Gillette Cup and in the early days of the John Player League. After he left the game he ran a post office, like his brother. Now retired, he concentrates on golf, shooting and snooker.

I was there to see the Championship won and it was fantastic. I was up there for a couple of days. Nothing better. We always thought we could win it when I played but in truth we never got close. By the time we did nearly get there, in 1981, I was long retired.

I enjoyed my cricket. A century against India, including Bishen Bedi, and an all-round performance against Gloucestershire in the Gillette Cup spring to mind. My cricket was really better suited to the one-day game than the Championship.

But I'm not sure whether I'd enjoy it now. I think it's much harder today with all the one-day cricket, which hadn't even started when I began my career.

The fielding is so much superior these days. And the batsmen are much better at chasing down scores. They can pace it better than we did. But I don't think they bowl any better. They certainly don't bowl a length as well as they did in my day.

No one seems able to bowl a maiden over. We don't seem to have any pace bowlers. [England's] Steve Harmison hardly ever seems fit, and when he is he doesn't seem to want to bowl. It's a disappointment because, at the England level, they get all this time off. But it's a very different game, what with fielding restrictions and being wided for bowling two inches outside the off-stump.

TONY GREIG (1967–78)

Born: Queenstown, South Africa, 6 October 1946

Tony Greig, the former Sussex and England captain, was one of the biggest personalities, as well one of the biggest players, in world cricket in the 1970s.

He played one match for Sussex in 1966 but announced himself properly the following year when, against Lancashire's Brian Statham, Ken Higgs and Peter Lever, all England bowlers, he hit 156. He won his county cap in 1967, scoring 1,193 Championship runs and taking 63 wickets. He was tall, fair, powerful and personable, and it was clear that a cricketer of substance had arrived. He also had confidence and a certain presence, which would help him in his captaincy and in his career as a TV broadcaster beyond that.

The son of a Scottish father – he is distantly related to the former Rangers and Scotland footballer John Greig – and a South African mother, he had been recommended to Sussex by Richard Langridge who, like many Sussex cricketers before and since, was spending time in the Republic.

Greig hit the ball powerfully, especially when driving, and bowled medium-pace, achieving swing and bounce. He started his Test career against Australia in 1972. By the time it finished, prematurely, he had scored 3,599 runs at 40.43 and taken 141 wickets at 32.20.

These are impressive figures, certainly better than those for Sussex, proving that he had the character to rise to the challenge. Two of the best of his eight Test hundreds were scored under intense pressure – his 110 in Brisbane against the fury of Lillee and Thomson in 1974/5 and his 103 against India in 1976/7, when he had a high temperature.

He was an outstanding captain of England in 14 Tests, before his involvement with Kerry Packer in the setting up of World Series Cricket brought it to an end in 1977. He was a less successful Sussex captain and left the county in 1978.

If the cap fits. Tony Greig packs his bags ahead of England's tour of the West Indies in 1974. The all-rounder spent a decade at Hove and captained Sussex between 1973 and 1977. *(Sussex CCC)*

It was pretty late in Australia when the news [about the 2003 Championship win] came through. I was absolutely delighted. My first instinct was that I wanted to be there to celebrate, but it was a bit too far away. I will be over in England in late summer 2004, though, for the Champions Trophy, and will make sure I pop down to Hove.

It's a disappointment for me that we never won anything in my time at Sussex. We got to the Gillette Cup final shortly after I started, but lost it and then lost it again when we returned to Lord's a couple of years later.

I was captain by the time we made it to Lord's yet again, in 1973, but we lost then too. And by the time we won the trophy in 1978, I'd already left.

I know Tony Pigott is no longer at the club but in my view a lot of the credit should go to him. After all, he's the bloke who appointed the captain and the coach.

IMRAN KHAN (1977–88)

Born: Lahore, Pakistan, 25 November 1952

When he was a skinny youngster at Worcester in 1971 he was told by teammate and opening batsman Glenn Turner that he was wasting his time pitching the ball short, because he had the wrong build to be a fast bowler. But Imran Khan became one of the fastest and most terrifying of them all. More than that, in a period of great all-rounders, he was the champion, capable of winning matches with bat or ball. He was the finest of all Pakistani all-rounders and, along with Maurice Tate, the greatest to represent Sussex, for whom he first played in 1977.

He had been an outstanding university cricketer at Oxford and then moved to Worcestershire. But he found life there a little quiet and was attracted to Sussex because of its proximity to London. He was at his peak when, in 1981, he almost inspired Sussex to the Championship, opening the bowling with Garth le Roux, and again in 1982, when he captained Pakistan on their tour of England. He did help Sussex win the Gillette Cup in 1978 and the NatWest Trophy eight years later, when he scored 50 not out.

He was such an outstanding player that his atrocious time-keeping was tolerated. He last played for Sussex in 1988 when he appeared in just four Championship matches, though he was still a key member of the one-day side. But he continued to play for Pakistan and captained them to victory in the 1992 World Cup.

When I played for Sussex the title was very elusive, so I was delighted with the news. The world of politics is keeping me very busy but I do talk to John Barclay, our great captain in 1981, from time to time.

That was my happiest year with the club. John was made captain that season and he was the perfect man for the job. He was very positive, always looking for the win. And he had a great relationship with the players. He could always take a joke, even from the junior players.

I have very happy memories of my years with Sussex, even though my career there got off to a disappointing start. My first full season at Hove was in 1978 and that was the year Arnold Long was made captain. He was a very nice man but not a good captain because he was too negative. He didn't want to take risks because not losing seemed more important then trying to win.

There was other bad news. Sussex had sacked John Snow in 1977, the year I joined the club. It was very disappointing because I had looked forward to bowling with such a great fast bowler who passed on lots of helpful tips to me.

John was at his peak when I first toured England as a very young member of the Pakistan team in 1971 and the following year I enjoyed his great battle with Dennis Lillee in the Ashes series. Men like these made me want to bowl fast. I got to know John more during World Series Cricket.

The other blow at the start of my Sussex career was when, in 1978, Tony Greig left the club. I liked his approach to the game and he was one of the reasons I joined the club in the first place. But I still had many, many happy days at Hove. I will always remember Ian Gould teaching me Cockney.

IAN GOULD (1981–90)

Born: Slough, Berkshire, 19 August 1957

His nickname, 'Gunner', was a reference to his footballing allegiances, for he supports Arsenal when he's not following the horses, but it might also have referred to his quick-fire Cockney wit, which is a feature of his umpiring today.

Ian Gould was, in every sense, at the centre of the glorious Championship charge of 1981. He was an agile wicketkeeper, an aggressive left-handed batsman, either opening or in the late middle-order, and the possessor of a rare cricketing nous which the captain, John Barclay, accessed on a regular basis.

Gould started his career with Middlesex, for whom he played between 1975 and 1980. When that county signed Paul Downton, and when Sussex lost Arnold Long at the end of the 1980 season, Gould, who wanted to remain in the south, moved to Hove. He played in the side that picked up one-day trophies in 1982 and 1986. He was made vice-captain in 1985 and captain in 1987 before he returned to Lord's to lead Middlesex second XI in 1991. He was a good enough cricketer to play for England in 18 one-day internationals and was a central figure in their 1983 World Cup campaign.

To be perfectly honest I thought they [Sussex] could be in danger of relegation [in the 2003 County Championship]. I went through their side at the start of the season and thought they could struggle to stay up because they might have difficulty bowling out sides on flat wickets. I was delighted to be proved wrong. It really was a great effort. I was umpiring elsewhere at the time and felt a bit emotional when the news came through.

Mushy proved to be a great signing. Speaking as an umpire, he certainly keeps you on your toes. But he's always laughing and joking and so different to how he was at the end of his Somerset career.

I was umpiring at Edgbaston when Sussex played badly and got beat by Warwickshire. The captain and coach were in a desperate state and I thought there might be some blood-letting afterwards, and I gather there was. That's the great thing about Adams and Moores. They've created a great dressing room. It reminds me of the one we had at Middlesex, where we weren't afraid to nail each other when things needed saying.

Ian Gould in action in 1983. 'Gunner' played for nine years at Hove and is a first-class umpire these days. *(Sussex CCC)*

In 1981 we were led by a great man, John Barclay. We were a team of individuals and it was mayhem sometimes in that dressing room. It might have gone tits-up early on but for 'Trout', who pulled us all together so well.

We were the best side in the country that year and would have won the title if we had beaten Notts, which we would have done if Mike Bore had been given out lbw to Imran. It was knocking the lot out. If I'd given that not out decision I would have retired on the spot.

My greatest memory of that season was beating Derbyshire at Eastbourne. The match was going nowhere when Imran suddenly produced one of the most inspired spells of bowling I've ever seen, swinging a very old ball all over the place. He took four wickets in five balls as Derbyshire lost their last five wickets for next to nothing. We still had to score 234 in two and a half hours, which is knocking along a bit, but we got there with five balls to spare thanks to a brilliant century by Immy. Great days.

4

LEADING FROM THE FRONT

Chris Adams' Story

S
ir Edmund Hillary was a duffer when it came to encores, and as Chris Adams gazed out over the County Ground in bleak midwinter he seemed to have a certain empathy with the famous explorer and mountaineer. 'I really do feel a bit like the bloke who climbed Everest and wasn't too sure what to do next,' he said, giving his unshaven chin a rueful rub.

It took six years for Peter Moores and myself to reach the summit. Now we have to find another one. I keep asking myself what now? I suppose we should say we'll win it again, and a few one-day trophies as well. But breaking it down and planning it can be difficult after everything we've achieved. I suppose we should all have a sense of euphoria after what we have done. But everyone is too busy thinking about next year and how we can follow it.

At the beginning of December 2003 it was confirmed that Sussex would open the defence of their title against Surrey at The Oval, followed by a home fixture against Lancashire. That helped to concentrate minds around Eaton Road.

Adams might not have Brearley's 'degree in people', as Rodney Hogg had it, or Ray Illingworth's prodigious tactical acumen, but he is a strong, natural leader; and he is at his best leading by bold example.

The Middlesex captain, Andrew Strauss, one of many vanquished opponents last season, said:

Chris is one of the most competitive captains on the circuit. You know you're in a fight from the moment you toss up. In a sense he captains like he bats. He's very positive, aggressive and a bit 'in your face'. He was blessed with a good team, the best last season, when they deserved their title. Tactically, there's not much out of the ordinary but he's pretty sound and he soon recognised that in Mushtaq he had a terrific bowler who had to bowl a lot of overs to be at his most effective.

Adams himself said:

My first coach at Derbyshire told me that it takes seven years to make a batsman and, coming into my seventh year as skipper of Sussex, I think the same can be said about this job. The whole basis of my captaincy revolves around me leading from the front. When the chips are down I'll be the first out there, leading the way.

It is an irony, therefore, that Adams should enjoy his greatest success as a captain at a time when his own cricket was ravaged by poor form and self-doubt. For more than half the 2003 season his batting was in disarray and his confidence in pieces.

By the middle of July I was in a proper state. Mentally, I don't think I could have been in a worse situation. I had all sorts of problems with my batting. Whether it was my feet, my hands or my head, I just didn't know where to put them. For the first time since I could remember I was finding batting difficult.

I felt a bit like the golfer whose swing has fallen apart, who can't hit the ball straight but who, at the same time, is in denial because he used to hit the ball perfectly straight. You try every variation you can think of but after a while the confidence saps away. My batting had lost all its rhythm.

Then we played Leicestershire at Grace Road. I made a duck and 16. And a decision. I decided that the only way out of my slump was to go into the nets and hit a thousand balls every day. That's exactly what I did. And in the process I injured myself and had to pull out of the one-day side suffering from tennis elbow. But it worked. It got me out of my malaise. I stopped questioning where I was technically right and wrong, and decided to just hit balls and more balls until I felt right. And to come out of it and score a hundred against Surrey and two in the same match against Lancashire almost gave me more satisfaction than if I'd scored 1,500 runs in the season. I had shown myself that I still had that fight and desire.

And I've got to say that throughout these problems the lads were great. They made it clear that they were happy with my leadership and that they would score the runs until my form returned.

In the still reflection of a chill, December morning, Adams realised that his preparation for the season had not been rigorous enough: 'If I'm honest I would have to say that I didn't do enough work, in pre-season or in early season. But it was my benefit year. And we had just moved house. I had a lot of stuff going through my mind.'

Adams recovered his form so successfully that he scored 966 runs in the Championship at 35.77, with four centuries. He finished a modest sixth in the county's batting averages, but that disguised the essence of his contribution: that he scored his runs when they were desperately needed.

It was a feature of the Sussex season that they scored consistently well, providing a stage for the juggler from Sahiwal, Mushtaq Ahmed. But the consistency of Matt Prior, Tim Ambrose and Robin Martin-Jenkins in the middle-order was often preceded by the failure of the specialists. Tony Cottey held the top order together in Hove's spring and early summer sunshine, and Murray Goodwin found his best form as the whisper of autumn brought russet and gold to the campaign's final sets. Between these two periods, however, the batting often faltered before it was seized and held aloft by Adams. It was here that his character emerged; and it was here, in August and September, that Sussex evolved from being contenders to become champions.

There are all sorts of reasons why Sussex won the Championship. One very good one was that we were very rarely short of runs because everyone contributed at some stage. Look at Mark Davis's hundred against Middlesex,

Tucking in. James Kirtley, Tony Cottey, Chris Adams and Bas Zuiderent enjoy a snack at the pre-season photocall. *(Simon Dack/Brighton Argus)*

when he and Matt [Prior] dug us out of a hole. Mark had a very up and down season. He hadn't really established his authority on it. But that was his time, his turn. When he walked out that day we all just knew he was going to make big runs. But what do we do for an encore?

Adams asks the question again, shrugging cold shoulders inside his fleece before spooning a cappuccino's brown froth into his mouth. And then he reflects, as if analysis of past deeds will lend a clue to their reprise. Warwickshire at Edgbaston, Surrey at Hove, Lancashire at Hove and Old Trafford . . . these matches might feel as old as sepia stills now, but these were the fixtures that shaped a historic Championship.

It was the Warwickshire game in May, perhaps more than any other, that proved pivotal.

It happens everywhere. Instead of coming out with it you get little conversations between individuals within dressing rooms. It was happening there, at Edgbaston, with us. The beauty of what happened at Warwickshire is that we nailed it there and then and told each other that it had to stop.

We lost a match we might have saved, getting bowled out for 106 in our second innings, and it was clear that, with the talent on display, we were under-performing. It was there and then that we decided that if something needed saying we should come out and say it, because we were all grown men. And I'll always have more respect for the bloke who comes out and says what he's thinking, even if I don't agree with it, than the one who sits quietly in a corner keeping his real feelings private.

From here, we moved on. And I must say that we had a great leader in Mushy, whose whole philosophy is about speaking openly and everyone being honest with each other. He spoke at Edgbaston and it mirrored everything that we were thinking.

We've got some young players here but they're mature enough to say what they think, and that's the key to our success. The talent was always there. You don't get a contract unless you've got talent. But I think Peter and I created the right environment for people to play in. We have people living in reality here, instead of what Mooresy calls the 'land of bullshit'.

We had a landslide opinion at the end of the Warwickshire match that we weren't going to let ourselves down again, that we were going to bind together and that performances were what mattered most.

After that we played Zimbabwe. But in our next Championship game we had a good win over Notts at Horsham, with Mushy getting 12 wickets, and we were on our way.

Six weeks later, though, Adams came in for criticism from Sussex, as well as Surrey members, for his tactics against Surrey at Hove. The match was drawn, with Sussex taking one more point than Surrey. But the prevailing mood was that Sussex might have won had Adams been more positive. The feeling niggled that Adams, instead of seizing an opportunity, had cowed before Surrey's might and been over-cautious. He decided to come off for bad light when his side, at 69–2 in their second innings, led by 143 runs with 37 overs of the day still to be bowled. When Sussex resumed the following day, there was no declaration until they were 302–5 and all life had been wrung from the game.

Anyone expecting Adams to hold his hands up in a gesture of *mea culpa* is doomed to disappointment. He has no regrets to this day.

Tactically, I think I got it spot on last season, and I haven't always done so. When we came off for bad light against Surrey I heard that Alistair Brown went into the pressbox and said that we were scared. But I would have described our approach as being cautious.

My philosophy in that game – and I wasn't on my own because I'd canvassed the whole team – was that while Sussex could not have won the Championship on that day, we might have lost it. So instead of trying to force a win from a precarious situation we opted for caution and the chance, the following day, to bat Surrey out of the game.

People forget that for two days we had thrown everything at them. We had them on the rack several times. We really rattled them. But because they're such a great team, they clung on to the game. And if I had been [Surrey captain] Adam Hollioake on that third day I would have been thinking 'Hang on, we're going to win this match.'

They had Saqlain. And Jimmy Ormond, who was bowling well in gloomy conditions. It was the right decision and I stand by it. Look at all the fuss that has rightly been made over England winning the rugby World Cup. And then look at the tactics employed by Clive Woodward. There were times when it was right for England to run the ball wide and go for tries, and times when the forwards had to keep ball and go for possession and narrow victories. That was exactly the philosophy I had, that there was a right time to be bullish and play this aggressive, attacking cricket.

But when we played the champions at Hove, in the situation we were in, I didn't think it was the right time. From Surrey's reaction to that result, looking at the way they behaved, I began to believe that the Championship was on.

Adams was also criticised for saying, on several occasions, that Surrey were the title favourites. This was a consistent tactic to keep the pressure off his players. Surrey had won the title in three of the previous four seasons. It was only right, he felt, that the pressure should be on the team with all the stars, and not on a club that had been around for 164 years and never won the Championship. Inside the dressing room, however, it was different.

I was banging the drum and reminding everyone that the Championship was there to be won and that if anyone didn't believe it he shouldn't be there.

But I didn't really believe that we would win it until, with 12 minutes to spare, we got Warren Hegg out and beat Lancashire at Hove. I went back to the dressing room and thought right, we can only lose the title from here.

Leading from the front. Chris Adams hammers the ball through the covers against Essex. (Simon Dack/Brighton Argus)

We were all singing 'Sussex by the Sea' that night. Heggy heard us celebrating and turned round, probably making a mental note because we still had the match in Manchester to come.

To their credit, Lancashire came in with a late charge. The four days we spent at Old Trafford in September, when we just had to draw to win the title, were the most draining I have experienced in county cricket. It was an awful time. We knew we were that close, that we couldn't really lose it. We lost time to bad weather and kept saying to ourselves, 'That's another hour out of the way.' We were counting the clock down.

When we did get on Lancashire proved just what a class act they were and we lost by an innings. They had also told the Surrey lads that they were going to stuff us. But our attitude wasn't really right in that match.

It was right for the next game, the final match of the season, against Leicestershire. Sussex needed just six points for the title. It was the match that would see Mushtaq's 100th wicket of the season, Murray Goodwin's epic and undefeated 335, the greatest day in the club's history . . . and it ended with Christopher John Adams, his flannels sodden with champagne, leading the revelry from the dressing room balcony.

❖ ❖ ❖

Adams, one of the most destructive players in the game, was taught to bat by imagining he was rocking a teddy bear to sleep. The man who led Sussex to historic glory in 2003 is generous when asked to name those who inspired him. He mentions his parents, John and Lyn; his brother David, with whom he first played on a sloping back garden in Whitwell, Derbyshire; Mike Stone, who ran the Derbyshire Cricket Association team and persuaded him to turn his back on football and go to Repton; his old Derbyshire coach Phil Russell; and even his first county captain, Kim Barnett, with whom he had a such a well-documented falling-out. But pride of place goes to Benita White, a 67-year-old Chesterfield woman who ran the local Cricket Lovers' Society and who taught the eight-year-old 'Grizzly' how to play cricket. 'She's a fantastic lady and it was through her that this whole thing started,' said Adams as he prepared for the 2004 season. 'My father decided that my brother and I needed proper coaching and saw this advert in the local paper. Benita took us under our wing and said, 'Right, we're going to make cricketers of you.'

Benita, who journeyed to South Africa to see Adams make his Test debut five years ago, said:

If you visualise how you hold your bat, you've got your arms in a round, with your elbows stuck out, and when you're batting, the action that you do is rock your bat back and forward, as if you're rocking your teddy bear to sleep. Kids remember things like that. Like making the letter P or the number 9 with your arms and bat.

Benita – who also coached the young Ian Blackwell, so she knows a thing or two about smiting – has given up coaching but hopes to see her star pupils in action again this summer after a year of illness.

The funny thing is that of the two I thought David, Chris's brother, would do better because he was technically much more correct. But Chris, who I remember as a little stocky lad who had more power than those around him, had this incredible determination and worked and worked at his game all the time. I'll be down to see him again next summer, though I don't think he needs my help any more.

Adams was born in the mining village of Whitwell, close to the Yorkshire border in north Derbyshire. His father was a Yorkshireman and Yorkshire was the county Chris wistfully wanted to play for during his dark and difficult days with Derbyshire.

John Adams was the Football Association's regional coach in the north and played cricket for Staveley. His two sons followed him into the team and at 13

Chris won the club's open single-wicket competition, bowling spinners with precocious accuracy and turn. When he played for England Schools' Under-15s it was as a spinning all-rounder. But by now his thoughts were turning to football.

I didn't really gel at Chesterfield Grammar School, and at 16 I decided I would leave, after completing my O-levels, and take up a YTS football option. I played centre-half and had three offers on the table, from Chesterfield, Scunthorpe and Barnsley. I was also offered a month's trial by Sheffield Wednesday, then in the old First Division. It was then that Mike Stone played a big part in my career. Mike approached my parents and told them that I could do my A-levels at Repton. It was there that I broke Richard Hutton's run-scoring record.

Adams was sitting in his study one day when he was approached by the housemaster who told him two men had arrived to see him; they were the chairman and captain of Derbyshire County Cricket Club.

They offered me a three-year contract, either straight away or after my final year at Repton. I talked with the school and decided to go straight away. The school got me there in the first place in the hope that I would play professional sport, which would be good for them. I was never there for the academic side of things.

Adams first played for Derbyshire when he was just 18. In his solitary Championship innings in 1988 he scored an encouraging 21 at The Oval against a Surrey attack led by Sylvester Clarke. He was impressive in the dressing room too. His friend and teammate Tim O'Gorman remembers a senior professional in the side, who was having a shocker, complaining bitterly about the game.

Chris rounded on him and told him in no uncertain terms that he was lucky to be earning a living playing the greatest game in the world in the fresh air and that he could be working in an office or even down a pit. This told us two things about Chris, who was just 18 at the time. First, he truly loved the game and second he was prepared to stand up for himself.

The following year Adams began to establish himself as an exciting batsman and an outstanding fielder. He played in seven Championship matches and scored a vigorous 79 against a Lancashire attack of Wasim Akram, Phil DeFreitas, Ian Austin and Mike Watkinson. He also played for England Under-19s along with a young seam bowler called Dominic Cork.

Adams was given his first full season in 1990 and responded with 932 first-class runs at an average of 31.06. He also announced himself to a wider audience when he came on as a substitute fielder for England against India at Old Trafford and took two catches, one an outstanding effort at short-leg to dismiss Navjot Sidhu off the bowling of Angus Fraser.

When he was awarded his county cap in 1992, establishing himself as one of the cleanest strikers in the game as he scored 1,109 first-class runs at 41.07, he appeared destined for a long and exciting career at the Racecourse. It was not to be.

In 1995, following the departure of John Morris and Peter Bowler from an unsettled dressing room, Adams, too, asked to leave. He repeated his request in 1996, though no one could question his contribution on the field as he scored 1,742 runs at 52.78. Derbyshire, who were second in the Championship that year, said no and no again when he offered to buy himself out of his contract. He threatened to take the club to the European Court.

Derbyshire lost so many of their personnel in 1997 that they might have been playing their cricket inside the Bermuda Triangle. Like Sussex, 200 miles away, they were in disarray. Their captain, Dean Jones, the coach, chairman, cricket chairman, secretary and commercial manager all departed. So, too, did Adams, finally released at the end of the season with one year remaining on his contract.

A lot has been said about my time at Derby, and the 10 per cent that wasn't great has overshadowed the 90 per cent that was fantastic. I will always be grateful to the club for what they did for me. But I'd signed a five-year contract at the start of 1994 because the captain, Kim Barnett, had made all sorts of promises that my career would be taken care of. He knew how passionate I was about playing for my country and I was led to believe that this would happen one day, provided I scored the right number of runs.

But one year down the line I felt – along with a couple of other batsmen – that the pitches at Derby favoured the seam bowlers. For one thing, I felt this was not getting the best out of the team. We had this fantastic array of seamers whom we would have backed to bowl well on any pitch. Meanwhile, we weren't scoring enough runs.

A better option would have been to play on good batting surfaces, score lots of runs and let our bowlers do the business. Green seamers, though, were the order of the day and it meant that batting was very much a matter a chancing your arm. That's not an excuse for not scoring runs. I told the club that if that was their policy, then fine, but in that case would they let me go somewhere else where I would have a chance of scoring a bigger volume of runs and even of forcing myself into the England reckoning. An

England A tour would have done. I just wanted to feel that I was another step up the ladder towards a Test cap.

The reaction I got from Derbyshire was one of disbelief, even bitterness, that I felt that way. And I spent the next two years fighting a losing battle with the county's establishment while my career went nowhere. Other players the same age, meanwhile, were receiving recognition.

Kim was getting very close to Dominic Cork at this stage and in my opinion the conditions were being created to suit Dominic's bowling. It was Dominic's career that seemed to be the important thing for Kim and Derbyshire. Again, I had no complaint about that. I just felt that if that was the case, I wanted to go. I had a great deal of respect for Kim as player and captain. He had taken one of the smaller clubs to the heights of winning one-day trophies and competing in the Championship. But I felt it was time to leave and he felt differently and that led to a bitter fall-out between us.

Adams had a much better relationship with Dean Jones when the Australian became captain in 1996. But Jones left the club the following year and Adams, feeling increasingly isolated and no closer to an England call despite his magnificent summer the year before, redoubled his efforts to get away.

I'd made my mind up to leave in '97, but Dean told me to give it another year. But then he left early that season, one of a number of people to leave that year, and I knew I had to go too. Playing for Sussex never entered my head. In my heart of hearts I wanted to play for Yorkshire. That was my passion. My Dad was a Yorkshireman and I was born just a mile from the Yorkshire border. It was a big, successful club, it had a certain mystique and that's where I wanted to go.

It was then that Adams received a phone call from the Sussex chief executive, Tony Pigott. Pigott knew Adams was disaffected and had got his phone number from O'Gorman.

I met Tony in July, at a service station off the M1. It was a couple of days before Derbyshire played Sussex in the quarter-finals of the NatWest Trophy. I went along to the meeting thinking there was no way I was going to sign. Sussex were a bottom-of-the-table side. They were in a situation where their season couldn't get any worse. They were struggling to win a game and had just had a massive revolution. But I sat and listened and, in half an hour, Lester sold the club to me. He talked about a new dawn, a fresh and exciting era.

Signing on. Chris Adams signs his five-year contract after Tony Pigott persuaded him to leave Derbyshire and head to the south coast. *(Simon Dack/Brighton Argus)*

He told me everything I wanted to hear. Peter Moores was captain but he'd been offered the coaching job. Tony's big idea was to sign Shane Warne as captain, myself to strengthen the batting and a couple of youngsters to help build for the future. But the Shane thing didn't happen. I don't think it was ever going to. He had a big friend in Robin Smith and was always going to join Hampshire if he came into county cricket. So a month after signing my contract with Sussex, I was offered the captaincy.

Before he signed for Sussex there was that NatWest match between his counties, old and new. He scored an unbeaten 129 in a Derbyshire total of 327–8, though this was trumped by an astonishing innings of 158 by Rajesh Rao.

Robin Marlar was the Sussex chairman, but the driving force at the club was Don Trangmar, who was to become chairman. Don made the journey to Derby, mainly to watch Sussex but also to keep an eye on me to see if I could really play. I think I satisfied him on that score.

The money at Sussex was good but it wasn't the best offer on the table. Another factor in my decision to go to Hove was that David Gilbert had joined the club from Surrey. I thought David could help get me international cricket because it seemed to me that whatever he said seemed to carry a lot of weight in the media. I thought that if I could just get this guy on board and behind me it could only be a good thing.

Tony was a great driving force. But in retrospect the worst decision he ever made was to bring David to the club. David said quite openly that he was only coming to take Tony's job and that's exactly what he did. It was like suicide for poor Tony, who is still a good pal of mine. He thought it would never happen but it did, while I was away on tour with England.

In 1998 the improvement in the Sussex side was immediate. Having finished bottom the previous year, they were seventh in the Championship and qualified for the new Super Cup competition. Adams was the only batsman to pass 1,000 runs, and his average was 42.92. There was a new and vigorous spirit in the side. And the rebuilding continued. The following year Sussex were 11th, missing out on the new first division of the County Championship that would start the following season by just three points. But it was a year of personal triumph for Adams, who scored almost 2,000 runs in all competitions and led the side to the second division title in the National League, as well as the semi-final of the Benson and Hedges Cup.

He signed a new six-year contract with the club and at the end of the season he was selected for England's tour of South Africa.

The following year, though, was one of desperate anti-climax. Sussex finished bottom of the County Championship's second division and were relegated in the National League. After all the investment and rebuilding, on and off the field, it seemed that they were back to where they had been in 1997.

It was a particularly troublesome season for Adams following a difficult winter in South Africa. The tour management backed him by playing him in all five Tests, but he scored just 104 runs from his seven innings at an average of 13. Having waited so long to be given his England chance, he wondered whether he would get another.

He was fined £500 by the ECB for pushing Essex's Danny Law during a Benson and Hedges Cup tie at Chelmsford in April, and three weeks later he was involved in a heated exchange with the umpire, David Constant, at Hove. The club backed him, but there was a warning from chief executive Gilbert that this could not go on. He admits now that he and coach Peter Moores might have lost their jobs that year.

The England experience was a tough one and I came back from South Africa wanting to fight the world and prove that I could play. It happens to a lot of players and because of my temperament I became a very aggressive player that year. I was desperate to put right the opinion people might have had of me.

While I was in South Africa my younger daughter, Sophie, had three epileptic fits in 24 hours. One is quite common, I was told, two is worrying and three is very worrying. The doctor told me that he didn't know what was going to happen but that I should prepare myself for the worst. That was enough for me to jump on the next plane home.

The next two or three days were quite unpleasant, but then she woke up one morning and I could tell, just looking at her eyes, that she was OK again. I phoned David Graveney, the chairman of selectors, that evening and told him that I really wanted to rejoin the tour. I wanted to go to Zimbabwe and fight for my place. Otherwise, I felt, I might not get another opportunity. He said he would get back to me. Then I was told to stay where I was, but if someone got injured they would recall me.

Going through a Test series in which it didn't happen, and then playing only two one-day internationals, was a disappointment because I felt I went on tour as the best one-day player in the country. That might explain why I was angry and frustrated in 2000. I have matured since then, though the experience has been a tough one. One of the reasons I did well for Sussex in 2003 was that I realised that, in all likelihood, England wouldn't come calling again. I can never give up entirely on that idea, and the sight of Martin Bicknell running in last year was most encouraging. But I know it probably won't happen again for me.

The two incidents in that 2000 season were regrettable and I was at fault, initially, on both occasions. But I must say that both Danny and Connie reacted poorly. And that got me in more trouble than was necessary.

The handling of the Law incident was farcical. Adams pushed Law in the back but neither umpire saw it and the clash should have been settled over a beer at the end of the day. Law himself would have settled for an apology. But his case was taken up by his captain, Nasser Hussain – who had just spent the winter with Adams in South Africa – and a three-page report was sent to Sussex.

In the end it took a disciplinary panel, the Professional Cricketers' Association, two Sussex senior executives and three Essex cricketers, as well as Adams himself and his solicitor, to resolve the matter.

The ECB decided to take no action over the Constant affair. In the Championship match against Warwickshire at Hove Adams was twice given out lbw. After the second occasion, when Ashley Giles was the bowler, Adams asked the Warwickshire players what they thought of the decision and then marched into the umpires' room to see Constant. The umpire was clearly shaken by the confrontation but later accepted an apology.

When we finished bottom in 2000 it was the worst time for me at Sussex. Supporters were fed up because we had gone from the top to the bottom of Division Two in six weeks. But a year later we showed everyone that we could go the other way when we won promotion.

In 2001 Sussex won nine matches, two more than any other county, to win the second division title. The batting was led by openers Richard Montgomerie and Murray Goodwin, but Adams, despite missing two matches early in the season, passed 1,000 runs once more.

The enthusiasm of Adams and Moores, reflected in the spirit and zest of the entire team, was a harbinger of what was to come. In 2002, a difficult season following the tragic death of Umer Rashid, Sussex finished just above the drop zone. But it was a summer of consolidation and their sixth position was the best they had achieved for 18 years. Adams, after scoring a double century against Lancashire, missed most of June through injury but still finished top of the batting averages. And then there was the next season. It was 2003.

5

INSHALLAH!

Mushtaq Ahmed's Story

It was not inappropriate that Mushtaq Ahmed, the miracle from Sahiwal, emerged as the outstanding Sussex player in the *annus mirabilis* of 2003. The club's history is enriched by its exotic Asian associations. The Indian princes Ranjitsinhji and Duleepsinhji, the Nawab of Pataudi, Imran Khan and others dazzle like silk saris among the white flannels of the native yeomanry. But such names evoke a sense of frustration too. The greatest players to journey to Hove from the subcontinent were Ranji, Duleep and Imran. All three clutched at the main prize but ultimately saw it slip past them, often in heartbreaking circumstances. The anguish was palpable. Mediocrity can feel more comfortable than the glimpsed glory of second place.

Then came Mushtaq. Bearded, bouncy, chuckling Mushtaq. Past his best, some said. He had left Somerset in disappointing circumstances in 1998 and his international career had wobbled downhill since the turn of the century. He moved to Sussex after a spell playing league cricket in Staffordshire, for goodness' sake. Ian Peebles, that wonderful leg-spinner and humorist, once observed that his was at once the most difficult of the cricket arts to master and the easiest to lose. And Mushtaq looked in need of the lost property office.

Leg-spinners, as we all know, are a rum lot at the best of times. Bowling full-tosses and long-hops, kicking the turf and shaking their heads, they can be the stuff of a captain's worst nightmare. Sussex folk, for whom Ian Salisbury's frustrating career is still an uncomfortably fresh memory, knew all about the problems. Mushtaq, though, was simply a revelation, dumbfounding batsmen and some experts alike. Whirring in with arms flailing, for over after over, he was like some toy cricketer advertising long-life batteries. And before each delivery, in an unconscious tribute to his hero Abdul Qadir, he would lick his fingers delightedly, like a small boy with jam-smeared hands.

After a while the batsman wore the troubled countenance of someone in the middle of a lengthy cross-examination by the late George Carmen QC. Playing a successful shot merely left him with the nauseous sensation that he was being set up for the next difficult question. Some got out very quickly. Others played him with patient care, until they realised that the scoreboard had stopped and the life was being squeezed out of the innings. They would attempt to move things along; and get out.

Match after match, month after month, Mushtaq's forensic probing propelled Sussex towards their historic destiny. It was a team effort, of course, and the immense spirit of the side was most evident. It was the consistency of the run-making that allowed Mushtaq to bowl as he did, and the quality of the close catching that made the most of the bowler's accuracy. But still, it must be said, Sussex would not have won the Championship without Mushtaq Ahmed. He took 103 Championship wickets in 2003. Ten times he took five wickets in an innings and five times he had ten in the match. But it was not just the wickets and the delivery of the Championship. Mushtaq communicated his joy to the crowds, for enthusiasm such as his is infectious. He also reminded everyone that quality leg-spin, an art form in itself, is one of the true delights of the game. The news of his deeds travelled far beyond the confines of Eaton Road. He was recalled to the Pakistan team and played two Test matches and a one-day international, though with little success. By the beginning of 2004 he had given up even domestic cricket in his home country for a while to be with his dying father in Lahore.

'We won the championship four months ago now,' he recalled, 'but I still think about it every day and thank God for it. Sometimes God will put you in a dark place to test you. But I waited for the sunrise and it came.'

Small boys at Hove – and they can almost look Mushtaq straight in the eye – know the meaning of 'Inshallah' ('God willing'). They call their hero 'Mushy' but their wide, dancing eyes would suggest that the familiarity of their address does not represent a lack of respect. He is the most popular cricketer at Hove.

Traditionally, Sussex have always managed to produce seam bowlers, but the twirly men have been a little thin on the lush grass at the County Ground, even since overseas players poured into the market place in 1968. Sussex, who already had Murray Goodwin on their books as an overseas player, decided that a spinner should fill the remaining vacancy, but Mushtaq was not the county's first choice. Their original targets were Stuart MacGill, the Australian leg-spinner who signed for Nottinghamshire, and Harbhajan Singh, the Indian off-spinner who was also being pursued by Lancashire. But when MacGill's representatives asked for £100,000 and Harbhajan made it clear he was going to Old Trafford, Sussex picked up interest in Mushtaq.

On the negative side, he was approaching 33, was not in the Pakistan side and had suffered that anti-climactic end to his county career at Taunton five years earlier. So a big question mark sat over the man described by former Australia captain Mark Taylor as the greatest leg-spinner he had ever seen. On the positive side, he had proved his fitness by playing a couple of matches for Surrey as Saqlain Mushtaq's locum the previous season, he had a point to prove, his absence from the Pakistan team was not necessarily a bad thing and the asking price was roughly half what MacGill wanted.

One of the matches he played for Surrey had been against Sussex at Hove. He went wicketless but was still impressive. In September 2002 he was signed by Sussex as their second overseas player. The captain, Chris Adams, said at the time: 'He's got an exceptional first-class record and has taken 183 wickets in 50 Tests. He comes across as someone who is very hungry to perform and prove a point, both here and to the selectors in Pakistan.' Both Adams and the director of cricket, Peter Moores thought he would be good; they had no idea how good.

The first Championship match, against Middlesex at Lord's, ended in defeat after Sussex had the better of matters for the first three days. But Adams was convinced. 'After Lord's we knew we had something to work round in Mushy. We knew we had that X-factor we had been searching for. Mushy was suffering from a septic nail in the second innings and it was amazing that he could even hold the ball, let alone bowl it.'

When he took 11 wickets against Warwickshire at the end of June he had taken 52 in just seven Championship matches and there was excited chatter about his becoming the first bowler to take 100 Championship wickets since 1998, when both Andy Caddick and Courtney Walsh achieved the feat. 'Peter [Moores], the Sussex coach, made a big gamble by offering me a job and I felt determined to repay him,' he said. 'And I always wanted to get 100 wickets in a season. I had gone close before. It was something very special for me. But the unity and togetherness of the team was what won it. Even the 12th man was an important part of that unity. The Lancashire game at Hove, which we won, was the game I think about most. It was very crucial because they wanted to win the Championship too.' So how did he do it? He agrees with Adams that he is not a prodigious spinner of the ball. This is a bowler who needs long spells to wear batsmen down, to undermine their spirit and unpick their technique. 'But I turn it enough to worry batsmen and try to make it so they don't know which way I'm turning it,' he said. 'Lots of variation is my big thing, both with the pace of the ball and with my different actions. I bowl a leg-break with a googly action, for example. And I like lots of overs to get into a rhythm.'

Behind the stumps, Matt Prior had a close-up of the Pakistani's arsenal.

I was a bit worried at first, nervous that I might make a mistake. But Mush is such a great pro. He came up to me early on and said, 'OK, just you and me, one to one, after nets.' And that is what we did. For about an hour we would work together so that keeping to him, instead of being tricky, would be a delight. Then I would bat against him and he would have fun trying to beat me.

Mushtaq Ahmed in familar pose during his home Championship debut in the win over Kent. (Simon Dack/Brighton Argus)

The thing that makes Mush such a great signing for Sussex is that his contribution doesn't stop on the field. Away from play he is good at giving the young players advice about dealing with people, about living away from home and coping with all sorts of pressures. He has so much wisdom.

As for the bowling, that is something else. It's his variation which is the key. He will float one up for the drive then bowl a quicker one that skids on. The googly is often aimed a little wider of the off-stump to come in, while the leg-break drifts in towards the stumps. Then he bowls the top-spinner and the flipper, changing his pace and his line. And then he will bowl them all again with different actions. The batsmen either hit out and get out, or go into their shell, surrounded by close catchers, often blocking and getting a bat-pad. A huge amount of pressure is being created.

Then there is his batting. He's very serious about his religion and his family, but when he was younger I think he enjoyed a party. Well, his batting represents his party time now. He really enjoys himself at the crease and he made some useful fifties for us. He's got some real wristy talent. The way he stepped outside his off-stump to flick an off-stump delivery from Wasim Akram to fine leg for four in last year's Twenty20 Cup tie was a fantastic shot which will live with me for ever.

But how long will the miracle last? Of course, if he never bowled another ball his place in the Sussex pantheon would already be assured. But it is expected that he will be the side's main attacking bowler once again in 2004, and the workload could test a man who will enter his 35th year in midsummer. Then there is the question of his future in international cricket, surely in doubt once more. His strong desire to return to the Pakistan fold was a big factor in his bowling last season. Without that will some of his desire ebb away?

I want two more good years playing for Sussex. England is my second home. I've had ten years here. I played for Somerset for five seasons and had three tours with Pakistan. And then there was a season or two I played some league cricket.

If I play two more years I will be coming up to 36. Then, maybe, I will do some coaching. I would love to help others bowl leg-spin. And I can teach batsmen how to play spin too. But I don't want to be playing for too long. I don't want to hear people saying, 'What shall we do with the Mushy?' and asking, 'Why is he still playing?'

In bleak midwinter, Chris Adams warmed himself with memories of Mushtaq's achievements in the summer of 2003. Then he attempted to analyse his qualities.

Mushy is not one of those explosive bowlers, like Muralitharan, who might take five for seven in five overs, although he can knock over the tail pretty quickly. He is not an extravagant turner of the ball. He doesn't give it a real rip, like Shane Warne. The majority of his wickets are lbw or bowled. That would suggest that he is not one of the biggest turners because if he was he would find it difficult to hit the stumps. But he's a master at bowling at the right pace, varying his flight and putting the ball in the difficult areas. His control is superb. His game is not so much about bowling magic balls as tying batsmen down until they make errors.

When he returned to Test cricket with Pakistan in the winter he found it difficult to take wickets. But in that environment you have to take a wicket in six or seven overs or you're whipped off. I learned early on that I had to get him to bowl and bowl for him to get his returns.

I think our management got him right when it came to tactics and motivation. Even when he was injured and wanted to come off, we persuaded him to stay on and bowl because we needed him.

Mushtaq, the son of a cotton grower, made his first impression on English cricketers when he was just 17. It was during Mike Gatting's notorious tour of Pakistan in 1987/8. It is a series better remembered for the controversial umpiring in Lahore and Faisalabad than the actual cricket.

Pakistan's wrist-spin was dominated by Qadir in those days. But Mushtaq made an impression when he returned figures of 6–81 for the Punjab Chief Minister's XI in his home town of Sahiwal. England, expecting a more extended batting practice before the second Test in Faisalabad, were bowled out for 279.

> Qadir was my hero. I watched him on TV when I was a boy. I was the wrong height to be a fast bowler. So I decided to be a leg-spin bowler. But a spinner can still have a fast bowler's aggression. Qadir was a great role model for a young spinner.

The next time we heard about Mushtaq was during the 1988 Youth World Cup in Australia, where he took 19 wickets. Then, in the domestic season of 1988/9, he took 29 wickets in five matches in the Patron's Trophy at the miserly average of 20.00. By the end of the season he had taken 52 wickets. He also made a sizeable impression in the under-19 series against India, in which he took 26 wickets at an average of 19.76. His batting was also developing, for his wickets were garnished with a couple of fifties. He made his first appearance for Pakistan in a one-day game in Sharjah in March 1989. But his big chance came in January 1990, when he was flown to Australia to replace Qadir. He made his Test debut at Adelaide.

It was a difficult start. Australia dominated and it took a memorable second-innings sixth-wicket stand of 191 between Imran Khan and Wasim Akram to save the match for Pakistan. Both Mark Taylor and Dean Jones scored heavily, and the latter, using his feet to counter Mushtaq's spin, scored a century in each innings. Mushtaq muffed a difficult return catch offered by Jones and finished the match with 1–141 in 48 overs. There was worse to come.

In the next match of the tour Pakistan played Victoria at Melbourne and Mushtaq was twice warned by the experienced umpire Robin Bailhache for following through down the pitch. When he continued to transgress, the umpire instructed the captain, Ramiz Raja, to remove him from the attack. Pakistan refused to accept this judgement and Intikhab Alam, the manager, was brought onto the field. But instead of bringing some discipline to the proceedings, Intikhab allowed his players to walk off. He even led them from the field himself. Play eventually resumed after an uncomfortable compromise – Ramiz claimed that he had not heard the final warning.

It got better for Mushtaq, though not in that series, in which he took just five wickets at 42.40. By the time of the 1992 World Cup, Mushtaq had become central to his team's one-day plans and he took 16 wickets in that tournament, a tribute to his control. Wrist-spinners are not normally the most reliable of bowlers in tight and tense one-day internationals. In the final, against England, he picked up the wickets of Graeme Hick, totally deceived by a googly, Graham Gooch and Dermot Reeve. His figures were 3–41 as Pakistan won by 22 runs. When he returned to Pakistan the government presented him with a plot of land.

I was so happy to help win it with Imran Khan as captain because he was the man who changed my career. I remember being expensive and not taking the wickets and Imran came over to me, put his arm round my shoulders and told me to always be brave. He told me that I could always win matches but that I should not be afraid if people hit me. It was a big boost. That was when I decided to go for it whenever I bowled and not to be afraid to buy wickets.

He toured England with Pakistan in 1992, taking 15 Test wickets at 31.66, and Somerset made their move for him that summer. It was an inspired choice. Brian Rose, Somerset's cricket chairman, said: 'The whole process of signing him took about five minutes. Mushy was so keen to come. He has been the model overseas player. He wins matches for the club and adds members.'

In his first summer at Taunton he was Somerset's player of the year. He took 85 first-class wickets at 20.85 and scored almost 500 runs, and until their form faltered, Somerset even nurtured their own hopes of a first Championship. Peter Anderson, the county's long-serving chief executive, said:

Mushy was a pure joy. He was a bubbly, extrovert character at the County Ground, who was as popular off the field as he was on it. He loved talking cricket and often held court after matches. The younger players lapped it up because he was a Test star. At Taunton the wickets were designed to suit Andy Caddick in those days but it didn't matter to Mush. He could bowl on any wickets. There was some bounce for him here, though, and he made the most of that.

The following year Somerset were hit hard by Pakistan's decision to demand his return earlier than expected, in July, for their tour of Sri Lanka. Mushtaq had not been at his best at the start of the season – tired, perhaps, after a busy international winter – but he had just taken 12 wickets against Worcestershire, indicating a return to the high plains of the previous summer.

There was nothing disappointing about 1995. Mushtaq took 95 first-class wickets, his best return in county cricket until 2003, and took five or more

Another frenzied appeal from Mushtaq Ahmed, this time in the title-clinching win over Leicestershire. *(Simon Dack/Brighton Argus)*

wickets in an innings on seven occasions. He bowled more overs, 952, than anyone else in the country that year, which spoke as much for his stamina as for his enthusiasm. In the seven matches Somerset won he took 58 wickets, a decisive contribution.

He did not play for the county in 1996 because he was touring England with Pakistan, for whom he topped the Test averages with 17 wickets in three matches. Mushtaq was a central figure in the two victories at Lord's and The Oval. He returned to Taunton in 1997. Perhaps he was jaded after yet another busy international winter, or it could have been the effects of the knee injury, which never healed properly, but he was less effective than before, taking 50 Championship wickets. The following year was his last with the county and it was a disappointing end. He played just six Championship matches, taking 14 wickets. The knee still troubled him and he was also concerned about his wife's confinement. He was rarely seen at Taunton and his chuckling good humour had disappeared.

When he did play he appeared to have lost his old conjuror's skills. Batsmen were not so easily deceived. He had also lost his place in the Pakistan side. In addition, it was noted by some that this social animal's evening schedule was not necessarily restricted to his ability to play cricket under lights. It seemed certain that he would never play county cricket again. He recalls:

I had played for Somerset for four years, and they were good ones. But what happened in 1998 was my fault. And I regret is very much. There was a change of coach, which did not help. But I must take the blame. I didn't have a good time. Mentally, I was just not there. But I was very upset to be away from my family at a difficult time. I would say that my last season with Somerset was the first time in my career that I wasn't really enjoying my cricket, and enjoying it is very important to me. Because I am professional, I have to consider the money. But I really love playing the game.

When there is rain I hate it. Some cricketers like having a rest in the dressing room but I do not, because it destroys my opportunity to play cricket. How can you say you are the best spinner in the world when you are sitting in the dressing room? And that last year at Somerset was the only time I didn't have my usual feeling about the game.

Anderson said:

When he came down with Sussex last season [2003] he received a wonderful welcome from everyone. Because of what he had achieved and because everyone loved him. And if he apologised to me once, he apologised a hundred times for the way his career tailed off.

I think he got distracted with a few things that were happening off the field with Pakistan cricket. There were accusations of gambling with some players. It was a difficult time for him. And he enjoyed a drink or two at the time. But, overall, we remember him most fondly for making such a big impact in his few years at Taunton. And even more than his marvellous leg-breaks I remember his enthusiasm, the fact that he really wanted to play. That's something you can't say about all county cricketers.

He has settled down as a mature family man and he seems to be taking his religion even more seriously these days. It's all helping his cricket.

He certainly seems an aeon or two away from the troubled young man who toured the West Indies in 1993. He justified his billing as a match-winner when he took 5–86 and 3–43 in the 114-run win over Jamaica and 6–43 against the under-23 side in Grenada. But it was during this match that he was arrested, along with Wasim Akram, Waqar Younis and Aqib Javed, on charges of 'constructive possession of a banned drug'. He was released after the charges were dropped but then missed the first Test because of a back injury.

Even after the disappointment of his Test comeback against South Africa in late 2003, Mushtaq is determined to play again for his country.

Inshallah, I always say, but if God wills it, I will play again for Pakistan. I have come back once and I can do so once more. I never give up because this game is my passion. And what I do in England is noticed in Pakistan.

Moores, who played against Mushtaq in the Somerset days, is convinced that leg-spinners age well.

I think they get better all the time. They're still getting better when their bodies give out. It's a wonderful craft.

I don't have to pay to get into Hove, but I think I would do so to watch Mushy. I just love watching him bowl. Leggies, big leggies, googlies, top-spinners, flippers . . . they just roll off his fingers.

The big thing he's given us is that we now know we can bowl sides out on flat pitches. He's been brilliant. And it's not just the wicket-taking. He gets his wickets by containment. He doesn't bowl bad balls. He gets them in the business area and that allows us to get men round the bat and create real pressure.

Mushtaq's extraordinary season was completed when he was named Player of the Year by the Professional Cricketers' Association. Previous winners include Malcolm Marshall, Brian Lara, Richard Hadlee and Mike Procter. He feels that he is bowling better than ever before.

You must remember that players in county cricket are much better at playing leg-spin now. This is the time of the electronic media when everyone is watching TV and coaching videos. When I played for Somerset the batsmen were not so good at playing me.

Coaches know all sorts of things about how to play spin and because of TV people are watching you a lot. It's difficult to have secrets. Because of this there is always pressure to learn new things to trick batsmen.

Mushtaq, one senses, will not have to learn that much. There is always a fresh little deceit hidden away in his bushy beard. Besides, he beats batsmen in the mind as well as through the air and off the pitch.

The season of 2003 will be remembered for many things. There was Murray Goodwin's unbeaten 335 in the final match, followed by the moving balcony scene when the Championship was celebrated. There was the strike bowling of James Kirtley and fightback to form of the captain, Chris Adams. Most of all, though, there was the sight of the remarkable Mushtaq, prancing to the stumps for yet another testing delivery, which was usually followed by a theatrical appeal. Mushtaq was the maker of an astonishing summer.

SIX YEARS IN THE MAKING

Peter Moores' Story

As the Sussex players tumbled down the dressing room steps to join their captain on the outfield moments after the Championship had been won, it didn't seem right that Peter Moores wasn't leading them out for that joyous, impromptu lap of honour. After all, no one had contributed more to the greatest moment in the county's history. Ask any player, official or long-suffering supporter and they would all say the same.

But no. Moores preferred instead to savour an unforgettable occasion on the players' balcony, surrounded by his fellow coaches, Mark Robinson and Keith Greenfield, and support staff. 'It was a fantastic moment, but the players had done all the hard work out there in the middle all summer and they deserved to take the credit at that moment,' he said. Of the hundreds of pictures of the champagne-soaked celebrations that were taken over the following days, only a few showed Moores up at the front, basking in the adulation of the crowd, most of whom, like him, were still trying to come to terms with Sussex's achievement. He tended to be tucked in at the side or the back of the photographs, a reluctant hero perhaps. Yet it was their coach that the players, almost to the man, sought out first for a congratulatory bear-hug in the moments after Murray Goodwin scored *that* boundary. They all knew, like the rest of us, that had it not been for Moores, Sussex's search for English cricket's Holy Grail would have extended into a 114th year and beyond.

For Moores, the county's finest achievement wasn't something that had miraculously come together in the space of five summer months. It was the culmination of six years of planning that began in 1997 when he replaced his great friend Alan Wells as skipper. With so many experienced players on their way out of Hove, there were few alternatives when Wells was relieved of the captaincy. Perhaps it was a case of being in the wrong place at the right time, although Moores, who had been vice-captain for one season, never saw it that way. After joining the county in 1985 from Worcestershire he had witnessed Sussex's gentle decline at first hand, working under five coaches, four captains, three chief executives, two committees – and one groundsman. Now, though, he had the opportunity to shape Sussex's future from a position of authority rather than as a mere foot soldier with 12 years' experience but little influence on the day-to-day running of the county's cricketing operation.

It turned out to be one of the shortest captaincies in the county's history. After one season he had been replaced by Chris Adams, but there was no bitterness on the part of Moores. He still loved keeping wicket, and had the captaincy not been thrust upon him during that turbulent winter of 1996/7, and had he not eventually been given the job of coach, he could easily have played on for another four or five years in that unostentatious but utterly reliable way of his. He maintained a level of physical fitness that shamed teammates ten years or more younger than him (and still does to this day), and, most importantly of all, he still had the enthusiasm and ability to sustain his playing career into his fourth decade. Perhaps he might still have been playing in 2003 had things worked out differently, although it's highly unlikely he would have been part of a Championship-winning team.

But now fresh challenges lay ahead. Desmond Haynes' uncomfortable 18-month reign as coach ended in August 1997 and Tony Pigott soon appointed Moores as his replacement. Pigott's decision-making during his time as chief executive was occasionally suspect, but he got this one right even though it was eventually to put a strain on their friendship.

The decision was not made on a whim, either. The pair had been room-mates for many years during their playing days, expounding their theories on the game during many a late-night hotel bar pow-wow. Pigott happily admits he did most of the listening. Now he was anxious to harness Moores' unquenchable enthusiasm, as well as the technical knowledge that he had accrued since taking his first steps into coaching as a 21-year-old, some 14 years earlier. 'He was the obvious choice,' said Pigott.

That season he had as captain was always going to be difficult. We'd lost six capped players and although Peter helped recruit some good replacements in Neil Taylor and Mark Robinson, we were still very inexperienced. But by the end of the season, after Des Haynes left, we were picking the side together and Peter was spending more and more time on the coaching side of things, so it seemed the right move.

As expected, Sussex finished bottom in the Championship in 1997, but the season ended on a personal note of triumph when Moores took a hundred off Nottinghamshire's bowlers. He played two more first-class games at the start of 1998 and wore the gloves for the last time at Arundel on a cheerlessly cold afternoon at the beginning of May when Sussex lost to Hampshire in a

Peter Moores keeps a close eye on proceedings from his favourite vantage point on top of the Gilligan Stand. *(Simon Dack/Brighton Argus)*

Sunday League match. Two days later he announced his retirement from playing so that he could concentrate on coaching.

There were still some doubters to convince, not least Robin Marlar, who had been openly critical of his appointment as skipper during the pre-revolution days at the end of 1996. Moores still remembers a lunch date early in Marlar's reign as chairman and his as captain.

It was a couple of days before the 1997 season. He couldn't stress enough the importance of a good start. 'Don't let the wheels come off' were his immortal words. About a week into the season we lost to the British Universities in the Benson and Hedges Cup. I had to avoid him for a few days after that!

We didn't get off on the best footing and I had to earn his respect in those early days as captain and then coach. He was a one-off and there was no doubt that he was one of the main catalysts for change at the club. Without all of that perhaps I would never have got my chance to lead the side, which was a tremendous honour, and then coach as well, which I was really keen to move into. Maybe Robin perceived me as part of the old regime, but he fought his corner in the same way as me and I always admire that in anyone.

As reinforcements to the playing staff, such as Adams and the prolific Australian Michael Bevan, arrived at Eaton Road, so expectation levels rose, albeit modestly. In 1998, Moores' first full season as coach, the hard work and planning paid off. Sussex rose from last place to seventh in the Championship and qualified for the Benson and Hedges Super Cup, a one-off one-day competition for the top eight finishers. By the end of the season Moores had a new title as well – cricket manager. His role and that of David Gilbert, who was taking more responsibility for off-the-field matters, were now more clearly defined.

The improvements on the field continued in 1999. Although Sussex just missed out on a place in Division One when the Championship was split into two leagues, they celebrated their first trophy for 13 years by winning the National League second division title with 13 victories in their 16 games. They reached the semi-final of the Super Cup, and although they slipped four places in the Championship, they still won six games – the same number as the previous year. The season had only just ended when Pigott departed and was replaced by Gilbert.

Of the seven chief executives or their equivalents with whom Moores has worked during nearly two decades at Hove, his relationship with Gilbert was the most difficult. As a former Australian Test cricketer who became a successful coach in his own right with Surrey, Gilbert was eminently qualified to give his opinions on how the club's cricket operations should be run and wasn't afraid to voice them.

We were on the right track at that time, but I just felt too much power had been vested in the cricket management and that worried me. It looked as if the captain [Adams] and coach [Moores] were running the whole club, which, in my opinion, was palpably not the right thing.

A year later, at the end of the disastrous 2000 season, it looked as though matters might come to a head. In the space of a few weeks Sussex tumbled from the top of the second division to the bottom. Their inglorious collapse coincided with the absence of the prolific Bevan on international duty and ended with a two-day defeat by Gloucestershire in the final game. An hour or so later the players and their coach filed sheepishly onto the committee room balcony for the end-of-season presentations. Moores bravely predicted a big improvement in 2001 to widespread disbelief from the members gathered below. The big question now was whether he would still be there to try and keep his promise.

To the surprise of many, chairman Don Trangmar and Gilbert held their nerve, although there was pressure from within the club and outside for change. There had been enough blood-letting in the previous three years and this was the time for a show of faith. Moores remembers:

Behind closed doors we were dragged over the coals. But in public Don was very supportive, which I was grateful for at the time, although I never feared I would lose my job, because when you start thinking that you are going to be sacked, you never do or say what you believe. The relationship between the coach and the chief executive is the most important in the club, after coach and captain, and, in hindsight, I would have done things a bit differently with regard to David. I always saw David as very ambitious and a bit of a political animal. He was someone else whose respect I had to earn, but that was all part of the learning process as far as I'm concerned. He brought structure and discipline to the club, which I admired and which the club needed, and he was straight-talking, which is something else I like in a person. We had some very strong exchanges about the way things should be done. Put it this way, there wasn't much laughter between us and we were never what I would call mates. I felt at the time he could have communicated better, but he was pushing for what he thought was right. He taught me a lot, though, and in hindsight I should have handled certain situations better and I expect David feels the same. If we sat down now and had a beer we'd probably laugh about it, and I know he was as pleased as anyone when we won the Championship.

The management's faith in Moores didn't prove to be misplaced. Dave Gilbert made a shrewd overseas signing in Murray Goodwin as replacement for Bevan, and youngsters like Tim Ambrose and Matt Prior – two key members of the 2003 Championship-winning team – were given their chance by Moores, who quickly recognised their potential as wicketkeeper-batsmen. The club even agreed to the coach's request to take the players to Grenada for a two-week pre-season training trip. It proved one of the best decisions they ever made.

It was fantastic preparation for us. Back home everyone was kept indoors because of the rain, but we had two great weeks where we worked and practised really hard. It's no coincidence that we hit the ground running that season.

The wheel eventually turned full circle. In September 2001, 12 months after the ignominy of the two-day defeat by Gloucestershire, which condemned Sussex to last place, they beat the same opponents to win the Championship's second division and clinch promotion for the first time. The tremendous team

Planning for the future. Chris Adams, coach Mark Robinson and Peter Moores at Sussex's pre-season photocall, April 2003. *(Simon Dack/Brighton Argus)*

spirit and work ethic fostered by Moores and Adams, which was evident even in pre-season in the Caribbean, shone through. Moores' achievements were also beginning to be noted elsewhere. In the winter he had coached the England A team on their tour of the Caribbean, where they were beaten just once in the West Indies' domestic competition, the Busta Cup.

Back home, competing with the bigger counties for the first time since the divisional split was always going to be difficult and expectation levels were lowered accordingly. But even before a ball had been bowled the club was stunned by the deaths of all-rounder Umer Rashid and his brother on 1 April 2002 during the county's second pre-season visit to Grenada. The tightly knit squad were thousands of miles from home and their loved ones, trying to come to terms with the tragedy; those were desperate moments. To no one's surprise, the situation brought out the best in their coach. The job of telling the Rashid family once the dreadful news was confirmed fell to Moores, and it must have been one of the hardest things he'd ever done in his life. He comforted devastated players, organised the squad's early return home and then led the club's mourners at the funeral a few days later. All this while trying to come to terms himself with the loss of a player he'd brought to the club three years earlier and nurtured carefully. Within a few days the new season had begun, but Rashid was never forgotten. When the Championship celebrations got under way 18 months later, Moores and the squad made a point of dedicating the victory to Rashid's memory and that of long-serving scorer Len Chandler, Moores' navigator on countless away trips, who died just a few weeks before the end of the season.

In 2002, despite winning only three matches, Sussex became the first promoted county not to lose their first division place the following season, their top-flight status secured with a game to spare. Again, the county recruited carefully that winter, making one significant signing in Mushtaq Ahmed. While Adams predicted a top-three finish, Moores was slightly less bullish: 'If we get on a roll then who knows, but the minimum we're going to do is act like winners, talk like winners and play like winners.' It turned out to be a more prophetic pre-season prediction than his captain's.

Not that Sussex played much like winners at Edgbaston in their third game of the season. Far from it, in fact. They were routed for 106 in less than two sessions and lost heavily. It brought a rare public rebuke from their coach and even more stinging criticism within the confines of the dressing room. 'Something was wrong, we all knew that and after the Warwickshire game it almost felt as if the lads wanted a big bollocking, but I didn't want to give them that opportunity, well not straight away anyway,' said Moores.

Some of the players were rested for the following game against Zimbabwe and Moores was forced to defend his weakened selection against the tourists, but the day before the next Championship match against Nottinghamshire at Horsham the squad reconvened. According to Moores, it was there that they 'left the land of bullshit and returned to the land of reality. . . . That afternoon we sorted a few things out, it's fair to say, about levels of commitment to what we were trying to achieve and their own personal performances. They were asleep as a side, but that day we woke them up.' Seasoned Sussex watchers could hardly believe the transformation from the team that had limped listlessly to defeat in Birmingham to the one that demolished Nottinghamshire at Cricketfield Road a fortnight later. Sussex had some momentum and Moores was determined it wouldn't be lost.

There were no complaints when they were beaten in the next game by reigning champions Surrey, but they were quickly back on track at Tunbridge Wells against Kent: 'At The Oval we were beaten by the better side and we suffered because no one could make a hundred, but we went at Kent all the time. We had started to play with the arrogance of a champion team.'

For the following three weeks Moores and his players switched their attention to the new Twenty20 Cup, but the coach must have been thrilled that the squad showed that same intensity when they returned to Championship action against bogey side Warwickshire, whom they hadn't beaten at Hove for over a decade, at the end of June.

On the first morning there was such a buzz about us, even before we'd started the game. Mushtaq got another load of wickets in that game and after we'd won it I honestly felt we would at least finish in the top three, anything other than that with the position we were in would have been a disappointment.

And so to Arundel and another victory, this time over Essex, which was followed a few days later by a fourth successive win at Leicester. The momentum was building.

The whole focus of the side was changing by then. We were totally committed to winning every game, losing didn't come into it. We still knew Surrey were going to be hard to stop, but we were also aware that they would have to work hard to maintain the pace we were setting.

Sussex were on a roll, but Moores still had the form of individuals to worry about, not least his captain, who had struggled for runs all season. At Leicester, during a practice session lasting nearly two hours, Adams went back to basics, encouraged by his coach, who happily stood 22 yards away giving him throw-down after throw-down. The next game against Nottinghamshire ended in a draw after a first day washout, but there was no loss of momentum.

Everything about our batting on that second day, when we were trying to make up time after the rain and score quickly, was fantastic, the shot selection, running between the wickets – everything. The captain got 46, but it was a proper innings. He was ready to come to the party.

Party-time, as far as Adams was concerned, came in the showdown with Surrey at the start of August when he made his first hundred for 15 months. But he ended the game roundly criticised for his tactical approach after coming off for bad light on the third day and then delaying Sussex's declaration until tea on the final afternoon, condemning the meeting of the top two to a sterile draw. Moores said:

We had two opportunities in that game to nail Surrey and we blew them and we knew we wouldn't get a third because they are a quality side. Chris Adams sat the squad down and we all decided that we couldn't win the Championship by winning that match, but we could have lost it if we'd gambled by batting on when the light wasn't too good and their bowlers had their tails up. Our confidence was still intact and I suppose there was an element of making them suffer a little bit by keeping them in the field for so long on the last day. It was a psychological ploy because they had made us suffer so much in the past.

Five games to go and Sussex knew they would never have a better chance of making history. Moores called the squad together on the eve of the next match against Lancashire, knowing that a victory would effectively end their opponents' own chance of sneaking up on the rails.

I told the lads that the most important thing now was for them to enjoy what they were trying to achieve. There was already enough pressure without adding to it. But funnily enough I was convinced we would beat Lancashire. In fact, I was never so sure about a game all season as I was that one. We hadn't lost at Hove, we were playing well and you could tell the players wanted to prove a few people wrong after all the stick we'd got following the Surrey match.

Moores was right. Sussex did win, albeit with only 12 minutes to spare, although as the coach joined in another rousing rendition of the team anthem 'Sussex by the Sea' he might have sensed that Lancashire captain Warren Hegg, incensed by some of the umpiring decisions, was already plotting revenge.

In the next game at Colchester, there was little for Moores to do except enjoy an awesome performance from his side: 'Murray Goodwin and Richard Montgomerie set the tone in the first session. They opened the door and we piled in and, as a coach, all you can do then is just admire the way we played.'

There wasn't much for the coach to admire on the Hove scoreboard a fortnight later, just after lunch on the second day of the penultimate home match against Middlesex. The county were 107–6 and it seemed as if the idea of what they might achieve was starting to prey on fragile minds: 'I remember walking around the ground and it was all doom and gloom. Everyone thought we'd blown it. I don't know why, but funnily enough I still had the feeling that someone would get us out of trouble.' That someone turned out to be Mark Davis, who made a career-best 168 and totally changed the match. Two days later the county were cruising to a seven-wicket win and the calculations were being done. Two games to go, ten points between Sussex and history. 'We knew then that something would have to go horribly wrong for us not to win it.'

In many ways the penultimate game at Old Trafford seemed to be the ideal fixture for a team on the verge of immortality. Ever since the breathless victory over Lancashire at Hove a month earlier, Moores knew that Sussex's only remaining title rivals would be desperate to right a few wrongs. The challenge should have served to concentrate Sussex minds. Instead they ended up losing by an innings with a session to spare, despite the loss of the equivalent of nearly a day's play to rain.

In hindsight, all that rain didn't do us any good. The mood seemed to be that the draw was the obvious result because of the time we'd lost on the first two days. But the pitch broke up quite quickly and we lost an important toss. I think we might also have underestimated how much Lancashire wanted to win that game. They felt some of the umpiring decisions when we'd beaten them at Hove had gone against them and they wanted to redress the balance. We had to bat through the last day and I knew that would be difficult. The pressure was mounting and the wicket was doing a bit. In the end we could have no complaints, we'd been well beaten by the better team.

Sussex gained revenge of sorts the following day when they delayed Lancashire's National League title-winning celebrations with a nine-wicket win, a rare highlight in another disappointing limited-overs campaign. It was just the confidence boost the squad needed as they returned south to prepare for the finale against Leicestershire three days later.

I knew the lads would be nervous. They wouldn't have been human had they not felt some pressure, but I was determined that we were going to win it with a bit of style. I didn't want us scraping over the finishing line. There was Surrey's record of ten wins in a season to try to equal and more than anything I wanted people to say that we had deserved to be the champions.

Leicestershire played the role of party-poopers pretty well until moments before lunch on the first day, when Mushtaq Ahmed bowled Brad Hodge to take his 100th wicket.

That was like scoring the opening goal just before half-time in the World Cup final. Mushy got a standing ovation and then another one when we came in for lunch. The dressing room was on fire. We had learned to play under pressure and from that moment on I knew we would win the game. In the second session, when we bowled them out, we were absolutely cooking. All you can do as a coach is sit there and revel in it.

The finest moment of Peter Moores' career came the following day and then the celebrations began in earnest. The fact that there was still a game to be won became something of a glorious irrelevance as the squad enjoyed their moment of triumph, first in the dressing room and later in the Sussex Cricketer pub. A bleary-eyed Moores woke the next morning in the spare bed at the home of physio Stuart Osborne, five minutes before he was due on

Radio Five Live: 'I just about got through that interview, God knows how. I was still very drunk.' A few hours later, inspired bowling by Jason Lewry had secured an innings victory and the celebrations could start all over again.

There was always a fair chance that one member of the Moores family would end up making a career out of cricket. Peter's enthusiasm for the game was nurtured by his father, Bernard, almost from the moment he could swing a home-made bat or catch the ball. It no doubt helped that there were plenty of siblings who shared his interest in sport – seven of them in fact. The Moores family – Mum, Dad, five brothers and three sisters – grew up in a three-storey townhouse in Macclesfield. Although not particularly famous for producing sporting luminaries, Macclesfield was also the birthplace of Jonathan Agnew and Matthew Fleming, the Kent all-rounder who played one-day cricket for England and has never hidden his ambition to conceal the fact that he comes from Macclesfield: 'Peter is one of the few professional athletes burdened with Macclesfield on his passport. He has my sympathy.'

Moores' brothers, Tony, Stephen, James and Robert, shared Peter's early love for sport and in particular cricket. 'We had the same bedroom, which provided a great venue for a rugby or football game involving large stuffed mice, usually played when we should have been in bed,' said Stephen. 'The other good thing about the house was the backyard and the entry, which was the ideal size for cricket, about four foot wide and 20 foot long with the bottom half of the entry door the wicket. Many great Test matches were played in that entry – usually England v West Indies, occasionally Lancashire, but never Sussex!'

When he was 12, Peter was given Alan Knott's *Book of Wicketkeeping* as a birthday present. It made a big impression on the young Moores.

> By then cricket was no longer just a game, but a way of life for me. Knotty was a hero of every young cricketer at the time and reading that book really got me interested in the skills of wicketkeeping. It sounds a bit daft, but that book got me started. It was a big influence on my career.

By the age of 14 he was keeping wicket in the first XI at King's School in Macclesfield and playing age-group cricket for Cheshire, his potential having been spotted by Ian Wilson, the master in charge of cricket at King's.

> It was remarkable how quickly he was accepted in the first XI, not only for the quality of his wicketkeeping but also as a cricket-mad character. As a

youngster coming into a team of older lads, many of whom had to earn their place in the side the hard way, Peter had to have something special, and he definitely did.

For the next four years Moores enjoyed an outstanding schoolboy career as a wicketkeeper-batsman and by the time he left in 1981 he was captain of King's and had earned a place in the England Schoolboys side after a successful trial. And, alongside his undoubted ability, it was his approach to the game, according to Wilson, that stood out: a dedication to fitness – he worked on improving his physique with home-made dumbells made out of old detergent bottles filled with sand – and a willingness to learn about the game at every opportunity.

He played for England Schoolboys under the captaincy of Hugh Morris, but it was an impressive performance in the annual match between King's School and MCC in the late summer of 1981 that gave Moores the opportunity to take the next step.

Freddie Millet, who did a lot for schools' cricket in Macclesfield, always ran the MCC game. They were quite impressed, so Freddie took me down to Lord's for a trial at the end of 1981. It went well and they took me on.

Among the 1982 intake at headquarters were Mike Veletta, who played Test cricket for Australia, and Dermot Reeve, who was to become a teammate of Moores at Hove a few years later and remembers Peter's enthusiastic approach, even to mundane tasks like selling scorecards on big match days or bowling to MCC members.

One player could always be found still practising when the light had faded or Don Wilson, who was our coach, had given the lads the all-clear to shower and exit. Most of the boys could hardly walk by the end of the day and were counting the minutes until Don's final whistle, but 'Action' – as we nicknamed Peter – was still bubbling over with enthusiasm.

In Wilson, the 1982 intake had an enthusiastic and knowledgeable tutor. The previous summer Ian Botham had laid waste to the Australians, eight years after he'd been on the Lord's groundstaff. 'Just look what Botham did,' Wilson would remind his pupils. 'That could be you.' Perhaps he was stretching the point a little, but Moores warmed to Wilson, his love of the game and the importance he placed on fostering good team spirit. The boys were paid the princely sum of £32 on a Friday afternoon and then Wilson would hold court in the indoor school bar at Lord's. Moores would normally be the last to leave, happy to make sure there was always a full glass in front of the coach as long as the stories kept coming.

Three months into the season, his career took an unexpected turn. Mark Vaughan, the regular understudy to David Humphries at Worcestershire, broke his nose and Lord's recommended Moores to the county. 'I had one trial game and they took me on for the rest of the season, basically I just switched contracts.' The success Worcestershire enjoyed in the late 1980s was still a few years away when Moores pitched up there for the first time in July 1982, but the foundations were already being laid. In his first season he helped the county win the Second XI Championship for the first time in 20 years. Cutting their teeth alongside Moores in that successful side were the likes of Richard Illingworth, Phil Newport, Tim Curtis – all of whom played for England – and Damian d'Oliveira. Basil d'Oliveira cast a paternal eye over his son and the rest in his role as club coach, while Phil Neale had just succeeded Glenn Turner as the county's third captain in as many years. At various times the second XI was captained by Vanburn Holder, now a respected umpire on the first-class circuit, and Curtis. Moores played ten matches for the Championship-winning team and had established himself as deputy to David Humphries by the end of the season. 'Peter Moores was a successful and enthusiastic wicketkeeper,' noted *Wisden*.

Moores' first-class debut came the following season against Somerset at New Road: 'I'll never forget it. I flat-batted Ian Botham through the covers for four first ball and he got me out next ball!' He played seven times that season and made a further four appearances in 1984, but by then Worcestershire had identified Yorkshire's Steve Rhodes, rather than Moores, as the long-term replacement for Humphries. Moores was distraught, but Neale and d'Oliveira wrote letters of recommendation to all the first-class counties after releasing him at the end of the 1984 season, and Sussex responded with the offer of a trial the following March.

By then he was already taking his first tentative steps into coaching. In the winter of 1984/5 he spent weekends playing for Harare Sports Club in Zimbabwe, the rest of the week teaching the game to the well-heeled pupils of a privately run college some 80 kilometres up country from Harare. 'It was a tough introduction because of the amount of coaching you had to do. That was what the job entailed basically.' The following off-season offered a more daunting task when he coached Free State Country in South Africa. 'There was a very good standard. Even the club team I played for at weekends contained eight or nine players with first-class experience. They were no Western Province, but it was still a heavy duty job for someone who was 20-plus and still a bit wet behind the ears.'

Moores returned home from Zimbabwe, got blind drunk with Neil Lenham, an old opponent from schoolboy cricket, on the eve of his Sussex trial, and impressed sufficiently to be taken on after a month as understudy to Ian Gould. His Championship debut at Bristol in June was also his solitary appearance in 1985 and it was nearly two more years before he played for the county again. A serious back injury threatened to end his career before it had started. Only his own determination stood between him and the scrapheap.

I had a series of injections, but basically the whole of 1986 was a write-off. I remember going to see a doctor in Hastings just before Christmas who gave me the last injection and thinking that was it, my career was over. He told me if I was to have any chance of playing again I would have to swim 50 lengths every day before the start of the season. I had to be very disciplined in my rehabilitation but I didn't mind that. In fact, I loved it. I got really fit and never really suffered from a bad injury again.

In 1987 Moores established himself as first-choice wicketkeeper, and in John Barclay, and then Paul Parker, he found captains who shared his passion for the game even if their enthusiasm wasn't always mirrored in the rest of the Sussex dressing room.

John made a good impression on me pretty much straight after I got into the side. I still remember an incident in my third or fourth game. Imran Khan had only been bowling for three overs with the new ball when John sidled up to me at the end of an over and asked me whether I thought he should take him off. I couldn't believe it. Here was the captain asking me whether we should replace someone who, at that time, was one of the best bowlers in the world. I couldn't answer him, I was speechless. But that day I vowed that when anyone asked for my thoughts on the game I would give them.

As he established himself as a player, so his interest in coaching blossomed.

Even back then I knew that if possible I wanted to coach full-time. The plan was to play on until I was 40 and then coach, hopefully at first-class level. During the winter I was virtually full-time at Hove in the indoor nets in the Gilligan Stand. It was great experience because one minute you would be coaching a group of ten-year-olds and the next session might be with a 70-year-old getting his eye in again before the start of the season. There was lots of one-to-one coaching, which I liked, and it gave me a really good grounding.

❖ ❖ ❖

Even for someone with Moores' energy and enthusiasm, captaining and coaching the side was always asking too much, so the decision to retire from playing in May 1998 wasn't difficult. He finally hung up his gloves after 230 first-class matches, in which he scored more than 7,000 runs and took 502 catches. He played 235 one-day games, scoring just over 2,500 runs, with 213 catches. The last of his seven first-class hundreds, in the final match of the 1997 season against Nottinghamshire, probably gave him the most pleasure. His form with the bat that season, his only one as captain, had been disappointing, which was hardly surprising considering the burden he had to carry as skipper, coach, social organiser and occasional nursemaid to the younger players, whose development he saw as his number one priority. The standing ovation he received after that final hundred meant a lot to him.

Tony [Pigott] made me player-coach, but by the start of the 1998 season I knew I couldn't do both jobs as well as I wanted to. Fortunately we'd signed Chris Adams and Michael Bevan, so there was a lot more experience on the field. We just needed someone to organise things off it. I always saw coaching as the next step for me after playing, but it was still a bit of a surprise that it happened so quickly.

Now Moores had the chance to start implementing changes to the whole structure of Sussex cricket. It was a task he attacked with his customary zeal. He admired the motivational methods which Dermot Reeve, his old teammate on the MCC groundstaff, and Bob Woolmer were employing to bring success to Warwickshire. The game was changing at Edgbaston and elsewhere but Sussex, as had often been the case in pre-revolution days, were struggling to keep up.

We were forced into change in 1997. It doesn't always mean that change is good, but our record over the previous ten years suggested we needed to change our approach. If you always do what you always did you will always get what you always got. At the start of every season we would turn up without really looking at the facts, thinking it would be our year, but it never was, even though our dressing room had some of the most talented players in the country. County cricket was stagnant for years, but the whole culture started to change for the better thanks to people like Bob Woolmer and Dermot Reeve. They were the catalysts. In contrast, we at Sussex seemed to be closed off to a lot of what was going on around us in terms of fresh ideas and ways of doing things, and I wanted to try and put that right.

Moores was quite happy to steal ideas from other sports and to integrate them into his own fresh approach. The days when players disappeared at the end of the season and weren't seen again until the following March became a thing of the past. Year-long training was introduced. Players were encouraged to attend regular winter net sessions and embrace the training programme put together by sports scientists at Brighton University. Even players who were allowed to go abroad had to follow a strict fitness regime. When one returned from Australia overweight at the start of the 2001 season it was touch and go whether he would be allowed to go on the pre-season tour. Even then he was forced to endure gruelling early-morning runs up and down the hills near the team hotel in Grenada as punishment.

Sussex were among the first counties to embrace the video analysis system, which logs every ball of every game and provides a valuable tool in improving players' technical skills. The days when players would do laps of the outfield and then have nets in pre-season seemed light years away when Moores was leading the squad around Army assault courses or on orienteering expeditions with his boyish enthusiasm.

Of course, the bottom line remained performances on the field. From his early days as head coach Moores recognised the need to make the playing staff smaller, to encourage quality rather than quantity. In his first year Sussex had a squad of 24. In their Championship season it was down to 18 and is unlikely to rise above that number while Moores has anything to do with it. As the numbers decrease, so the wage bill has risen, topping £1m for the last two years: 'We believe in rewarding the players well, but as well as having talent – which every professional cricketer has – they have to buy into what we are trying to achieve in terms of every aspect of the game.' That includes playing their part in fostering a sense of togetherness in the dressing room which has become the envy of many of their rival counties.

His methods slowly began to get results. Apart from the unexpected blip in 2000 there was steady progress. In 2002 the club moved with surprising haste to offer him a new four-year contract and ward off interest from other counties, notably Warwickshire. He holds the level four national coaching certificate – the highest domestic coaching qualification – and is widely regarded as the best of the English-born coaches operating in the domestic game. If he ever leaves Hove, it could well be to replace Duncan Fletcher in charge of the England team.

For now his priority is crystal-clear. Having finally reached the summit of English cricket, the challenge is to keep motivating his players to do their utmost to keep Sussex there.

There is excellence in everyone and, as a coach, my job is to take the lid off and let people play with freedom and take away the fear of failure. That remains the biggest challenge, because not so long ago we always felt we were trying to keep the lid on.

Undoubtedly one of the cornerstones of Sussex's success has been the relationship between Moores and his captain Chris Adams. They have been through a lot together, but there remains a huge mutual respect. Their core beliefs about the game and what it represents are the same, and fundamental disagreements are rare.

Chris lets me do my job and I let him do his, and my respect for him as a captain is huge. I think both as a person and a cricketer he has matured a lot. You saw that in 2003. It is hard to captain a side when you're not playing well, but Chris put the considerations of the team first and I was thrilled when he came good with the bat in the second half of the season.

The feeling of respect is mutual.

Peter has been alongside me every step of the way since I came to Sussex in 1997. All of us, but most of all me, owe a lot to Peter on a team and personal level. He was reluctant to step forward and take credit for what we achieved last season, but I know how thrilled he is with what he and the players were able to achieve.

For Moores there are still never enough hours in the day. But now, in his new role as the county's director of cricket, he has the opportunity to shape the future of Sussex cricket from the professionals in the first team right down to under-tens, the youngsters who are starting to get a feel for the game at about the same age as he did.

You can't really compare coaching with playing. In many ways playing is easier – you turn up, perform to the best of your ability and go home. Coaching is all-encompassing, but you get huge satisfaction when it all comes together as it did for us in 2003. It's fun watching people improve. You haven't done it for them, but you have helped and that gives you a great buzz.

## 7

THE SUPPORTING CAST

Continuity of selection was undoubtedly one of the key elements in Sussex's Championship success. Of the 15 players used in 2003, a core of six played in all 16 matches: skipper Chris Adams, Mushtaq Ahmed, openers Richard Montgomerie and Murray Goodwin, all-rounder Robin Martin-Jenkins and wicketkeeper-batsman Matt Prior. Two players, Tony Cottey and Tim Ambrose, were only missing for one match.

Not all of the 15 produced match-winning performances, but when one was needed, inevitably a player stepped forward. 'We had players taking wickets and scoring runs at different times of the season, so no two or three players peaked at the same time,' said Adams. 'There was always someone who came to the fore – that was our strength – while the support the players gave each other was immense, especially when they were struggling for form.' Here are their stories.

JAMES KIRTLEY (VICE-CAPTAIN)

Born: Eastbourne, 10 January 1975. Sussex debut: 1995 (capped 1998).
First-class appearances for Sussex: 106. Runs: 1,276. Wickets: 409.

In the late summer of 2003 James Kirtley's hard work and unstinting belief in his own ability was rewarded. He finally made his Test debut for England against South Africa at Trent Bridge and then joined the celebrations as his beloved Sussex clinched their first Championship. 'It was an amazing time,' he said. 'Everything I've ever wanted to achieve in the game happened in the space of a few weeks.'

Unfortunately, a recurrence of a shin splints injury, which he first suffered playing in his second Test at the end of August, meant Kirtley was unable to take part in the decisive match against Leicestershire, although he was fit enough to lead the side in the field for an hour at the start of the third day. The ovation he received must have brought a lump to his throat, but Sussex supporters weren't going to miss the opportunity to show their appreciation for Kirtley's Herculean efforts, not just in the 2003 season, but in the previous

James Kirtley appeals for lbw in the win over Kent where he took six second-innings wickets and bowled himself into the England Test squad. *(Simon Dack/ Brighton Argus)*

seven, when, on more than one occasion, he seemed to be carrying the bowling attack almost single-handedly: 'The Leicestershire game was a tough one to miss out on. I tried hard to regain my fitness but it wasn't to be. However, I had the confidence to know that I'd made a contribution this year even though I missed nearly a third of the season because of international commitments or injury.'

A match-winning 6–26 in the early season win over Kent was witnessed by England selector Geoff Miller, but he was left out of the final XI for the two Tests against Zimbabwe on the morning of the match and returned instead to county duty. Those were cruel blows, but Kirtley hid his disappointment well and took 10 wickets in the wins over Nottinghamshire and Kent. Kirtley didn't appear in any of Sussex's last five Championship games as he established himself at Test level by playing in back-to-back Tests against South Africa. He took 13 wickets, including a match-winning 6–34 as England squared the series at Trent Bridge. But events at Hove were never far from his mind.

He finished one short of claiming 50 wickets in a season for the fifth successive year, a remarkable record that reflects both the consistency of his performances and his fitness: 'I have only missed eight matches in eight seasons and it was inevitable that at some stage injury was going to catch up with me, but there was no point in going for short-term fixes.'

Kirtley was with the coaching staff and other members of the squad on the balcony when Murray Goodwin hit the 'winning' runs. He has been alongside Peter Moores and his new-ball partner Jason Lewry every step of the way since the dark days of 1996, when he must have wondered whether he would have to move on to fulfil his ambitions in the game.

Yet he always believed he would help his county make history.

For someone who has been at the club for as long as me it's hard to explain just what it meant. It may have been six or seven years in the making, but I always believed I would be part of a Sussex team which won the Championship. I will never forget the expressions on the faces of the supporters and people who work behind the scenes on the day we won. It just brought home how much it meant to everyone.

MURRAY GOODWIN

Born: Harare, Zimbabwe, 11 December 1972. Sussex debut: 2001 (capped 2001). First-class appearances for Sussex: 50. Runs: 4,378.

Murray Goodwin has won his place in Sussex cricket lore as the man who 'won' their first Championship. Goodwin has taken Test hundreds off some of the best attacks in the world, but his phenomenal batting performance in the clincher against Leicestershire rated just as highly on a personal level. He had told his teammates when they huddled together on the outfield before the start of play that he wanted to hit *the* winning runs. He was true to his word, but far from finished. Four hours later he was acknowledging the umpteenth standing ovation on that unforgettable day after scoring 335 not out and breaking Sussex's individual batting record, which had stood for 73 years.

Sussex have arguably never had a better-value overseas player than Goodwin. He topped the averages for the second time in three summers with the county, although it wasn't until the second half of the season that he started to produce the weight of runs that helped underpin their charge to the title. Of his 1,496 Championship runs, which gave him the fourth-highest aggregate in the country, just 458 were made in the first nine games. He was finally up and running at Trent Bridge with 148 against Nottinghamshire, before another weak attack was mercilessly dealt with at Colchester, where Goodwin took 210 off the Essex bowlers, a career-best that he was to eclipse less than a month later. Although it came in a losing cause, perhaps his best performance was in the penultimate match at Old Trafford. Pinned by a bouncer from Lancashire's Peter Martin, which caused a cut requiring eight stitches and left his right cheek bone severely bruised, he made a defiant 118 and won the unstinting admiration of his teammates. Matt Prior, who batted with him in both innings, had no hesitation in declaring Goodwin's gutsy effort his individual highlight of the season.

Goodwin tends to choose his words carefully and keeps his emotions in check, but even he was overwhelmed by those memorable scenes at Hove and the part he had played in helping his adopted county make history.

Winning the Championship is up there with anything I have achieved in the game and breaking the county's batting record was a humbling experience, just to see my name up there with some fantastic players. To be honest I hadn't got any idea I was close to it, but just after I'd got past 300 Carl Hopkinson came on with a change of gloves to tell me what the record was and that we'd be declaring as soon as I got there. I just about had the energy to get the 30-odd runs I needed. The walk back to the dressing room at the end is something I will never forget.

As for the team, we kept playing good cricket throughout the season, so actually winning the Championship was no fluke. Of course we were lucky to have someone like Mushtaq Ahmed, but three players got over 1,000 runs and four others were close, which showed what an awesome team effort it was. When you have guys coming in at six, seven and eight and scoring big runs you can't begin to imagine how much it does for the confidence of the whole side.

In February 2004 he agreed a new one-year contract with Sussex.

Record breaker. Murray Goodwin acknowledges the applause after scoring the boundary that clinched the Championship. Seconds later he was engulfed by delighted teammates as the celebrations began.
(Liz Finlayson/Brighton Argus)

JASON LEWRY

Born: Worthing, 2 April 1971. Sussex debut: 1994 (capped 1996).
First-class appearances for Sussex: 110. Runs: 1,254. Wickets: 397.

He began the 2003 season wondering if it was to be his last in first-class cricket and ended it in the dusk of a late summer's evening, sitting in a semi-circle with his teammates on the Hove wicket, trying to take in just what they had achieved in helping Sussex finally win their first Championship.

As one of the few current players born and bred in the county, Lewry will always have a place in the affections of Sussex supporters, but they must have wondered whether his best days were behind him. Privately at least, Lewry shared those fears. After all, he'd finished 2002 so desperately short of confidence that he was bowling left-arm away-swingers around the wicket and 'wondering what the hell I was doing'. Twelve months later he was reflecting proudly on the part he'd played in helping his county make history.

He finished with 41 wickets but would have taken a lot more had he not been sidelined by injury for five games. His second lay-off came after he'd taken ten wickets, his best performance for nearly two years, at his beloved Arundel in the win over Essex. He returned for the last four matches and won the admiration of his teammates when he took 8–106 in the second innings in the finale against Leicestershire, not so much because it secured the victory that equalled Surrey's record of ten wins since the Championship was split into two divisions, but because it earned them a precious extra day off. As Lewry cheerfully admits, bowling 20 overs and taking eight wickets represented a remarkable physical achievement on his part, considering the extent to which he and the rest of the squad had been celebrating their title win the previous evening.

Jason Lewry, a regular wicket-taker in the successful Championship campaign, gives his all against Kent at Hove. (Simon Dack/Brighton Argus)

On that Friday morning it's fair to say I was still a bit worse for wear. I was driven to the ground and fell over getting out of the car, tore my trousers and hobbled into the ground with blood all over my knee. We did one gentle warm-up lap before play started but even that was too much for James Kirtley. He kept on running – right to the toilets by the hospitality boxes so he could be sick!

Everyone was in a bad way. We took a couple of early wickets but they batted well and after tea it looked like we would have to come back again for a fourth day. Chris Adams came up to me and said if I got Darren Maddy out he would run around the ground naked. Next ball, I got him out so he offered to do it again! He ended up doing five laps of the ground later that evening in front of the players. The other lads were just as pleased. They all kept coming up to me offering congratulations, not so much for the eight wickets but for making sure we'd given ourselves more time to get over our hangovers!

The game won, the players returned to the Sussex Cricketer pub to continue the celebrations.

Another unforgettable night, I have never known an atmosphere like it. To be honest my car didn't leave the car park at the ground for another three weeks. We seemed to be celebrating all the time. Even a few months afterwards people were still coming up to me offering their congratulations. Until it happened and you saw people in tears on the day we won it, you didn't realise just how much what we achieved meant to so many people.

Lewry was determined to enjoy the season as if it were his last. Perhaps his batting reflected that carefree approach more than his bowling. There were unexpected late order cameos in the first two games, which yielded important tail-end runs, and then, at Colchester, he produced the maiden first-class fifty which he'd been threatening for nine years. Meanwhile, from his regular station at mid-on, he got as good a view as anyone of the phenomenal impact made by Mushtaq Ahmed.

Mushy was just inspirational, simple as that. As the recognised strike bowlers, there is a lot of pressure on James Kirtley and myself to get the wickets, but we could actually bowl around him last season and that definitely helped us. He didn't bowl a better ball all season than the one that got him his 100th wicket.

TONY COTTEY

Born: Swansea, 2 June 1966. Sussex debut: 1999 (capped 1999).
First-class appearances for Sussex: 63. Runs: 3,438.

As a Welshman, helping his former county Glamorgan to Championship glory in 1997 ranks as Tony Cottey's proudest moment in the game. But becoming one of the handful of current players who have won the title with two different counties wasn't far behind. What's more, Cottey played an outstanding role in Sussex's success after four relatively lean years with the county. His 1,149 runs also ensured that his love affair with the game would continue into an 18th season after his contract was extended for another year.

It's doubtful that Cottey ever played better in his entire career than during one month in the high summer of 2003. His purple patch began at Hove at the end of June with 188 against Warwickshire, flourished at Arundel where he fell just two runs short of taking hundreds off the Essex attack in both innings, and continued a few days later with another century, this time against Leicestershire at Grace Road. He made seven consecutive fifties, one short of C.B. Fry's county record, which was established in 1900. As experienced a campaigner as Cottey knows just how the vicissitudes of the game can tease a player. He was just happy to prove wrong those beyond the boundary at

Hove who had always doubted his ability. He was happy, too, in sharing his Championship-winning experiences in those crucial last few weeks of the season with the more callow members of the dressing room.

> We became The Immortals – the first Sussex team to win the Championship – and it's a nice thought that when people look back in a hundred years' time they will remember what we helped achieve. It's something everyone who played their part can be proud of.

Of his own contribution, Cottey is more modest.

> Every season you are going to have periods when you feel in nick and other times when you can't buy a run. I had a purple patch and made the most of it, but as everyone who was part of what we achieved will say, the best thing about our success was that it was a team effort. Six or seven guys contributed with the bat and Mushtaq gave us that bit extra with the ball.

RICHARD MONTGOMERIE

Born: Rugby, Warwickshire, 3 July 1971. Sussex debut: 1999 (capped 1999). First-class appearances for Sussex: 83. Runs: 5,499. Wickets: 2.

By his standards, Richard Montgomerie had a lean year with the bat in 2003. Consistency had been his hallmark in his four previous seasons with Sussex, so it was a surprise that he made just one hundred in the Championship year, although it wasn't a surprise that it came at Horsham, a ground which has been good to him over the years.

Montgomerie's productive partnerships with Murray Goodwin at the top of the order were a feature of Sussex's promotion success in 2001. In 2003 they posted just two century stands, but the 202 they put on against Essex at Colchester was certainly among the most entertaining in the three years since they began opening the Sussex innings together. The other century partnership came against Surrey in the top-of-the-table encounter at Hove, where their 149 set up the platform for Chris Adams to mark his return to form.

But in one facet of the game Montgomerie was almost unsurpassed, both among his teammates and in the country as a whole. Only two players took more than his 22 catches, the vast majority of Montgomerie's taken in his specialist position at short leg. Without his outstanding reflexes and spring-heeled reactions it's doubtful whether Mushtaq Ahmed would have reached a century of wickets.

Montgomerie has been at Hove long enough to remember the bad times, notably when they finished 2000 bottom of Division Two, and he could have been forgiven for thinking the team faced another year of struggle in 2003 after their ignominious surrender to Warwickshire, the county for whom he played junior cricket, in mid-May. They bounced back with a spectacular win over Nottinghamshire in their next match, fortified by Montgomerie's solitary hundred of the season. It was then, even at this relatively early stage of the season, that he felt Sussex might win the title.

> Mushtaq and James Kirtley were bowling beautifully and the batting was starting to fire. I thought then that we had a chance, but our most important win was against Lancashire and undoubtedly the defining moment of the season was the Middlesex home game. We were down and out twice, but came back to win. It was a game I will remember for the rest of my life.

While Montgomerie acknowledges the part every one of his teammates played in the success, he reserves special praise for Peter Moores, the person who knows almost as much about Montgomerie's game as the player himself: 'His attention to detail and dedication were outstanding. He and Chris Adams deserved the success more than most because they are the ones who suffer most when we lose.'

TIM AMBROSE

Born: Newcastle, New South Wales, 1 December 1982. Sussex debut: 2001 (capped 2003). First-class appearances for Sussex: 30. Runs: 1,821.

The Aussie accent is still unmistakable, but Tim Ambrose now considers himself a son of Sussex and, after the role he played in their Championship success, the county's supporters proudly regard him as one of their own. He hadn't turned 21 when the title was secured, but his performances in 2003 marked him down as a player of genuine international potential.

It wasn't so long ago that Sussex were desperately struggling to fill the void left by Peter Moores' retirement. Now, in Ambrose and Matt Prior, they have two outstanding young wicketkeeper-batsmen, either of whom would comfortably hold down a place at most rival counties. Prior began the season in possession of the gloves, but Ambrose took over wicketkeeping duties against Warwickshire at the end of June and never looked back.

There were many highlights for him in 2003. Together with Prior, and watched from the boundary by his father Ray, who had flown over from Australia for the occasion, he was awarded his county cap during the Surrey game at Hove. There were crucial contributions with the bat at No. 5, notably at Arundel, where his unbeaten 93 saw Sussex home. In both innings he helped Tony Cottey, with whom he shared a house during the summer,

Tim Ambrose whips off the bails and stumps Leicestershire's John Sadler. Tony Cottey admires his teammate's handiwork from slip. *(Simon Dack/Brighton Argus)*

construct match-winning partnerships. He was happy to admit afterwards it was one of the funniest experiences he'd ever had on a cricket field. 'Cotts kept me going by telling me stories between overs, most of them dirty!' There were eight other half-centuries and perhaps the only disappointment was his failure to convert one of them into a precious hundred, but they will no doubt come on a regular basis as his talent continues to blossom.

With the guidance of Moores and the pressure for his place from Prior there was never any doubt that Ambrose's wicketkeeping skills would improve as the season wore on. The biggest compliment his teammates and those admiring his neat and tidy glovework from beyond the boundary can pay him is to say that, like all good stumpers, you hardly noticed his presence. There were 29 catches and seven stumpings, most of them off Mushtaq Ahmed, whose exotic variations he picked more easily than a succession of hapless batsmen.

All smiles. Tim Ambrose celebrates with Matt Prior after stumping Leicestershire's John Sadler. *(Simon Dack/Brighton Argus)*

Ambrose is a young head on experienced shoulders, and having enjoyed Sussex's success, he has a taste for more.

After all we went through together as a team you can't describe the elation when we finally won the Championship. There were some pretty amazing performances, but if I had to pick out one it has to be Lancashire at home when every one of us played his part.

Early in the season he declared his intention to play for England rather than Australia when he becomes qualified by residency at the end of 2004, and there is no doubt he has a bright future. 'I'm definitely a Sussex man now. I love living here and I will always be grateful to Sussex for giving me my chance so early.'

MATT PRIOR

Born: Johannesburg, South Africa, 26 February 1982. Sussex debut: 2001.
First-class appearances for Sussex: 48. Runs: 2,180.

No one epitomised the spirit of adventure in Sussex's 2003 success better than Matt Prior. It would have been easy for him to retreat into introspective mode when his role in the side changed halfway through the season. Instead, in his first game freed of wicketkeeping responsibilities, he made a hundred against Warwickshire and followed it with two more in the second half of the summer as he passed 1,000 runs for the first time, a considerable achievement for a No. 7 who often had to bat with the tail. But it wasn't just the weight of runs, it was the way he scored them. A strike rate of 74.96 put even his captain, who is no slowcoach, in the shade and there were 18 Championship sixes, again more than any of his teammates.

There's no doubt that his most important contribution came in the win over Middlesex at Hove. At 105–6 the county were in danger of following on, but in partnership with Mark Davis he launched a thrilling counter-attack that saw 195 runs added for the seventh wicket. His contribution of 148 was only five runs short of the career-best he'd made a fortnight earlier against Essex, when, for the second time in the season, he reached three figures by clearing the ropes. On both occasions Sussex supporters were left wondering wistfully when they'd last witnessed such a display of Bothamesque hitting from one of their favourites. To round off an outstanding summer, Prior earned a place in England's winter academy and was soon getting approving glances from Rod Marsh, the Academy director, who knows a thing or two about the wicketkeeper's art.

Even then, as memories of Sussex's success began to fade, Prior was finding it hard to believe that at 21 he'd already won two major honours in the game.

I remember Mark Robinson, who was my first room-mate, telling me when I came onto the staff in 2001 that I would be very lucky to win the Championship. Now I've helped get us promoted to Division One and we've won the biggest prize of the lot.

I would like to have kept wicket more, but I accepted that whoever was doing the job better had to play. One of the papers described me and Tim

Taking cover. Matt Prior is in the firing
line against Essex at Arundel.
(Simon Dack/Brighton Argus)

[Ambrose] as friendly rivals. Well, they got that half right because we are mates and we have a huge laugh about our so-called rivalry. We are best friends but there is a lot of respect for each other as well.

Early in 2004 Prior committed himself to the county for a further four years by signing a new contract. He went to the England Academy, was selected for the A team tour to India and vowed to reclaim the wicketkeeper's gloves on his return to Hove for the new season: 'Staying at Sussex wasn't a difficult decision to make. I think the Championship win is the start of something big, not a one-off.'

ROBIN MARTIN-JENKINS

Born: Guildford, Surrey, 28 October 1975. Sussex debut: 1995 (capped 2000). First-class appearances for Sussex: 84. Runs: 3,735. Wickets: 199.

Confidence is such a vital part of any professional sportsman's make-up. Just ask Robin Martin-Jenkins, who was at a low ebb early in the 2003 season. His first five Championship appearances had yielded just nine wickets and 180 runs, and for the first time in his Sussex career, his

place as the county's principal all-rounder was under serious threat. In a C&G Trophy game at the end of May against Middlesex he was withdrawn from the attack after bowling two expensive overs. But something happened in the short journey from Lord's to The Oval, where Sussex faced Surrey in their next Championship game two days later. His spirits soared as the rhythm suddenly returned to his bowling action, and his renewed confidence was reflected in some outstanding batting. He scored half-centuries in both innings at The Oval and did the same again when Sussex completed a rare double over Kent in their next fixture. By the end of that game his teammates were making somewhat flattering comparisons with Don Bradman, and even The Don might

All-rounder Robin Martin-Jenkins made some crucial contributions with bat and ball during the season. *(Aaron St Clair/Brighton Argus)*

have approved of the stylish way he flayed the Nottinghamshire attack to score his only century of the season a few weeks later.

Of all the Sussex bowlers, Martin-Jenkins benefited most from the emergence of Mushtaq Ahmed. Chris Adams was able to keep him fresh by using him in short spells, none more effective than the 3–9 burst that undermined Kent's second innings in the win at Tunbridge Wells. In James Kirtley's absence he often had to open the attack and proved to be a canny operator with the new ball. It was no coincidence either that a reduced workload, certainly in Championship matches, enabled him to stay injury-free and play in virtually every game, both in four-day and limited-overs cricket. Then there was the ongoing improvement in his mental approach to batting, which he partly attributed to trying hard not to get out, even if it was for only ten minutes in the nets. The days when he would give his wicket away with reckless regularity seemed to be a thing of the past in 2003.

Like James Kirtley and Jason Lewry, R.M.J. can still remember the bad old days of Sussex cricket. It made the champagne taste that bit more special.

Six years ago if someone told me that one day we'd win the Championship, I would have called them a liar. The success we enjoyed seemed a long way off then. But every year the squad has improved and once we got on a roll and started to win a few games you could tell we were going to go very close, if not win it. Fantastic memories – I'll never forget the faces on the crowd when we did our lap of honour in the Leicestershire game. I've been part of Sussex cricket for a long time but even I didn't really appreciate how much it meant to so many people.

MARK DAVIS

Born: Port Elizabeth, South Africa, 10 October 1971. Sussex debut: 2001 (capped 2002). First-class appearances for Sussex: 41. Runs: 1,172. Wickets: 67.

It was no surprise that the player who spent most of the 2003 season in the shadow of Mushtaq Ahmed was the side's other slow bowler, Mark Davis. But ask his teammates to name the individual performance that turned Championship dreams into reality and, to a man, they would nominate Davis's career-best 168 against Middlesex in the penultimate home match. Until then Davis's contribution to the Championship success had been fairly modest. When his captain needed one end to be tied up, he could usually rely on the off-spinner to do it, but in ten matches he took just 14 wickets at a cost of over 50 runs each, although his 3–44 return in the second innings against Essex at Arundel was crucial in the context of a close match. In the first half of the season the fourth-bowler slot tended to go to Kevin Innes, but

Mark Davis was often overshadowed by fellow spinner Mushtaq Ahmed, but the popular South African made match-winning contributions with bat and ball. *(Simon Dack/Brighton Argus)*

once the sun appeared and wickets dried out Davis came into his own and played in the last five matches, proving to be an excellent foil for Mushtaq while retaining his happy habit of taking important wickets.

But it was as a batsman that Sussex needed him when he walked out to face a fired-up Middlesex attack with his side 105–6. While Matt Prior blazed away at the other end, Davis opted for crease occupation. A day later he was still batting, having helped his side turn a losing situation into a winning one.

'That was the best example of how, when we needed it most, someone came up with a big performance for us,' said Chris Adams. 'He'd had a pretty lean time with the bat but he kept promising us that he'd get a big score and he was true to his word. He is the epitome of the team man and is so highly regarded by his teammates.'

A few weeks later Davis found it hard to stop the tears as he joined Adams and Murray Goodwin on the outfield, moments after the Championship had been secured. He said:

> It was a very emotional moment for me and definitely the highlight of my career. The feeling when we won it and everyone did a lap of honour will stay with me for ever. I didn't have a great season with the ball, but after my innings against Middlesex I felt I had made a contribution. When the side needed it I chipped in, but it was a fabulous team effort overall that won us the Championship.

KEVIN INNES

Born: Wellingborough, Northamptonshire, 24 September 1975. Sussex debut: 2002. First-class appearances for Sussex: 21. Runs: 666. Wickets: 38.

A maiden first-class hundred, a unique place in the record books and a Championship winners' medal – not a bad season for a player who, 12 months earlier, wondered whether he had any future in the game at all. No one has been more invigorated by the seaside air than all-rounder Kevin Innes. He bravely decided to cut his losses with Northamptonshire, the county for whom he'd played second XI cricket at the age of 14, before the start of the 2002 season, even though his contract had another year to run. Essex didn't fancy him, but Sussex saw something when he arrived at Hove for a trial, and within a month he was making his Championship debut.

Innes' big breakthrough came a year later at Horsham in the win over Nottinghamshire, when he became the first 12th man in history to make a hundred. Twenty minutes later, as he scurried around the dressing room attending to 12th man duties, he reflected on his achievement, James Kirtley having taken his place as the nominated team member after returning from the Test squad. 'If I could bottle the emotion I felt when I reached my hundred and sell it I would be a very rich man, it was a very special moment for me.'

Magic moment. Kevin Innes
celebrates his maiden first-class
hundred against
Nottinghamshire.
(Liz Finlayson/Brighton Argus)

Horsham proved to be the high-water mark of Innes' season. He played in the next two games and also appeared at Leicester and Trent Bridge, but by then his bowling was badly hampered by a groin injury, which would need an operation at the end of the season, and he didn't play in any of the last five matches. Still, Innes was an integral part of the celebrations and happy to reflect on how his career had been transformed by his switch to Sussex.

> The coaching staff, in particular Peter Moores, have helped me so much. A couple of years ago I wasn't getting much of a chance at Northampton and even though I didn't think I had much of a future it was still a big decision to leave my home county. But here I am, a Championship winner. It was an unbelievable few months.

BILLY TAYLOR

Born: Southampton, 11 January 1977. Sussex debut: 1999.
First-class appearances: 28. Runs: 183. Wickets: 71.

Less than a fortnight after helping Sussex to glory, Billy Taylor had decided to leave the county and take up the offer of a three-year contract with Hampshire. It wasn't a hard decision to make. Taylor had enjoyed the celebrations and could reflect that he played a big part in the county's success with 21 wickets in his seven appearances, but the club couldn't give him any assurances that he would play more regularly in the future, and the opportunity of long-term security and regular cricket with his native Hampshire proved too tempting: 'It was disappointing still not to be considered one of the main bowlers at Sussex, but my time with the county finished with a massive high, helping them to win the Championship.'

Taylor has operated in the shadow of Sussex's regular new-ball pair of James Kirtley and Jason Lewry since he came to the club in 2000 after impressing in a trial match, and he often had to wait for injury to either of them or, in Kirtley's case, an England call-up before getting his chance. So it was in 2003. He played in successive matches at Horsham and The Oval, where he bowled without luck against a top-quality batting side, but it was only when Kirtley established himself in the England set-up at the beginning of August that he got an extended run in the team. His most important contribution was undoubtedly the second innings spell he produced against Lancashire at Hove when he took four wickets and bowled unchanged for 17 overs in the afternoon session on the final day to break the back of Lancashire's innings. It was a performance full of guts and no little skill, but

Taylor has always had those qualities in abundance. Nineteen of his wickets were taken in the last five matches, while his unbeaten, career-best 35 in the win over Middlesex came in a last-wicket stand of 106 with Mark Davis, the fourth highest in the county's history.

Now he is preparing for new challenges with no regrets: 'Being part of winning the Championship was fantastic, but this is a good move for me. I will miss Hove, especially the supporters and members who I think appreciated that I always tried my best.'

PAUL HUTCHISON

Born: Leeds, 9 June 1977. Sussex debut: 2002. First-class appearances for Sussex: 8. Runs: 52. Wickets: 13.

Few current cricketers have won Championships with two different counties. Sussex had two of them in 2003, but within weeks of the season's end, it was down to one after Paul Hutchison left Hove with a year remaining on his contract. Like Billy Taylor, the former Yorkshire left-armer felt a move would enable him to play more regular first-team cricket, and he joined Middlesex on a two-year contract, his third county in four years.

A succession of injuries meant Hutchison had played a peripheral part in Yorkshire's 2001 triumph. In 2003 he appeared just four times and in one of those games he was replaced by James Kirtley, who had been released by England, after bowling just five overs with the new ball against Kent at Tunbridge Wells. At least he felt he'd made a greater contribution to Sussex's success than Yorkshire's.

Coach Peter Moores worked hard to remodel Hutchison's action, and he left Hove a much better bowler than when he arrived, while concerns over his fitness record had largely disappeared. But, even after Taylor's departure, he accepted there were no guarantees that he would have a bigger role at Hove in the future.

The last two years have been very frustrating, but I wouldn't swap them for anything. It was disapointing that I didn't play a bigger part in helping win the Championship but I felt more part of it than when I was at Yorkshire. We seemed to build momentum all through the season and there were any number of fantastic individual performances which helped us, while the team spirit was the best I have ever known anywhere during my career.

Michael Yardy's brave half-century couldn't prevent defeat against Surrey at The Oval. *(Simon Dack/ Brighton Argus)*

MICHAEL YARDY

Born: Hastings, 27 November 1980. Sussex debut: 2000. First-class appearances for Sussex: 34. Runs: 1,486. Wickets: 3.

Restricted to just two Championship appearances, Michael Yardy nevertheless made an important contribution to Sussex's success and might have been able to establish himself on a regular basis had his valiant vigil in the game against Surrey at The Oval helped secure his side a draw. As it was, he was last man out with 5.2 overs remaining after defying a Test-quality attack for over five hours. For Sussex's next match he lost his place to Tony Cottey, who had now regained his fitness.

Yardy returned at the end of July to make a stylish 47 at Trent Bridge when Tim Ambrose suffered a knee injury, and in those two innings at least, the nuggetty left-hander proved – as much to himself as to anyone else – that he has what it takes to prosper at first-class level. He hasn't got the range of strokes of some of his teammates, but he sells his wicket dearly and his determined, hardworking approach clearly appeals to his captain Chris Adams: 'There are lots of guys in our team who like to play their shots but we also need guys who can play stodgy innings and guts it out and Michael is capable of doing that.'

It was hardly surprising that Yardy picked out Murray Goodwin's heroic effort against Lancashire at Old Trafford, when he battled on after being struck above the eye by Peter Martin to make a century, as his individual highlight of the season. As a player who'd come up through Sussex's junior ranks, Yardy relished the moment when history was made: 'To be able to win it in front of our own supporters was extra special.'

Carl Hopkinson, Bas Zuiderent and Shaun Rashid were the only members of the squad not to play in a Championship match. Zuiderent and Rashid were released at the end of the season.

8

CONFOUNDING THE ODDS

The bookmakers were sure. So were the cricket writers, the ex-players and the coaches when their opinions on how the County Championship would unravel were canvassed before the start of the 2003 season. The champions' pennant would either continue to flutter over The Oval or, at a pinch, be raised above the majestic pavilion at Old Trafford. Sussex? They were generally considered 33–1 outsiders and some bookmakers were even offering 50–1 against the oldest first-class county winning the blue riband for the first time. No one has yet been found, inside the county or beyond, who considered those odds too good an investment opportunity to turn down.

Too much reliance on James Kirtley, the soothsayers said. No evidence that Mushtaq Ahmed was as potent a force as he had been during his first stint in England with Somerset. Not enough depth in the batting. 'Will improve, but won't win much,' said Bob Woolmer, who coached Warwickshire to back-to-back titles in the mid-nineties and knows about these things. His prediction was one of the more generous ones.

How wrong they were. And how Sussex enjoyed proving them wrong. The county written off by everyone outside the Hove dressing room finished a hefty 34 points clear of their closest rivals, Lancashire. Large portions of humble pie all round. At least Lancashire, whose own long wait for another outright Championship was extended into a 70th year, had the scant consolation of an innings win over Sussex in the penultimate match of the season at Old Trafford. But that only served to ensure that Sussex would make history in front of their own supporters. Over three unforgettable days at Hove against Leicestershire in mid-September things were rounded-off nicely – Murray Goodwin broke the county's batting record and Mushtaq Ahmed became the first bowler since 1998 to take 100 wickets in the Championship.

Captain Chris Adams had been in bullish mood before the season got under way. Apart from the luck of a genuine pace merchant, he felt the squad of 18 – the smallest in the country – was the strongest he had captained and also the best balanced: 'This is as excited as I've felt for a long time. We're maturing as a squad and the way it has evolved there are now a lot more guys who are prepared to lead from the front rather than relying on one, two or three big players.' Adams called Mushtaq Ahmed his 'secret weapon' and there was a hint of what was to come at Hove on the opening weekend of the season.

While Sussex missed out as the first round of Championship games got under way in unseasonably warm weather over the Easter weekend, Mushtaq was flexing his fingers and bamboozling the students of Cardiff UCCE in the final warm-up match at the County Ground. He finished with figures of 11–49 as Sussex completed an easy win inside two days. For many of his new teammates, the Pakistani leg-spinner was something of an unknown quantity. Of the squad, fewer than half had played against him during his Somerset days and now, as he got to work in the nets, they were soon to encounter the problems that would confound countless batsman all over the country as the summer wore on. Robin Martin-Jenkins remembered his first encounter with Mushtaq as a gangling 19-year-old playing only his second match for Sussex in the Sunday League at Bath.

My first two balls were fizzing leg-breaks, which comfortably turned past my prodding bat. The third was, to my mind, short and outside off-stump. Just as I shaped to play the cut shot that was sure to send the ball crashing to the cover boundary, the ball broke back between my bat and pad and sent the bails flying. My main recollection of that innings was being amazed at the sound of the ball as it came towards me. It made a kind of buzzing noise like a swarm of wasps.

How grateful Martin-Jenkins and his teammates were that Mushtaq was on their side as the season unfolded.

There were times, particularly in the first third of the season, when it looked as if the bookmakers and the pundits had got it right and that Adams' confidence was wildly misplaced. Sussex finished poorly in their opening game at Lord's and positively awful at Edgbaston, where their second innings capitulation on the final afternoon prompted something of a first: a stinging public rebuke from coach Peter Moores, whose usual style when the wheels come off is to administer the reprimands within the the confines of the dressing room.

There were games when Sussex put their supporters through the emotional wringer before all was safely gathered in. Wins in the final session of the match were achieved on five occasions, most memorably at Hove in August when Lancashire were beaten with just 12 minutes to spare. It was breathless stuff but here was further evidence of a side growing in self-belief and increasingly sure of their own destiny.

Mushtaq Ahmed runs away in triumph after snaring his 100th victim of an incredible summer. *(Simon Dack/Brighton Argus)*

Hanging around. The life of a professional cricketer is not all glamour. Mushtaq Ahmed, James Kirtley, Peter Moores and Chris Adams try to keep warm at the pre-season photocall. *(Simon Dack/Brighton Argus)*

On other occasions the cricket Sussex produced simply overwhelmed their opponents. Those who witnessed it can seldom have seen a more ruthless performance from the county than the one that swept aside Essex in three days at Colchester in mid-August. This was the game that convinced the squad the title was now theirs to lose, a view reinforced 48 hours later when bottom-of-the-table Leicestershire confounded everyone, including themselves, by drawing with Surrey after following on 335 runs behind. The Sussex players, following events on Ceefax as they played a one-day game against Nottinghamshire, could scarcely believe it. Surrey won only once in the last 71 days of the season as their Championship defence imploded. Sussex took over at the top of the table at the end of that round of matches and their position was never threatened again.

MATCH 1 – LORD'S, 23–26 APRIL

Sussex 239 and 204, Middlesex 116 and 330–7. Middlesex (17pts) beat Sussex (4pts) by 3 wickets.

Sussex were winning this game right up until Middlesex's eighth-wicket pair, Ben Hutton and Simon Cook, came together and took advantage of a tiring attack with an unbroken stand of 42, which secured victory 35 minutes after tea on the final afternoon. Sussex would have won had Mushtaq Ahmed not been suffering from a badly infected finger. He finished with four wickets on his first-class debut for the county, but Sussex's bowling hero was James Kirtley. He took 4–87 in the second innings, including two wickets with the new ball, to leave Middlesex 288–7, but as he tired, Cook clubbed him for three boundaries in one over before Hutton swept Mushtaq to score the winning runs.

It was not quite the scenario Chris Adams had imagined when he won the toss. In spring sunshine, Lord's was looking its magnificent best and batsmen on both sides eyed a short boundary on the Grandstand side with considerable relish. Murray Goodwin and Richard Montgomerie appeared to have negotiated the new ball successfully, but then three wickets fell in six overs, including Tony Cottey for the first duck of the season. Two of the first three went to Queenslander Joe Dawes, who got considerable help from a green-tinged pitch in two spells from the Pavilion End either side of lunch.

Adams and Tim Ambrose effected a recovery of sorts with a fourth-wicket stand of 51 in 14 overs, but the innings went into decline when off-spinner Paul Weekes took a sensational return catch off a bludgeoning straight drive from Adams in the last over before lunch. Ambrose composed a 92-ball half-century, but his was one of five wickets to fall for 40 runs in 15 overs during the afternoon and at 172–9 the innings had gone into a tail-spin. An hour later, though, things looked a lot different after James Kirtley and Jason Lewry had put on a county record 67 for the last wicket, Lewry belting 45 off 43 balls.

A precious bonus point had been secured and at least now Sussex's bowlers had something to defend. Kirtley and Lewry, sharing the new ball for only the second time since May 2002, began to enjoy themselves just as much as the Middlesex seamers had done. Kirtley removed home captain Andrew Strauss and Lewry bowled the dangerous Owais Shah before nightwatchman Cook became Mushtaq's first victim of the season. Middlesex resumed on day two on 74–4 and within 90 minutes they had been dismissed for 116. Three wickets fell in ten balls in the middle order before Mushtaq mopped up the tail, as he was to do on so many occasions during the summer. Kirtley was outstanding and only the laws of gravity denied him a fourth wicket when a ball to Chad Keegan rattled both bails, one of which was perched precariously on its groove. Amazingly, neither fell to the ground as bemused players and umpires gathered around the stumps.

Sussex's first-innings lead of 123 should have been enough to set up victory, but if anything their batting second time around was more feckless than it had been on day one, and this time there were no heroics from numbers 10 and 11 to rescue them. Apart from Montgomerie, all of the top order got starts, but only Robin Martin-Jenkins showed the necessary determination against accurate seam bowling in awkward conditions as he reached the 16th half-century of his career in just over two hours of watchful occupation. The impressive Keegan – wearing a fetching Alice band – finished with 4–36 from 21 overs, but a ninth-wicket stand of 40 between Martin-Jenkins and Kirtley took Sussex's lead beyond 300. Surely that would be enough on such a sporting pitch.

The third day dawned cool and overcast, and when the forecast rain finally swept in during mid-afternoon, Middlesex had given themselves a fighting chance. Sussex added just ten more runs before Lewry fell to Dawes, which left the hosts with a target of 328. Strauss and Shah overcame the early loss of Sven Koenig to put on 117 for the second wicket, but Sussex appeared to have made a crucial intervention when Kevin Innes trapped Shah in front – one of 15 lbw decisions in the match – shortly before rain forced the players off.

An absorbing final day saw the balance swing from one side to the other. Strauss made a composed 83 before becoming one of Kirtley's victims, but Middlesex bat deep and there were contributions all the way down. Kirtley looked like being Sussex's matchwinner, but with Mushtaq's threat negated by his injury, he lacked support and Middlesex were able to celebrate a win in their first match since promotion.

Adams wasn't too downhearted. 'If we keep putting ourselves in the position we were in here we will win a lot of games this season,' he said. 'With 14 points for a win there is more of an incentive and I can see there being a lot of ups and downs. Mushtaq did well considering the pain he was in; to see him bowling in such agony was quite distressing just to watch.'

MATCH 2 – HOVE, 30 APRIL–3 MAY

Sussex 279 and 198, Kent 185 and 159. Sussex (19pts) beat Kent (3pts) by 133 runs.

James Kirtley effectively bowled himself into the England Test squad with his best return for two years as Sussex gained an eventful first win of the season with over four sessions to spare.

England selector Geoff Miller was Chris Adams' house guest during the match and the captain admitted that he had taken the opportunity to press Kirtley's claims again over dinner. The next day Kirtley took 6–26 as Kent subsided from 94–2 to 159 all out. This took his haul in two matches to 16, not bad for a bowler who has always regarded himself as notoriously slow out of the blocks. 'I'm not a good starter so it's nice to get off to a bit of a flyer,' remarked Kirtley. 'There were certain things that I wasn't quite happy with against Middlesex. I wanted to get some more efficiency into my action and it's nice that it paid off in this match.'

No one at Hove for the opening day of the new season could complain about the entertainment served up. A typically green-tinged early-season pitch encouraged seam movement and it was no surprise that Kent bowled first after winning the toss. Although no one played a substantial knock in Sussex's 279, there were useful contributions all the way down the order. Chris Adams struck ten fours in what was his only half-century in his first nine Championship innings, while Tim Ambrose, Mushtaq Ahmed and Jason Lewry, who clearly fancied himself as a batsman after his cameo at Lord's, all contributed as Sussex scored 190 of their runs in boundaries.

Alamgir Sheriyar finished with 5–65 and it wasn't long before another left-armer, Lewry, was making incisions into the Kent batting when he removed Michael Carberry for just one. Kirtley bowled England man Rob Key, but Kent appeared to have steadied the ship through Greg Blewett and Matthew Walker. The second day was even more eventful. Sixteen wickets fell before a classy innings from Murray Goodwin effectively won the match.

Walker and Blewett were removed in successive overs and Kent lost their last seven wickets for 80, although Walker could consider himself unfortunate because he should not have been on strike when he was caught at slip off

Kirtley. Two deliveries earlier he had pushed the ball into the covers for a single but ended up with five when Kevin Innes' throw deflected off the stumps and went for four overthrows. Walker was told to stand his ground by umpire John Hampshire and later admitted that the incident had affected his concentration. Mushtaq Ahmed took three wickets and quickly finished off the tail.

The batsmen never felt truly settled, which made Goodwin's effort more impressive. He took the game away from Kent in a stand of 82 for the fifth wicket with Robin Martin-Jenkins, but just when Sussex appeared to be building an impregnable position, they lost five wickets in adding just eight runs, three of them to Mark Ealham, whose skiddy medium-pace was ideally suited to the surface. Goodwin fell for 96 in the last over of the day to an ugly swish across the line at off-spinner James Treadwell, his only false shot.

The innings was wrapped up quickly on the third day, leaving Kent a victory target of 293. Kirtley effectively settled the contest in an eventful over that included two wickets, a wide, one missed catch and another spectacular one, and ended with Jason Lewry and Tony Cottey on their way to the casualty department. Ed Smith, who'd given Kent hope in a third-wicket stand of 62 with Blewett, spooned a catch to cover and two balls later Lewry pulled off a spectacular one-handed intervention off a top-edged pull from Geraint Jones. Unfortunately, Lewry collided with Carl Hopkinson's right knee while taking the catch and ended up with a broken nose. Hopkinson was only on the field as a substitute for Tony Cottey, who'd injured his thumb fielding earlier in the over.

Kent were in terminal decline now. Kirtley took three more wickets in between three stoppages for rain and was in the Test squad three weeks later, while Mushtaq's googly bamboozled Mark Ealham after he'd battled for 16 overs for his 15.

COUNTY CHAMPIONSHIP TABLE 5 MAY 2003

	P	W	L	D	Btg	Blg	Ded	Pts
Nottinghamshire	2	1	0	1	5	6	0.75	28.25
Essex	3	0	0	3	5	8	0.00	28.00
Warwickshire	3	0	1	2	11	6	0.25	27.75
Middlesex	2	1	0	1	1	6	0.00	25.00
Sussex	2	1	1	0	3	6	0.00	23.00
Lancashire	2	0	0	2	9	6	0.00	23.00
Surrey	2	0	0	2	6	4	0.00	18.00
Leicestershire	2	0	0	2	3	6	0.00	17.00
Kent	2	0	1	1	1	6	0.00	11.00

MATCH 3 – EDGBASTON, 9–12 MAY

Warwickshire 422 and 285–7dec, Sussex 367 and 106. Warwickshire (22pts) beat Sussex (7pts) by 234 runs.

Only Mushtaq Ahmed's first five-wicket haul for the county and the batting of Matt Prior and Tim Ambrose offered Sussex any succour as their winless run at Edgbaston was extended into a 22nd year. Needing to bat for 55 overs to save the game after Warwickshire had declared shortly after lunch on the final day and set a nominal target of 341, Sussex were dismissed for their lowest total since September 2000. In mitigation, a hitherto benign pitch suddenly started to misbehave, particularly at the Pavilion End, where nine of the wickets fell, five of them in a new-ball burst from Mel Betts, which helped reduce Sussex to 43–7 at tea. But it was no minefield. Only Tony Cottey, who was ninth out for 55, and James Kirtley, who kept him company for 13 overs in the final session to give Sussex hope of salvation, showed the necessary application.

Director of cricket Peter Moores rarely criticises his players in public, but on this occasion they had no excuse. After a second defeat in three games he declared:

> The players have to come up with some answers as to how they are going to perform at a level and with a commitment which is acceptable to Sussex day in, day out. They shouldn't look for those answers anywhere else apart from inside themselves.

Mark Davis replaced Kevin Innes in the only change to the team which had beaten Kent, but it was Mushtaq who dragged Sussex back into contention on the first day after Jonathan Trott, a former South Africa Under-19 batsman with a British passport, had become the first Warwickshire player since Brian Lara in 1994 to score a century on debut. The leg-spinner took six wickets in 48 overs as Warwickshire subsided from 194–1 to 307–8 before their last two wickets and then plundered a further 115 when Sussex's attack lost its discipline on the second morning.

The reply was dominated by a stand of 125 on the third day between Prior and Ambrose, a record for the county's seventh wicket at Edgbaston. Earlier Cottey had passed 13,000 first-class runs and nightwatchman Kirtley improved his average to an enviable 97 before he was dismissed for the first time in five innings. However, at 235–6 Sussex were in danger of conceding a hefty first-innings lead. Both youngsters played with increasing confidence against an attack that lacked the menace it had shown in murky light on the second day. Prior, in particular, relished the chance to attack when the bowlers tested him against the short stuff. Both made half-centuries but disappointingly neither could convert them into three figures. Sussex conceded a lead of 55, but Jason Lewry took two wickets before the close to keep his side very much in the game. Or so it seemed.

Then, on the fourth morning, the wheels came off. It was hard for seasoned Sussex watchers to remember a more insipid bowling performance by their side. In 38 overs before the declaration, Warwickshire raced along at six an over, and Jim Troughton and Ian Bell won't have scored easier centuries. Even Mushtaq suffered. Troughton twice pulled him 30 rows back into the deserted Raglan Stand and Bell also hit two sixes, off Davis and Martin-Jenkins. Bell and Troughton's stand of 182 in 37 overs for the fourth wicket was a county record in home games against Sussex. Martin-Jenkins removed Dominic Ostler and Dougie Brown with successive balls, but it said much for the bowling that the hat-trick delivery disappeared to the cover boundary. Unfortunately, Sussex's woes were only just beginning.

COUNTY CHAMPIONSHIP TABLE 19 MAY 2003

	P	W	L	D	Btg	Blg	Ded	Pts
Surrey	4	1	0	3	15	10	0.00	51.00
Warwickshire	4	1	1	2	16	9	0.25	49.75
Lancashire	4	0	0	4	18	12	0.00	46.00
Middlesex	4	1	0	3	5	10	0.00	41.00
Essex	4	0	0	4	6	11	0.00	36.00
Nottinghamshire	3	1	1	1	6	9	1.00	32.00
Sussex	*3*	*1*	*2*	*0*	*7*	*9*	*0.00*	*30.00*
Leicestershire	3	0	0	3	4	8	0.00	24.00
Kent	3	0	1	2	6	9	0.00	23.00

MATCH 4 – HORSHAM, 21–24 MAY

Sussex 619–7dec and 52–0, Nottinghamshire 421 and 247. Sussex (22pts) beat Nottinghamshire (7pts) by 10 wickets.

Sussex had match-winners throughout the side as their season began to turn around following this crushing victory over Nottinghamshire. Three players scored centuries, with Kevin Innes making history at the same time as he achieved an unforgettable personal milestone. But it was Mushtaq Ahmed who produced the outstanding individual performance. Sussex wrapped up their second win just before tea and moved into third place in the table. Mushtaq followed up his 6–163 in Nottinghamshire's first innings with 6–81 in the second as the visitors, following on 198 behind, lost six wickets in the first hour on the final day and were bowled out for 247. Richard Montgomerie and Murray Goodwin knocked off the runs with the minimum of fuss.

It wasn't as if the surface had started to misbehave on the last day. In fact, with warm sunshine replacing the biting wind of the first three days, batting conditions were at their best. It was just that Notts couldn't cope with the twin threat posed by Mushtaq and James Kirtley, who shared six wickets between them in 14 overs to snap the visitors' resistance. Mushtaq's match haul was the best by a Sussex spinner for seven years, while for Kirtley it was a happy end to a week that had begun with disappointment when he was left out of the England side for the first Test against Zimbabwe at Lord's. Under new regulations, Kirtley was allowed to return to county duty in place of a nominated substitute, in this case Innes. While Kirtley was driving south from Lord's on the second morning, the player he was shortly to replace became the first 12th man in Championship history to make a century. What's more, Innes' 103 not out was his maiden first-class hundred and came after a sensational stand with Matt Prior that utterly demoralised Nottinghamshire's attack. The pair built on the foundations laid by Montgomerie, who had scored his third successive hundred at Cricketfield Road on the first day. The following morning Sussex plundered 203 runs in the session, with Prior and Innes adding 157 for the seventh wicket. Prior went into overdrive after a relatively sedate first fifty, going from 98 to 133 in the space of two overs before lunch when he cleared the rope four times in ten balls, reaching his hundred with a six into the pavilion off Kevin Pietersen. Shortly after the interval Innes was raising his bat to acknowledge a standing ovation after reaching his hundred with his 13th boundary. A stand of 84 in 21 overs with Mark Davis further deflated Nottinghamshire's spirits as Sussex made their biggest total in any match between the two counties.

Ten minutes later Kirtley had returned and Innes was reflecting on his moment in the sun as he attended to 12th man duties. 'It was very strange for me in the nineties,' he admitted. 'There was a mixture of excitement and nervousness. And then to get to a hundred . . . well, what a great feeling. If I could bottle how I felt and sell it I would be a rich man.'

It was breathtaking stuff, but the entertainment didn't stop there as Pietersen belted 166 off just 137 balls with four sixes and 17 fours, winning a sensational personal battle with Kirtley, whom he struck for a six and three fours in an over to areas of the field where the Sussex man is infrequently deposited. Bilal Shafayat hit three sixes off Mushtaq in his run-a-ball 71, but even a total of 421 wasn't enough to save Nottinghamshire from the follow-on. Darren Bicknell and Jason Gallian put together a century stand for the first wicket on the third evening, but a refreshed Mushtaq, far more effective than Notts' Australian leggie Stuart MacGill, quickly dismissed Gallian the next morning, and Sussex moved in for the kill.

Worryingly, as far as Sussex's opponents were concerned, Mushtaq confessed afterwards that he was only starting to warm to his task: 'There is more to come from me. I don't set targets, but I know that if I work hard and am honest with myself and my teammates then I will take wickets and perform well.' With 28 victims in four games, he was already firmly on course to make history.

COUNTY CHAMPIONSHIP TABLE 26 MAY 2003

	P	W	L	D	Btg	Blg	Ded	Pts
Surrey	5	2	0	3	19	13	0.00	72.00
Warwickshire	5	1	1	3	19	12	0.25	59.75
Sussex	4	2	2	0	12	12	0.00	52.00
Middlesex	5	1	0	4	6	13	0.00	49.00
Lancashire	4	0	0	4	18	12	0.00	46.00
Essex	5	0	1	4	8	14	0.00	41.00
Nottinghamshire	4	1	2	1	11	11	1.00	39.00
Kent	4	0	1	3	10	12	0.00	34.00
Leicestershire	4	0	0	4	4	11	0.00	31.00

MATCH 5 – THE OVAL, 30 MAY–2 JUNE

Surrey 480 and 233–3dec, Sussex 307 and 293. Surrey (22pts) beat Sussex (6pts) by 113 runs.

Surrey dominated throughout after winning an important toss, but Sussex were only 20 minutes or so away from denying them victory thanks to a superb rearguard action by Michael Yardy – the best innings of his career – that only ended when he was last out with 5.2 overs remaining. The left-hander, brought into the side because of injury to Tony Cottey, defied a Test-quality attack with men around the bat chuntering into his ear for over five hours, an effort that said much for his mental strength as well as his technical ability. He did not deserve to be on the losing side.

It had been hard work for Sussex from the moment Adam Hollioake let his batsmen have first use of a typical Oval shirtfront. Surrey's task was made easier when Billy Taylor was forced out of the attack in the 16th over with a thigh strain. Both Taylor and James Kirtley had struck during a new-ball spell, which Peter Moores thought was the best he'd seen from his side for two years. Surrey were 22–2, but that was about as good as it got for Sussex. Graham Thorpe confirmed he was back to his world-class best with 26 fours in a chanceless century that featured a masterclass against Mushtaq Ahmed. Surrey's 480 was about par considering the circumstances, but the score would have been a lot lower had Ian Salisbury (playing against his former county) and Saqlain Mushtaq not added 75 for the ninth wicket on the second morning.

James Ormond then undermined Sussex's reply with four wickets. Sussex lost Richard Montgomerie, Yardy and Chris Adams for a combined total of ten runs. However, they found salvation in the batting of Tim Ambrose and Robin Martin-Jenkins, who was running into the best form of his career. They put on

91 for the fifth wicket after Murray Goodwin fell for 60, while some typically aggressive strokeplay by Mushtaq at least earned his side a precious third batting point. In the first real heatwave of the summer, Hollioake did not enforce the follow-on so his bowlers could rest up, but the loss of 41 overs on the third day to bad light and unexpected drizzle almost scuppered the Surrey captain's careful calculations. Ian Ward was badly dropped by Mushtaq off his own bowling on 84 and celebrated by scoring his second hundred of the season with 18 fours and a six as he helped Jonathan Batty put on 137 for the first wicket.

The stoppage for bad light hastened Hollioake's declaration and although Sussex, needing an unlikely 407 to win, survived a testing mini-session in the gloom on the third evening, it wasn't long into the final day before Surrey were making inroads. Saqlain, who outbowled his Pakistan teammate Mushtaq, took three wickets in 12 balls to reduce Sussex to 85–4, but they were given hope by a fifth-wicket stand of 113 in 29 overs during the afternoon between Martin-Jenkins and Yardy, whose contribution to the partnership was just 18. Timing his shots superbly on both sides of the wicket, Martin-Jenkins hit 14 fours before Azhar Mahmood undid him with a reverse-swinging yorker. Matt Prior and Kevin Innes soon followed, but Kirtley kept Yardy company for ten overs and then Mushtaq drove the bowlers to distraction with a succession of unorthodox but highly effective shots, so much so that Saqlain bounced him in frustration!

Mushtaq did succeed in scattering the close field in a stand of 51 that used up 13 overs before he played back to Saqlain's quicker ball. Last man Billy Taylor had ten fielders for company and jabbed down the bat on the only delivery he faced before Ormond applied the *coup de grâce* in the next over with a beautiful delivery that nipped off the seam late to find the edge of Yardy's bat.

Moores was encouraged despite the disappointment of defeat.

We competed very well with a top-quality side for four days despite losing our opening bowler on the first morning. Michael Yardy's innings showed the sort of determination we have instilled into the side since the defeat against Warwickshire and he was desperately unlucky that it didn't save the game for us.

COUNTY CHAMPIONSHIP TABLE 2 JUNE 2003

	P	W	L	D	Btg	Blg	Ded	Pts
Surrey	6	3	0	3	24	16	0.00	94.00
Lancashire	5	1	0	4	21	15	0.00	66.00
Warwickshire	5	1	1	3	19	12	0.25	59.75
Essex	6	1	1	4	9	17	0.00	59.00
Sussex	*5*	*2*	*3*	*0*	*15*	*15*	*0.00*	*58.00*
Middlesex	5	1	0	4	6	13	0.00	49.00
Nottinghamshire	5	1	3	1	11	14	1.00	42.00
Kent	5	0	2	3	12	15	0.00	39.00
Leicestershire	4	0	0	4	4	11	0.00	31.00

MATCH 6 – TUNBRIDGE WELLS, 4–7 JUNE

Sussex 311 and 286, Kent 275 and 131. Sussex (20pts) beat Kent (5pts) by 191 runs.

Sussex quickly got over the disappointment of their Oval setback by completing a rare double over Kent to equal their total number of victories in 2002 with just six matches played. At this stage no one in the camp was contemplating anything other than the possibility of the top-three finish Chris Adams had predicted for his side at the start of the season, but there were lots of encouraging signs, not least the form of Mushtaq Ahmed. Kent clearly hadn't worked out a method of dealing with him in the six weeks since he'd taken 6–86 against them at Hove. This time he finished with nine wickets to make it 41 so far in the season, including two in three balls as his side wrapped up an impressive win 6.4 overs after tea.

Mushtaq took 4–56 in the second innings as Kent, chasing the biggest total of the match – 323 in 75 overs – succumbed for 131. Robin Martin-Jenkins, who also scored two half-centuries, completed an outstanding match by chipping in with 3–9 from seven overs, including wickets with successive deliveries as the home batsmen, struggling to cope with Mushtaq's probing variations, discovered that the supporting cast knew their lines as well.

With Mushtaq happy to operate for long spells, Adams had the luxury of rotating his other bowlers in short spells. 'I've bowled 40 overs fewer than at this stage of last season and I feel as fresh as a daisy,' explained Martin-Jenkins. 'Mushy's great for the team because it means the other bowlers can be rested for longer periods and keep coming in fresh. I'm sure we will all feel the benefit later in the season when we would normally be tired.'

Rain on the first day meant 44 overs were lost and with the ball moving about in the muggy atmosphere, it was hard work for Sussex's batsmen when the ball was pitched up. They closed on 142–5 with 62 from Adams, which hinted at a return to form for the captain. Sheriyar, Sussex's scourge earlier in the season, finished with four wickets, but not until Sussex's lower order had added another 137 for the last five wickets. Martin-Jenkins included eight fours and a six in his third successive half-century, while Kevin Innes and Mushtaq put on 62 for the ninth wicket.

While all this was happening James Kirtley was flying south from Durham, having been left out of the England Test team on the morning of the match for the second time. He was driven from Gatwick to the ground, had his limbs loosened by physio Stuart Osborne, bowled a couple of warm-up overs in the nets and came on to the field, pausing only to offer a word of consolation to his nominated replacement Paul Hutchison, who had made 18 important runs as nightwatchman and then bowled five overs with the new ball.

'Disgusted of Tunbridge Wells' was in his vocal element on the boundary at the Nevill Ground when Kirtley soon took two wickets. The feeling was that Sussex had stretched the interpretation of the new regulations regarding substitute players. Kirtley was on the ground when Kent began their reply, so why wasn't he bowling? But the key phrase is that they have to be 'ready to play'. Kirtley would have been risking serious injury had he been expected to change and start bowling without a proper warm-up.

Andrew Symonds and Matthew Walker put on 90 for Kent's fourth wicket, but both fell to Mushtaq before the close on the second day. Symonds holed out trying to clear long-off after he'd made 54 off 62 balls; he looked ominously good. It was a crucial turning point. Kent conceded a first-innings lead of 36, and by the end of the third day, which was interrupted by rain and bad light, Sussex had improved their advantage to 219 with five wickets left. Once again the new ball caused problems on a pitch now showing signs of irregular bounce, but Murray Goodwin and Tony Cottey, recalled to the side in place of the unlucky Michael Yardy, both scored fifties and Martin-Jenkins got his fourth in a row on the final morning with 11 fours and a six in a stylish 84, which he should have converted into a hundred. A sixth-wicket stand of 89 with Prior took the game away from Kent, even though Sussex then lost their last five wickets for 13 runs.

Now Mushtaq took centre stage once again. He had gone back to the team hotel the previous afternoon complaining of a stomach complaint, but all seemed right in his world when he began to bamboozle Kent's batsman on the final sunlit afternoon. At that stage of the season it was still hard to see Sussex challenging Surrey's supremacy, but there was no doubt they were building up a head of steam.

COUNTY CHAMPIONSHIP TABLE 9 JUNE 2003

	P	W	L	D	Btg	Blg	Ded	Pts
Surrey	6	3	0	3	24	16	0.00	94.00
Lancashire	6	2	0	4	26	18	0.00	88.00
Sussex	6	3	3	0	18	18	0.00	78.00
Warwickshire	6	1	1	4	23	13	0.25	68.75
Essex	7	1	1	5	9	20	0.00	66.00
Middlesex	6	1	0	5	10	16	0.00	60.00
Nottinghamshire	6	1	3	2	16	17	1.00	54.00
Kent	6	0	3	3	14	18	0.00	44.00
Leicestershire	5	0	1	4	7	13	0.00	36.00

MATCH 7 – HOVE, 27–29 JUNE

Sussex 545, Warwickshire 201 and 285. Sussex (22pts) beat Warwickshire (3pts) by an innings and 59 runs.

Sussex treasured this victory more than most during the Championship-winning campaign. It had been 11 years since their last success over Warwickshire, and painful memories of their embarassing surrender at Edgbaston seven weeks earlier were still fresh in the memory. But while the other three matches in the division were ending in draws, Sussex made up considerable ground on their rivals by completing an emphatic victory with over a day to spare.

'That was a big win for us,' admitted director of cricket Peter Moores.

A lot of us had suffered against them for a long time and it was nice to put the record straight. You could tell even before the start that the lads really wanted to win that game, there was a great energy in our performance and we played really well. Not many teams could have lived with us in that mood.

The county made a significant change to their team by relieving Matt Prior of wicketkeeping duties for the first time in nearly two years and handing the gloves to Tim Ambrose, who had kept impressively during the Twenty20 Cup matches played since the victory at Tunbridge Wells. Prior was disappointed, but he set about proving his worth in the side as a batsman by scoring his second century of the season. Sussex won a crucial toss and although they lost Murray Goodwin in the first over, their batsmen soon started to enjoy the true pitch and warm sunshine, none more so than Tony Cottey, who made a brilliant 188, his highest score for the county and his first century at Hove for four years. Cottey cut loose, hitting 31 fours with the confidence of a man who was running into the best form of his Sussex career. Prior embellished his efforts on the second day with some typically flamboyant strokeplay, while Richard Montgomerie and Tim Ambrose chipped in with half-centuries. Waqar Younis took 5–99, but it was his fellow Pakistani who was soon taking centre stage again. Michael Powell and Mark Wagh played confidently and took the reply to 104–1, but the remaining nine Warwickshire wickets fell for 97, four of them to Mushtaq and three to James Kirtley, who once again proved the ideal foil for the leg-spinner. Mushtaq wrapped up the innings quickly on the third morning and Warwickshire, 344 behind, were invited to face the music again.

Nick Knight and Powell put conditions into perspective for a while as they compiled an opening stand of 135, which at least suggested that the

Warwickshire's last man, Alan Richardson, has his wicket shattered by Mushtaq Ahmed. This was to become a familiar sight for Sussex supporters. *(Simon Dack/Brighton Argus)*

visitors were capable of prolonging their resistance into a fourth day. The breakthrough was made nine overs after lunch when Prior used all his wicketkeeper's reflexes to snap up Knight at silly point off Mushtaq, who then removed Powell and Wagh in successive overs. Ian Bell resisted for over two hours to make 37, but he became one of seven victims for Mushtaq. In only

Mushtaq Ahmed on his way to a seven-wicket haul in the second innings against Warwickshire. It was Sussex's first win over the Bears for 11 years.
(Simon Dack/Brighton Argus)

their third match together, off-spinner Mark Davis provided crucial support with the key wickets of Jonathan Trott and Tony Frost. It was left to Mushtaq to finish Warwickshire off after tea and he dismissed last man Alan Richardson for the second time in the space of seven hours. Mushtaq had 52 wickets from just seven games, Sussex were breathing down Surrey's neck at the top of the table and the Warwickshire bogey had finally been laid to rest.

COUNTY CHAMPIONSHIP TABLE 1 JULY 2003

	P	W	L	D	Btg	Blg	Ded	Pts
Surrey	7	3	0	4	29	19	0.00	106.00
Sussex	7	4	3	0	23	21	0.00	100.00
Lancashire	6	2	0	4	26	18	0.00	88.00
Essex	8	1	1	6	14	23	0.00	78.00
Warwickshire	7	1	2	4	24	15	0.25	71.75
Middlesex	7	1	0	6	14	18	0.00	70.00
Nottinghamshire	7	1	3	3	19	20	1.00	64.00
Kent	7	0	3	4	18	20	0.00	54.00
Leicestershire	6	0	1	5	8	16	0.00	44.00

MATCH 8 – ARUNDEL, 9–12 JULY

Sussex 359 and 257–4, Essex 340 and 274. Sussex (21pts) beat Essex (6pts) by 6 wickets.

A classic four-day contest played in glorious weather in front of good crowds ended with Sussex pocketing their fifth win in eight games as the season reached its halfway point.

Chasing 256 from 82 overs, the county were in trouble at 32–3 before Tony Cottey and Tim Ambrose – so memorably referred to in *The Times* as being 'like two petit pois in a pod' – put together their second substantial stand of the match. Cottey fell just two runs short of what would have been his second century of the match, but Ambrose finished unbeaten on 93 to guide Sussex to victory with 4.1 overs to spare.

Talk of winning the Championship had been banned in the dressing room, and, in public at least, Chris Adams still refused to concede that his side could sustain a genuine challenge to leaders Surrey, who were 26 points clear at the top going into the second half of the season. Yet his players continued to offer compelling evidence to the contrary.

The first day had been dominated by an absorbing duel between Mushtaq Ahmed and Nasser Hussain. Mushtaq finally got his man when the England captain, warming up for the series against South Africa, fell for 95, but only after Hussain, with his nimble footwork, had subdued the threat of the country's leading wicket-taker as well as anyone did all summer.

An enthralled Sussex crowd at picturesque Arundel saw their side complete another crucial win, this time over Essex. *(Simon Dack/Brighton Argus)*

Hot work. Matt Prior shelters from the fierce sun. *(Simon Dack/Brighton Argus)*

On a typically slow Arundel pitch it was hard work for the batsmen and Sussex were in the ascendancy when they reduced the visitors to 215–8, four of the wickets falling to Jason Lewry on the ground where he had made his Sussex debut nine years earlier. But Graham Napier came in at No. 9 to make an unbeaten 89, full of controlled aggression as Essex's last two wickets added 125.

The impressive Scott Brant made two incursions with the new ball as Sussex's reply faltered. Then the county's fortunes were revived by Ambrose and Cottey, who added 176 in 55 overs for the fourth wicket. After a cautious start, Cottey duly went to his second successive hundred with ten fours and a swept six off James Middlebrook, which took him to 99. The only disappointment for another 3,000-plus crowd was Ambrose's inability to convert his sixth half-century of the summer into a hundred. However, it needed an outstanding slip catch by Andy Flower to remove him. Just as their opponents' had done, Sussex's tail wagged enough to give them a first-innings lead of 19, but it was still anyone's game when the final day began with Essex 235 ahead with four wickets intact. For once Mushtaq was frustrated. Instead, Mark Davis removed Paul Grayson and Flower after they had both scored half-centuries. There were also two wickets for Lewry, including the crucial scalps of Hussain and Aftab Habib, who also made fifty. The rejuvenated Lewry soon wrapped up the innings on the last morning, taking 3–8 in 5.5 overs to complete a match haul of 10–124,

Nasser Hussain can see the funny side as Kirtley appeals for lbw. *(Simon Dack/Brighton Argus)*

his best figures for two years. But Sussex had to settle for a period of entrenchment after they lost both openers and their captain with just 32 runs on the board. There was barely a murmur from the crowd during a tense afternoon as Cottey and Ambrose put together their match-winning stand. Essex's spinners bowled round the wicket to restrict scoring opportunities, but the target was down to 52 when Cottey feathered a catch to the wicketkeeper.

Congratulations for Tony Cottey (right) from Tim Ambrose after his century against Essex. *(Simon Dack/Brighton Argus)*

Martin-Jenkins scored the winning boundary a few minutes before 6pm and then graciously allowed Ambrose to take centre stage as the players trooped off.

Ambrose is unusually self-effacing for an Australian and was happy to give all the credit for this latest Sussex win to his housemate.

> I have learned such a lot from the two occasions I have batted with Cotts this week and, as far as I'm concerned, he's a legend. We go into every game with such confidence at the moment and that makes a big difference. We know at least one person is going to produce a big performance.

COUNTY CHAMPIONSHIP TABLE 14 JULY 2003

	P	W	L	D	Btg	Blg	Ded	Pts
Surrey	9	5	0	4	38	23	0.00	147.00
Sussex	*8*	*5*	*3*	*0*	*27*	*24*	*0.00*	*121.00*
Lancashire	7	2	0	5	27	21	0.00	96.00
Middlesex	8	2	0	6	19	21	0.00	92.00
Essex	10	1	2	7	18	29	0.00	92.00
Warwickshire	9	1	3	5	27	21	1.25	83.75
Kent	9	1	4	4	26	26	0.00	82.00
Nottinghamshire	8	1	4	3	19	23	1.00	67.00
Leicestershire	8	0	2	6	16	21	0.00	61.00

MATCH 9 – LEICESTER, 15–18 JULY

Leicestershire 320 and 258, Sussex 416 and 166–5. Sussex (21pts) beat Leicestershire (5pts) by 5 wickets.

The gap between Sussex and leaders Surrey was trimmed to just five points after Sussex defeated bottom-of-the-table Leicestershire in the final session to record their fourth successive Championship win. It was another outstanding effort, typified by Tony Cottey, whose brilliant form with the bat continued, and the irrepressible Mushtaq Ahmed, who claimed another ten wickets to take his haul for the season to 65. Cottey made a century for the third match in a row to help establish a first-innings lead of 96, and then scored 58 as Sussex eased to their victory target, raising his aggregate to more than 650 runs from his last six Championship innings.

More significantly, as it turned out, skipper Chris Adams rediscovered his form with the bat. Not in the middle, where he made 0 and 16, but in the nets on the second day. 'Looking back, that's where it changed for me,' he recalled. 'I had a long net with Peter Moores and in the next game against Nottinghamshire I started to feel and play a whole lot better.' Leicestershire got first use of the best batting surface produced at Grace Road all season but looked in danger of squandering their advantage at 154–6. Then their evergreen captain, Phil DeFreitas, coming in at No. 8, led a fightback, adding 96 with Jeremy Snape for the seventh wicket before putting on 69 in 18 overs for the ninth wicket as he made his only century of the summer. It was a commendable effort by a 37-year-old in a temperature of 90°F, although it was no surprise when he didn't emerge to take the new ball a few minutes after losing his off-stump to Robin Martin-Jenkins. Despite DeFreitas's resistance it was still a praiseworthy bowling effort by a Sussex attack without Jason Lewry, who departed after delivering just six overs because of a side strain.

Sussex were 51–0 overnight, but their progress on day two was initially circumspect, with only 27 added in the first hour for the loss of Goodwin. Cottey and Richard Montgomerie asserted a measure of control in a second-wicket stand of 103, and although DeFreitas dragged his side back into the contest with two wickets in three balls as Sussex lost four for 54 in 16 overs, unhinging Cottey proved an altogether different proposition. Matt Prior gave him the support he needed and by the close they had taken Sussex into the lead. Cottey reached his hundred and, on the third morning, converted it into 147 before wearily offering a catch to the wicketkeeper. In over six-and-a-half hours he'd faced 281 balls, hitting 19 fours and a six. Even more disappointing was Prior's dismissal shortly afterwards, four short of his century. His innings, which contained 15 fours, was the most fluent of the contest.

With Lewry *hors de combat* and Adams protecting a sore wrist by fielding in the deep, vice-captain James Kirtley was charged with the responsibility of marshalling depleted bowling resources and he did a pretty good job. It helped, of course, that a wearing pitch was giving increasing assistance to Mushtaq, who took three more wickets on the third day. The last session ended with Leicestershire five down and ahead by a modest 66 runs.

For an hour on the final day it looked as though Sussex might be frustrated by the resolve of Trevor Ward, who extended his sixth-wicket stand with Snape to 63 from 24 overs. Ward was furious when umpire Peter Hartley upheld Mushtaq's cacophonous appeal for a catch at silly point and vented his frustration on a training ball, which he swatted from one side of the dressing room to another. Sussex didn't care. They had their breakthrough and Robin Martin-Jenkins struck twice in successive overs before Mushtaq completed his third ten-wicket haul of the summer.

Sussex were rarely troubled in chasing down a target of 163, the contest effectively settled by a fourth-wicket stand of 60 between Cottey and Ambrose. Another great victory, their third achieved in a final session, set up nicely the looming summit meeting between the top two.

COUNTY CHAMPIONSHIP TABLE 19 JULY 2003

	P	W	L	D	Btg	Blg	Ded	Pts
Surrey	9	5	0	4	38	23	0.00	147.00
Sussex	*9*	*6*	*3*	*0*	*31*	*27*	*0.00*	*142.00*
Lancashire	8	2	0	6	31	22	0.00	105.00
Middlesex	9	2	0	7	21	23	0.00	100.00
Warwickshire	10	1	3	6	32	24	1.25	95.75
Kent	10	1	4	5	31	29	0.00	94.00
Essex	10	1	2	7	18	29	0.00	92.00
Nottinghamshire	8	1	4	3	19	23	1.00	67.00
Leicestershire	9	0	3	6	19	23	0.00	66.00

MATCH 10 – TRENT BRIDGE, 25–28 JULY

Sussex 497–6dec, Nottinghamshire 296 and 291–4. Match drawn, Sussex 12pts, Nottinghamshire 8pts.

A first-day washout frustrated Sussex in their efforts to close the gap on Surrey at the top of the table. Fortunately, the weather intervened in the other games, the top three sides all settling for a full hand of bonus points from drawn matches.

This time it was Murray Goodwin and Robin Martin-Jenkins who emerged as Sussex's batting heroes. Adopting a positive approach from the start of what was effectively a three-day contest, Goodwin made his first century of the season after Sussex had won the toss, hitting 24 fours and two sixes in his 148. Tony Cottey's golden summer continued with another fifty, Chris Adams hinted at a return to form by making 46 and, on the penultimate day, Martin-Jenkins emulated Goodwin with his first hundred of the summer, dominating a fifth-wicket stand of 137 with Michael Yardy, who had replaced the injured Tim Ambrose in the middle order. The all-rounder's unbeaten 121 came off just 128 balls, with 17 fours and two sixes, before the declaration. Sussex had scored their runs at more than four an over and left themselves just over five sessions to bowl Nottinghamshire out twice. That was always going to be a tough proposition on a slow pitch with a temptingly short boundary on one side of the ground, but the bowlers appeared to relish the task. James Kirtley's exemplary control earned him five wickets and Nottinghamshire were sinking fast at 140–6 when Kevin Pietersen, not for the first time against Sussex, came to their rescue. The South African had made a swashbuckling 166 at Horsham earlier in the season. Now he forced Sussex onto the defensive for the first time in the match with 139, including 18 fours and two sixes, before he was eighth out early on the fourth morning, having added 114 in 22 overs with Paul Franks. Kirtley shared the other wickets with Paul Hutchison, who got a rare opportunity in the absence of the injured Jason Lewry and finally removed the dangerous Franks.

Following on, the hosts were soon 34–2, but that was as good as it got. Sussex were unable to separate Darren Bicknell and Russell Warren until after tea, as Warren went on to make a maiden century for his new county, finishing unbeaten on 114. Nevertheless, the county were ideally placed going into the crucial game against Surrey and had important players running into form.

'It all went pretty well until Bicknell and Warren came together,' admitted Peter Moores. 'We bowled well, but the pitch was very slow and negated Mushtaq a bit. He wasn't as effective as usual. But Murray and Robin batted superbly well and James Kirtley bowled brilliantly. I think if the game had run its course we would have won comfortably.'

COUNTY CHAMPIONSHIP TABLE 29 JULY 2003

	P	W	L	D	Btg	Blg	Ded	Pts
Surrey	10	5	0	5	43	26	0.00	159.00
Sussex	*10*	*6*	*3*	*1*	*36*	*30*	*0.00*	*154.00*
Lancashire	9	2	0	7	36	25	0.00	117.00
Middlesex	10	2	0	8	25	26	0.00	111.00
Warwickshire	11	1	3	7	34	26	1.50	103.50
Essex	11	1	2	8	22	30	0.00	101.00
Kent	10	1	4	5	31	29	0.00	94.00
Leicestershire	10	0	3	7	24	26	0.00	78.00
Nottinghamshire	9	1	4	4	21	25	1.00	75.00

MATCH 11 – HOVE, 30 JULY–2 AUGUST

Sussex 429 and 302–5dec, Surrey 355 and 114–1. Match drawn, Sussex 12pts, Surrey 11pts.

The contest between the top two attracted record gate receipts for a Championship match at Hove of over £20,000, but at the end Chris Adams had to defend his tactics after delaying his declaration until ten minutes before tea on the final day and setting Surrey a notional target of 377 in 34 overs.

Dissenting voices in the crowd – most of them from across the county border, it has to be said – felt Sussex had missed their chance of winning when they came off for bad light on the third day and 37 overs had been lost. But, in truth, Sussex squandered two match-winning opportunities much earlier when they had Surrey 126–6 and then 215–8 in their first innings. Adams was unrepentant, and as it turned out, he was right not to take undue risks. Sussex had rattled Surrey's gilded cage and the champions headed back to The Oval knowing that, if nothing else, they would find it hard to shake Sussex off their tail. 'Normally, when Surrey played us they were relaxed because they knew that at some stage over the four days they would take control the game,' said the captain. 'On the last day they got in our faces a bit and tried to unsettle us but I took that as a moral victory for us. It showed that we were breathing down their necks and were prepared to compete with them.'

Tim Ambrose (left) and Matt Prior were awarded their county caps during the match against Surrey. *(Tony Wood/Brighton Argus)*

On a personal level, it was a fantastic match for Adams. After a summer of toil with the bat he came good at last, and to do so in the most important game of the season gave him extra satisfaction. Richard Montgomerie and Murray Goodwin, the latter despite the discomfort of a dislocated thumb, put on 149 after Sussex had won the toss. This provided the perfect platform for Adams and it was hard to record a false shot as he scored his first hundred since May 2002. It was no surprise that Surrey launched a second-day fightback that saw the hosts lose their last seven wickets for 99, but Surrey then found themselves in dire danger of following on when they were reduced to 126–6 by a combination of Mushtaq Ahmed's wiles and the accuracy of Sussex's seamers. Relief came in the form of Mark Ramprakash, a thorn in Sussex's side throughout his career. Now he made his 65th hundred while the tail wagged sufficiently to enable the visitors to restrict their deficit to 74 runs.

It was hard work for Sussex on the third afternoon. The light was often poor and, as befitted the champions, the quality of Surrey's bowling bore a marked improvement on their first innings effort. Two wickets fell and the run rate barely got above two an over, so Adams' decision to come off when the light was offered wasn't that much of a surprise.

The final day was gloriously sunny, but the loss of a session had effectively cost Sussex the chance of setting a target that would insure them against a potentially damaging defeat and give them enough time to bowl Surrey out. Instead, Tim Ambrose and Matt Prior made unbeaten fifties before being awarded their county caps during the tea interval, while Saqlain Mushtaq and Ian Salisbury staged their own protest at Sussex's tactics by bowling seam-up instead of spin. Those spectators not indulging in a slow handclap headed for the beach. It was a disappointing end to what had been an absorbing contest until the final two sessions, but Sussex had established themselves as serious rivals for Surrey's crown.

COUNTY CHAMPIONSHIP TABLE 4 AUGUST 2003

	P	W	L	D	Btg	Blg	Ded	Pts
Surrey	11	5	0	6	47	29	0.00	170.00
Sussex	*11*	*6*	*3*	*2*	*41*	*33*	*0.00*	*166.00*
Lancashire	10	3	0	7	41	28	0.00	139.00
Middlesex	11	3	0	8	27	29	0.00	130.00
Kent	11	2	4	5	31	32	0.00	111.00
Essex	12	1	3	8	22	33	0.00	104.00
Warwickshire	11	1	3	7	34	26	1.50	103.50
Leicestershire	11	0	4	7	26	28	0.00	82.00
Nottinghamshire	10	1	5	4	23	28	1.00	80.00

MATCH 12 – HOVE, 14–17 AUGUST

Sussex 385 and 383–7dec, Lancashire 377 and 139. Sussex (21pts) beat Lancashire (7pts) by 252 runs.

Sussex strengthened their challenge by completing a breathless victory over Lancashire in front of an ecstatic crowd with just 12 minutes to spare after four enthralling days of cut and thrust. Their supporters, so used to mediocrity over the years, still didn't dare consider a Championship trophy,

Chris Adams on his way to the first of two hundreds in the crucial win over Lancashire. *(Simon Dack/Brighton Argus)*

Billy Taylor made crucial contributions with the ball throughout the season. *(Simon Dack/ Brighton Argus)*

but they were aware that victory over one of the county's two serious rivals meant there would never be a better chance.

Chris Adams appeared to have erred on the side of caution again when he delayed his fourth-day declaration until 12.35pm and set Lancashire 392, but it turned out that he got his tactics spot-on. Lancashire's only option was to bat out time for a draw, and Adams was able to persist with attacking fields throughout. Once again Mushtaq Ahmed was outstanding. He finished with 11–173 in the match, including 5–23 in 17.2 overs in the final session, to take his side to a sensational victory. Adams, too, played his part with centuries in both innings, but arguably the match-winning contribution – or certainly the match-turning one – came from unheralded seamer Billy Taylor, who did an admirable job as stand-in for James Kirtley who was making his Test debut. 'I have tried to be more aggressive this season and it paid off,' Taylor said afterwards. 'With four games left we really feel we can win the Championship and I want to make sure that I play my part.'

Taylor bowled 17 overs unchanged during the afternoon, including 4–20 in 33 balls – the best spell of his career – to break the back of Lancashire's

Mushtaq Ahmed is hugged by Chris Adams after removing England captain Nasser Hussain in the win over Essex. *(Simon Dack/Brighton Argus)*

batting before leaving the stage for Mushtaq to mop up the rest as fielders crowded round the bat. With the overs running out, the Sussex coaching staff – led by Peter Moores – positioned themselves around the boundary to make sure any balls that pierced the infield were quickly returned. They needn't have fretted. Lancashire subsided and retreated north muttering that they had been on the end of some questionable umpiring decisions and swearing revenge in the return at Old Trafford a month later.

Adams became only the fourth Sussex batsman to score two hundreds in the same game on more than one occasion. He batted for over ten hours in the match, a tremendous physical effort as temperatures climbed into the nineties. On the first day he battered 16 fours and five sixes in his 140 after Richard Montgomerie's half-century at the top of the innings. Mushtaq hit 60 in that bright and breezy way of his before almost single-handedly ensuring that Sussex had a small first-innings lead. Stuart Law seemed destined to take another hundred off the Sussex attack until he and the dangerous Carl Hooper were snared in quick succession on the second day. Mushtaq finished with six wickets and Sussex had a slender lead of eight runs.

If anything, Adams' batting in the second innings was even better. As Sussex battled to take control of the contest he settled for crease occupation and his first 50 runs took 137 balls. Then he opened his shoulders to launch a thrilling counter-attack, reaching his hundred off just 46 more deliveries. On the last day he fell just ten runs short of what would have been a second successive double-hundred against Lancashire, having hit 21 fours and five sixes. Montgomerie made another half-century and Sussex rattled along at six runs an over on the final morning. When the declaration came Sussex had given themselves 76 overs to bowl their opponents out. It was enough – but only just. The gap between Sussex and Surrey, who had just secured what turned out to be the final win of their Championship defence, was now just five points.

COUNTY CHAMPIONSHIP TABLE 18 AUGUST 2003

	P	W	L	D	Btg	Blg	Ded	Pts
Surrey	12	6	0	6	52	32	0.00	192.00
Sussex	*12*	*7*	*3*	*2*	*45*	*36*	*0.00*	*187.00*
Lancashire	11	3	1	7	45	31	0.00	146.00
Middlesex	12	3	1	8	32	31	0.00	137.00
Kent	12	3	4	5	36	35	0.00	133.00
Warwickshire	12	2	3	7	36	29	1.50	122.50
Essex	12	1	3	8	22	33	0.00	104.00
Leicestershire	12	0	5	7	29	31	0.50	87.50
Nottinghamshire	11	1	6	4	24	31	1.00	84.00

MATCH 13 – COLCHESTER, 20–22 AUGUST

Sussex 612, Essex 283 and 209. Sussex (22pts) beat Essex (5pts) by an innings and 120 runs.

This was the defining week of the summer. In the space of five days Sussex beat Lancashire and then routed hapless Essex with over a day to spare to move to the top of the table for the first time. Although Surrey regained pole position a couple of days later, their lead was down to a single point and Sussex still had a game in hand. The tide was turning.

Even the most rabid Essex partisan at Castle Park couldn't have helped but be impressed with the way the champions-elect dismantled their side. The tone was set during the first session, which ended with Sussex 161–0. As the players trooped into the pavilion for lunch, Essex's veteran opener Darren Robinson said to Tony Cottey: 'It's time for the *indoor* buffet now.' Even then, you would have got good odds on that morning session being Sussex's least productive during a day-long assault led by the merciless Murray Goodwin.

He helped Richard Montgomerie post 202 in just 45 overs for the first wicket. Montgomerie fell just short of his hundred, but there was never any doubt that his partner would reach three figures – and then some. Dropped at slip on 24, he made a career-best 210 from just 270 balls, including 101 between lunch and tea. It was breathtaking stuff and although Mohammad Akram, who was to join Sussex at the start of 2004, made inroads with the second new ball, Goodwin and Matt Prior accelerated thrillingly before the close. Goodwin had to play second fiddle as Prior smashed 15 fours before reaching his hundred with successive sixes off Graham Napier over a temporary stand at mid-wicket. Sussex finished the first day in a seemingly impregnable position at 521–8 and the next morning they added to their hosts' torment.

Prior finished unbeaten on 153 while No. 10 Jason Lewry's unorthodox but highly entertaining 70 was not only his maiden half-century but also the third career-best of the innings. Their total of 612 was their highest against Essex and the sixth-biggest in the county's history.

Robinson and Will Jefferson launched the Essex reply with a confident century stand, but events followed a predictable course once Mushtaq Ahmed had got to work on a pitch now showing signs of breaking up. He took four wickets as Essex subsided after their top three had all made half-centuries. Bowled out for 283, they followed on 329 behind. Chris Adams joked afterwards that his only contribution in this game was to win the toss. True, he had been castled first ball by a spectacular inswinging yorker from Akram on day one, but he was forgetting the outstanding pick-up and direct hit that ran out Robinson from mid-off in the first over on the third day. There wasn't a better piece of fielding all season.

Jefferson made another fifty, but Sussex slowly tightened the noose. Billy Taylor laboured diligently to take four wickets and the end came at 3.45pm. Even the notoriously hard-to-please Essex crowd gave Adams and his men a standing ovation as they trooped off.

Still Sussex's captain refused to believe that his side were now favourites. Instead he tried to deflect the heat off his players: 'We're playing without fear and the players are enjoying every minute of trying to make history, but the pressure is still on Surrey.' It appeared to be telling. The champions' failure to beat relegation-bound Leicestershire two days later meant Sussex went into the final three games as favourites.

COUNTY CHAMPIONSHIP TABLE 25 AUGUST 2003

	P	W	L	D	Btg	Blg	Ded	Pts
Sussex	13	8	3	2	50	39	0.00	209.00
Surrey	13	6	0	7	57	35	0.00	204.00
Lancashire	12	3	1	8	50	32	0.00	156.00
Kent	13	4	4	5	37	38	0.00	151.00
Middlesex	13	3	1	9	37	32	0.00	147.00
Warwickshire	12	2	3	7	36	29	1.50	122.50
Essex	13	1	4	8	24	36	0.00	109.00
Leicestershire	13	0	5	8	29	33	0.50	87.50
Nottinghamshire	12	1	7	4	24	34	1.00	87.00

MATCH 14 – HOVE, 5–8 SEPTEMBER

Sussex 537 and 108-3, Middlesex 392 and 250. Sussex (22pts) beat Middlesex (7pts) by 7 wkts.

Now the pressure was on, and for a while on the second day it appeared as if Sussex might buckle under the weight of expectation. With Surrey on their way to defeat at Canterbury, Sussex had the chance to put clear daylight between themselves and the rest, but at 107-6 chasing Middlesex's 392 it looked as though the limit of their achievement would be avoiding the follow-on. Then Matt Prior and Mark Davis came together in the most important partnership of the summer.

It was hard to tell there was any crisis at all as Prior led a thrilling counter-attack. His partner, a capable batsman so often in Mushtaq Ahmed's shadow during the season, emerged to make his career-best. Together they utterly transformed the match in a stand of 195 for the seventh wicket. Prior's 148 from 153 balls contained 25 boundaries, and by the end of the second day Sussex had gathered a full hand of bonus points. 'I remember walking round the ground on that second day and everyone was full of doom and gloom,' recalled Peter Moores. 'But Mark was due a score and somehow, even when

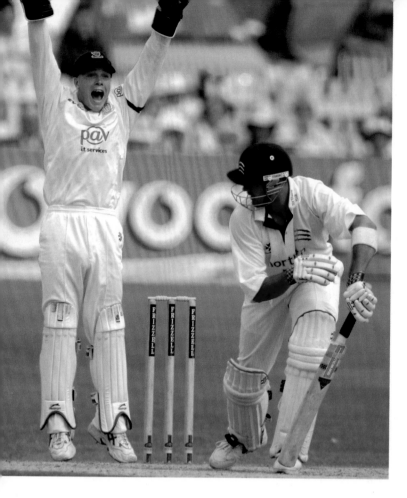

Tim Ambrose is confident that Middlesex's Owais Shah has become another victim for Mushtaq Ahmed. *(Simon Dack/ Brighton Argus)*

we were one hundred-odd for six, I thought we could claw our way back into the game. I don't know what it was, but I just knew.'

Middlesex's suffering continued the following morning. Davis completed a marathon innings of over seven hours' duration before holing out to long-on after facing 338 balls and hitting 17 boundaries in his 168. The tail-enders caught the mood after a cautious morning when only 86 runs were scored. Mushtaq had contributed 57 to a stand of 97 with Davis and now Billy Taylor made a career-best 35 not out and helped add another 106 for the last wicket. The former players, enjoying their annual reunion day, may have fretted that Sussex hadn't left themselves enough time to bowl Middlesex out again on a flat pitch, but they reckoned without the resolve of a bowling attack gathering themselves for one last push. By the end of the third day Middlesex had lost half their wickets and had a lead of just 12, Davis having completed an unforgettable day by removing the dangerous but reckless Owais Shah in the penultimate over. On the final morning Paul Weekes made a dogged half-century as Middlesex's last five wickets put on 98, but a target of 106 was knocked off in 97 minutes, with Richard Montgomerie leading the successful chase with an unbeaten half-century.

Four more second-innings wickets had left Mushtaq tantalisingly one short of his 100th for the season with two games to go. He'd produced another outstanding spell on the first day just when Middlesex captain Andrew Strauss and Shah, who both made superb centuries, were threatening to derail the Sussex express. They put on 219 in 46 overs, but from 309–3 the visitors folded to 392 all out. Mushtaq had to wait until the 27th over of a marathon spell from the Cromwell Road End for his first wicket, but he finished with 6–145 as the last five wickets tumbled in 27 balls for just 18 runs.

All of this left Sussex needing just ten points from two games to make history. Surrey, meanwhile, were all but out of the race after defeat by Kent. Lancashire maintained their slim hopes by beating Warwickshire. Now Sussex headed to Old Trafford.

Jason Lewry celebrates another wicket, this time in the win over Middlesex in September. *(Simon Dack/Brighton Argus)*

COUNTY CHAMPIONSHIP TABLE 9 SEPTEMBER 2003

	P	W	L	D	Btg	Blg	Ded	Pts
Sussex	*14*	*9*	*3*	*2*	*55*	*42*	*0.00*	*231.00*
Surrey	15	6	2	7	60	41	0.00	213.00
Lancashire	14	5	1	8	58	37	0.00	197.00
Kent	14	5	4	5	42	41	0.00	173.00
Middlesex	15	3	3	9	43	38	0.00	159.00
Warwickshire	14	3	4	7	43	33	2.50	146.50
Essex	14	2	4	8	27	39	0.00	129.00
Leicestershire	14	0	5	9	34	36	0.50	105.50
Nottinghamshire	14	1	8	5	28	39	1.00	100.00

MATCH 15 – OLD TRAFFORD, 10–13 SEPTEMBER

Lancashire 450–6dec, Sussex 251 and 180. Lancashire (22pts) beat Sussex (4pts) by an innings and 19 runs.

No Championship for Sussex – well not yet anyway – and no 100th wicket for Mushtaq Ahmed. Perhaps it was pre-ordained that the county would have to make history in front of their own supporters. They suffered a horrible attack of nerves at Old Trafford, where Lancashire exacted revenge for the defeat at Hove.

The county's timid approach deserved nothing more and they headed home to prepare for the final game still needing six points to make sure of the title. Lancashire, meanwhile, made it 63 points out of the last 66. It was hard not to agree with their supporters who contended that the rain that blighted so many of their matches in the first half of the season had cost them the chance of ending their own 69-year wait for an outright Championship success.

Rain appeared to be aiding Sussex's cause, too. On the first day 36 overs were lost and a further 43 on day two. But between the stoppages Lancashire batted well on a pitch that gradually deteriorated. Almost inevitably, Stuart Law took a century off Sussex for the third successive match and Mal Loye helped him add 241 in 62 overs with 144 before he was third out to give Sussex their first bonus point. Only another nine to go. The declaration came 75 minutes into the third day once Lancashire had gathered a full hand of batting points, but the Sussex attack badly missed James Kirtley, who was nursing sore shins and didn't play again for the rest of the season.

The pitch was still good, though. Sussex, and their growing number of supporters who had travelled north hoping to see history made, knew that one decent batting performance would be sufficient. If Sussex could avoid the follow-on there wouldn't be the time for Lancashire to force victory. All was going according to plan at 122–1. Fourteen overs later Sussex had stumbled to 157–7, the middle order routed by the burly John Wood, who removed Tony Cottey, Chris Adams and Tim Ambrose in a match-turning spell of 3–9. While wickets were tumbling like autumn leaves at the other end, Murray Goodwin settled down to score his third hundred of the season. It was certainly his bravest. On 87 he was felled by a bouncer from Peter Martin and suffered a badly cut forehead, which required several stitches. Bravely, Goodwin continued and carried his bat, the second 50 runs in his hundred coming off just 76 balls. A stand of 81 in 17 overs with Mushtaq, who made another half-century, at least enabled Sussex to scramble to a second batting point and eliminate Surrey from the title race. But they had lost two wickets after following on and it was always going to be hard batting all day on a fourth-day pitch that offered increasing turn to Lancashire's under-rated left-arm spinner, Gary Keedy.

More supporters had arrived from the south coast overnight, but they travelled in hope rather than expectation. Sussex began the final day needing another 170 to make Lancashire bat again, and Adams and Cottey made serene progress in the first hour to give them hope. But then Wood intervened decisively for the second time in the match, getting Adams caught off the splice before unseating Ambrose in his next over. Matt Prior got the four runs that took him past 1,000 for the season and Goodwin, his gash protected by a swathe of bandages, made a half-century in two hours of bristling defiance.

Keedy finished with ten wickets, while Mushtaq had none for the only time in the season. What odds would you have got on that? Sussex were beaten shortly after 3pm and there were no complaints from their captain.

We weren't as aggressive as we've been all season in the field, we went into our shell after the rain on the first two days and just looked to bat out time. Lancashire played exceptional cricket but if things went our way when we played them at Hove they turned around here.

Oh well. When you've waited 113 years for something, what difference are a few more days going to make?

COUNTY CHAMPIONSHIP TABLE 15 SEPTEMBER 2003

	P	W	L	D	Btg	Blg	Ded	Pts
Sussex	*15*	*9*	*4*	*2*	*57*	*44*	*0.00*	*235.00*
Lancashire	15	6	1	8	63	40	0.00	219.00
Surrey	15	6	2	7	60	41	0.00	213.00
Kent	15	5	5	5	42	44	0.00	176.00
Middlesex	16	3	3	10	46	41	0.00	169.00
Warwickshire	15	4	4	7	48	36	2.50	168.50
Essex	15	2	5	8	29	42	0.00	134.00
Leicestershire	15	1	5	9	36	39	0.50	124.50
Nottinghamshire	15	1	8	6	32	42	1.00	111.00

MATCH 16 – HOVE, 17–19 SEPTEMBER

Sussex 614–4 dec, Leicestershire 179 and 380. Sussex (22pts) beat Leicestershire (1pt) by an innings and 55 runs.

History is made.

FINAL COUNTY CHAMPIONSHIP TABLE 22 SEPTEMBER 2003

	P	W	L	D	Btg	Blg	Ded	Pts
Sussex	*16*	*10*	*4*	*2*	*62*	*47*	*0.00*	*257.00*
Lancashire	16	6	2	8	64	43	0.00	223.00
Surrey	16	6	3	7	63	44	0.00	219.00
Kent	16	6	5	5	47	47	0.00	198.00
Warwickshire	16	4	5	7	50	37	2.50	171.50
Middlesex	16	3	3	10	46	41	0.00	169.00
Essex	16	3	5	8	34	45	0.00	156.00
Nottinghamshire	16	2	8	6	36	45	1.00	132.00
Leicestershire	16	1	6	9	36	40	0.50	125.50

9

LEGACIES AND LEGENDS

THE NEARLY MEN

Life is full of Amundsens. Ask Scott of the Antarctic. Just when you think you're about to achieve something, you realise that someone else, somehow, got there first. It's maddening. Ask Sussex. They know all about being second. They have done it seven times. They have even managed it when they have looked the best side in the land. Every spring they set out on a mission and every autumn they discovered that someone had beaten them to it.

You will always find someone at Hove who will argue that Sussex won the Championship, jointly at least, in 1875, when they finished top alongside Lancashire and Nottinghamshire. But since the competition was only formally recognised in 1890 it is a difficult proposition to sustain. Now seems like a good time to abandon the notion. What is beyond dispute, however, is that Sussex have been second in the Championship on seven occasions; seven bridesmaids for seven summers.

The so-called Golden Age of cricket, in the early years of the last century, represented the first of the club's two great epochs. This was the Sussex of C.B. Fry and Ranjitsinhji, of Albert Relf and Joe Vine, and the county were second in the Championship in successive years in 1902 and 1903.

In the club's second great era, the late 1920s and early 1930s, they went one better. That is not to say they won the thing, but they came second in three successive seasons. This was the Sussex of Duleepsinhji and Maurice Tate, of Ted Bowley, Jim and Harry Parks, and John and James Langridge, and they were runners-up in 1932, 1933 and 1934. Little wonder they called it the Depression. They were second, too, in 1953, when the inspirational captaincy of David Sheppard dared to challenge the might of Surrey, and when the side included Ken Suttle, Ian Thomson and young Jim Parks, and John and James Langridge. They were last runners-up in 1981, under another captain with uncommon qualities, John Barclay, who could muster Imran Khan, Garth le Roux, Paul Parker and Gehan Mendis.

1902

It is surprising that Sussex did so well in the very wet summer of 1902, the season better remembered for the likes of Victor Trumper and Gilbert Jessop in a titanic Ashes series. Morale was poor and the captain, Ranjitsinhji, did not play for the club at all after the end of July. They could hardly argue that they were the best team that year. Yorkshire, the champions, won 13 matches and lost just once, while Sussex won seven and lost three. The scoring system then was one point for a win, one point deducted for a loss and nothing for a draw, with the points then calculated as a percentage of the number of matches played. When the two sides met at Hove, however, Sussex had much the better of things. Yorkshire scored 372, Sussex replied with 455 and Yorkshire were in trouble at 84–6 in their second dig at the end.

The batting that season was once again led by Ranji and Fry, the two outstanding batsmen in the country, who were awesome in tandem, though there was strong support from George Brann and Joe Vine. Against Surrey at Hastings Fry scored 159 and Ranji an unbeaten 234 as Sussex scored 705–8 declared. Ranji led the national batting averages with well over 60. But 667 of his 885 runs that year came from only four innings. After appearing in the match against Australia he seemed to disappear in a massive sulk, complaining about the attitude of a number of players. He had failed in the Tests against Australia and his poor form might be partly explained by the fact that his many creditors were in hot pursuit. The *County Annual* reported: 'Why he abandoned the team, with which he had been so closely connected, at the most critical stage of their season, is not pleasant to dwell upon here, but we are happy to report that a reconciliation has since taken place.'

In his excellent booklet, *Sussex – Seven Times the Bridesmaid*, Nicholas Sharp reveals the correspondence between Ranji and Newham, who was also the club secretary. Newham was desperate that Ranji should play on the club's western tour, against Gloucestershire at Bristol and Somerset at Taunton. Ranji, in his reply, said: 'There is a monstrously selfish spirit prevalent in the team . . . some of them are getting distinctly above themselves.' Although Ranji did not play for Sussex on their tour he did appear for the MCC against Australia at Lord's in August.

Cricket magazine, reporting on the match at Taunton, said: 'Again deserted by C.B. Fry and Ranjitsinhji, who were for the second time in the week taking a rest, and moreover, obliged to do without [Fred] Tate, who was suffering from rheumatism, Sussex did very well indeed to avoid defeat.' After the season had ended there was a whiff of reconciliation in the autumn air and Ranji invited four of the Sussex professionals to join him for a week's fishing and shooting in Yorkshire.

Sussex prospered that year because Fred Tate, close to the end of his career, had the season of his life. His off-breaks, delivered at just under medium pace and usually in marathon spells, proved most effective on the damp pitches and he took 153 wickets in 20 championship matches at an average of just over 14. The next highest was Albert Relf, with 56. Tate played his solitary Test match – against Australia at Manchester – in 1902, making his debut on his 35th birthday, and it is the stuff of cricket legend.

Archie McLaren, the England captain, moved Tate from his usual position in the slips to the leg-side boundary. Joe Darling immediately hit a skier to him, which he dropped. In a low-scoring game it was a crucial miss. England, set 124 to win, were 116–9 when Tate came to the wicket. He was bowled for four and England lost by three runs. A thrilling match is still remembered for Tate's dropped catch. He was inconsolable afterwards but, most prophetically, he turned to his friend, Len Braund, who had been bowling when he dropped the catch, and said: 'I've got a little kid at home who'll make it up to me.'

1903

In another extremely wet summer, Sussex came very close to winning the title. Lancashire complained in 2003 that their Championship challenge had been hit by the weather, and Sussex could have made much the same point 101 years ago. They won seven and lost two of their 15 games and had the better of a number of rain-hit draws. Middlesex, the champions that year, won eight and lost one. Both matches between the sides were washed out.

Despite Middlesex's success, Yorkshire were still regarded as the best side in the country and very much the team to beat. Sussex did it twice, and with some brio.

At Bradford, Sussex scored 558–8 (Fry 234, Ranji 93) and won by an innings and 180 runs. The match at Hove, by contrast, was a low-scoring affair. Yorkshire were bowled out for 72 and 96, while Sussex scored 132 and 37–6 to win by four wickets. Tate and George Cox senior returned match figures of 10–75 and 9–83 respectively.

Too often, though, Sussex dominated only to run out of time because of the weather. Against Surrey at Hove, for example, they scored 542–9 (Fry 200) and at The Oval, against the same opponents, they made 600–7 (Ranji 204, Vine 104). They declared on both occasions but the matches were drawn. They beat Lancashire by nine wickets when they scored 485 (Fry 181, Ranji 105) and in the return game scored 422–5 (Ranji 144 not out, Fry 98) to take a first innings lead of 211. But it was another damp draw.

In such a moist season the only wonder was that Fry managed to score 2,446 first-class runs. He made eight centuries, including two in the match against

Kent at Hove. Even Ranji, back captaining the side, couldn't match him that year. Ranji and Fry were not the only batsmen to watch in these times. When Gloucestershire came to Hove, Gilbert Jessop scored 286 out of 482 in less than three hours, reaching his century in 70 minutes and his 200 in two hours.

There was strong support from Brann, Joe Vine and Ernest Killick. But Sussex sometimes struggled to bowl sides out. The most successful bowler was Albert Relf, with 91 Championship wickets, supported by Cox (79) and Tate (62).

Sussex slipped back to sixth place in 1904 and Fry had so little luck with the toss that he eventually delegated the job to other members of the team.

1932

It was to be another 29 years before Sussex were second again. And it was another Indian prince, Ranji's nephew Duleepsinhji, who captained them in that year. Sussex were second in the three years from 1932 to 1934, and they had a different captain on each occasion. At the start of the 1932 season Duleep said that with one more bowler the Championship could be won. But, as students of jigsaw puzzles know only too well, it is the last piece that can prove most elusive. The bowler was never found; nor was the Championship.

There were no worries about the batting. It was led by the brilliant Duleep himself and was so packed with all-rounders that it had as much tail as a Manx cat. Maurice Tate, who had opened the batting for the county, often went in ten, followed by 'Tich' Cornford, who would himself go on to open the innings. This was Sussex cricket at its family best. There were John and James Langridge, Jim and Harry Parks and, of course, Fred's son and Ranji's nephew.

By now there were 17 teams in the Championship, playing 28 matches. Yorkshire, champions on seven occasions in the thirties, won the title with 315 points, winning 19 matches and losing two; Sussex finished with 262 points, winning 14 games and losing just one, to Yorkshire.

It might have ended more happily for Sussex if Duleep had been fit throughout, but he missed the final five games of the season when his health broke down. He was suffering from tuberculosis and would never play for the county again.

Sussex, at the point of Duleep's withdrawal, were 19 points behind Yorkshire with a match in hand. But the match against Yorkshire at Hove, played before a huge crowd, brought little good fortune for the home side. They were without Duleep, Ted Bowley and Bert Wensley (an important all-rounder), and six who did make it onto the field were not fully fit. Bowled out for 166 and 150, they were no match for the Yorkshire side of Sutcliffe, Leyland and Bowes, who scored 258 and 225–3.

Tate, still a great bowler, took 124 wickets at under 16, and Jim Langridge and Wensley also topped 100. It was a strong all-round side who played a great deal of very attractive cricket, but it was not quite enough.

1933

Without Duleep, a decline had been anticipated for 1933. But Sussex, under the captaincy of R.S.G. Scott, had a terrific season, winning 18 matches, more than ever before, ten of them by an innings. Yorkshire, champions again, won 19. The figures are a little misleading because Sussex played 32 matches and Yorkshire 30. That year the counties played at least 24 matches and the title was decided on a percentage basis.

The season is perhaps best remembered for the first-wicket stand of 490 between John Langridge and Ted Bowley against Middlesex at Hove. The runs were scored in a single day, in just 350 minutes.

The record against Yorkshire was most impressive, with two emphatic victories. At Hull, at the end of June, Sussex won by ten wickets. They scored 378 in their first innings (Jim Langridge 159 not out, John Langridge 75) and bowled out Yorkshire for 131, with Jim Langridge taking 4–34, before making them follow on. Yorkshire had already won the Championship by the time the sides next met at Hove in August. Sussex bowled out Yorkshire for 115 and 114 and won by an innings. They also did the double over Derbyshire, Gloucestershire, Northants, Somerset and Worcestershire, and were beaten only twice in this busy season.

Scott launched his captaincy with a century, striking the wonderfully named Valance Jupp, once a substantial all-rounder for Sussex but now, at 43, the captain of Northants, for seven sixes. The Langridges made more than 3,000 runs between them, 1,831 for John, 1,340 for Jim, and shared eight hundreds. Jim became the first player in the country to achieve the double and was selected for the tour to India that winter. The Parks brothers and Bowley also passed 1,000 runs although, without Duleep, the batsmen were sometimes accused of slow scoring. Bert Wensley took 117 wickets.

The best batsman that year was Tommy Cook. He scored 1,795 at an average of 47.23, including five centuries. Cook played football for Brighton and Hove Albion and was good enough to play for England on one occasion as a third division player. His batting in the mid-thirties almost saw him become a double international. He fought in both world wars, first in the Royal Navy, where he was decorated, and then in the South African Air Force, where he was seriously injured. Tragically, separated from his wife and suffering depression, he was to kill himself a month before his 49th birthday.

1934

The omens for 1934 were not good. Bowley, one of the finest batsmen in Sussex history, had played his last full season and Tate, who the previous season had failed to take 100 wickets for the first time since 1921, embarked upon his 40th year in May. But they almost won the Championship, leading the race from mid-May until mid-August. Yorkshire, such a force in previous years, faltered and ended the campaign sixth. This, many thought, would finally be Sussex's year.

Cook had an even better year, scoring 2,072 runs at 56, and John Langridge also passed 2,000 at 49. Jim Parks, his opening partner, scored five centuries, passed his 1,000 and averaged over 50. Harry Parks also passed 1,000 runs. Alan Melville, a stylish South African batsman, was now leading the side. Sussex once reached 500 and topped 400 on 11 occasions.

Tate was back to something near his best. Certainly, no one could question his fitness. He bowled more than 1,400 overs and took 137 Championship wickets at 19. He also proved an astute captain when he stood in for Melville. Jim Cornford took 81 wickets and Jim Parks and Bert Wensley had strong all-round summers.

So what went wrong? One key problem was the collapse of Jim Langridge's bowling form and confidence following a difficult tour to India. The elder Langridge, one of the finest all-rounders to represent Sussex, batted well enough, but his slow left-arm bowling faltered as it had never done before and as it would never do again. He lost his length and was frequently no-balled. His 48 wickets cost 28.35 (compare and contrast his 136 at 15 the previous summer). But it was the batting, which faltered towards the end of the season, that was probably more to blame for the club's third near-miss in as many years. Albert Relf, the coach, said: 'Sussex were beaten by the mentality of their batsmen. If their brains had been equal to their skill, all would have been well.'

The batting lost its enterprise, becoming introverted and full of self-doubt. There were also a high number of injuries and illnesses. Unbeaten until August, they then lost two matches.

Both Sussex and Lancashire played 30 matches. Sussex won 12 and Lancashire, the champions, 13. It was the end of the run. In 1935 Sussex slipped to seventh and the following year they tottered to 14th.

1953

Yorkshire had been the team to beat in the early years of the century, and the same was true in the 1930s. By the 1950s, Surrey, who won seven successive Championships from 1952, were in the ascendant. In 1953, however, Sussex gave them an awful fright.

Sussex had been 13th the previous year, and James Langridge, aged 46 and following three years of solid if uninspired captaincy, made way for the dynamic David Sheppard. Although he was only 24, Sheppard had already made his name as a batsman, scoring 3,545 runs in three short university seasons with Cambridge, including 14 centuries. In 1952 he had headed the national averages with 1,581 runs, including seven centuries, at 64.62.

He led by brave example, not only as an exceptional batsman but also as an outstanding close fielder. The Sussex fielding that summer was of a very high order. Sheppard scored almost 2,000 runs. Even more remarkable was the effect he had on everyone around him. They all, old and new, wanted to play for him.

The Langridges had survived the war, and so had Charlie Oakes and George Cox junior. It was the younger players, however, who set Hove alight. Young Jim Parks, Ken Suttle, Ian Thomson and Alan Oakman were all at the early stages of what would be fine careers. Five players made more than 1,000 runs – Sheppard, Suttle, Parks, Cox and John Langridge. The bowling, too, was invigorated. Two opening bowlers, Ted James and Thomson, in his first full season, took more than 100 wickets. There was some quality off-spin too, from Robin Marlar and Oakman.

The biggest match of the year came near the end of the season, on 29 August–1 September. Surrey, the champions, were the visitors to Hove. Sussex had already beaten them, by seven wickets, at Guildford, with Sheppard scoring a century and James taking nine wickets. Then a series of draws damaged their high ambitions. Now they had to beat Surrey once more, in their penultimate match, to have a chance of the title. Surrey lost three quick wickets but David Fletcher consolidated and guided his side to 220. Sheppard declared with eight wickets down once his side had reached the Surrey score. But Sussex could not bowl Surrey out a second time. The champions knew that a draw would suit their purposes. Every Sussex player, with the exception of the wicketkeeper Rupert Webb, had a bowl. In other circumstances they might have admired Peter May's elegant century a little more.

Sussex won 11 matches and Surrey 13 that year. T he table read: Surrey 184 points, Sussex 168.

1981

The season of 1981 was, arguably, the greatest heartbreaker of them all. Sussex were probably the strongest side in the Championship that year. Yet they were denied once more, this time by just two points.

The story of the season is best told in the captain John Barclay's highly entertaining volume *The Appeal of the Championship*, which is at once funny, self-deprecating and moving. Barclay, like Sheppard 28 years before, was an inspirational captain. Unlike Sheppard he was not an England player. But he was a brave and most obdurate opening batsmen who would usually take the sting out of the attack, a slip fielder with a safe pair of hand, and a thoughtful, loopy off-spinner who could cause problems in favourable conditions. Most of all, he had an indomitable enthusiasm and never stopped talking, pecking away, bird-like, until his zeal had been communicated to those around him. The players liked him and did everything in their power to claim the prize.

Barclay had drawn out his battle plans in the sand at Sydney's Coogee Bay during a break from captaining Waverley Cricket Club. Sussex's primary strength was the opening attack of Imran Khan and Garth le Roux. With Ian Botham, Kapil Dev and Richard Hadlee all playing, it was the era of great all-rounders. But Imran was the greatest of them, a point happily conceded by his rival, Hadlee, at Trent Bridge.

There was quality seam support, too. Ian Greig would play for England in 1982, and Geoff Arnold, who spent the bulk of his career at Surrey, had been perhaps the most skilful fast-medium bowler in the country in the seventies. Barclay and Chris Waller provided the spin.

The specialist batting, led by Paul Parker and Gehan Mendis, was less reliable than the bowling, but it rarely mattered because the depth was exceptional, with all-rounders Imran, le Roux, Greig, Paul Phillipson and Ian Gould, the wicketkeeper-batsman who had joined from Middlesex that year.

The most critical game of the summer was against Nottinghamshire at Trent Bridge, the only Championship meeting between the two sides that season. The pitches there had been prepared for Hadlee and Clive Rice, with plenty of grass left on. But when it was realised that Sussex had an even stronger pace attack, the skilful groundsman produced a turning wicket instead, one that would suit the England off-spinner Eddie Hemmings. He took nine wickets in the match, but even this could not swing it in his side's favour. Sussex had the better of it and deserved to win. If they had done so, the Championship would have been theirs.

Sussex scored 208 and then bowled out Nottinghamshire for 102. Sussex made 144 in their second innings, leaving Notts to score 251 to win on the final day. Notts lost their ninth wicket at 210, and even after the time lost to bad light, Sussex were favourites for a famous victory. Imran then beat Mike Bore, hitting him on the shin of his back leg. The Sussex players, and especially Imran, were convinced it was plumb. But umpire Peter Stevens – known to the Sussex players as 'Shaking' – gave not out. The match was drawn.

Sussex won their last four matches, taking 92 points. But so did Notts, taking exactly the same number of points to keep intact their slender lead. 'Our immediate reaction was not one of disappointment, rather of elation,'

Barclay said in his book. 'We had aspired to excellence and had played a lot of wonderful cricket along the way. It is only with the passing of time that the disappointment of not winning has grown. I can never quite put it to the back of my mind. The "what ifs" loom larger.'

CONSOLATION PRIZES

Marco Polo, in all probability, would have turned pale and made an excuse to avoid the journey. But then what would a mere Venetian merchant understand about the extraordinary lure of the Gillette Cup.

It was midnight on 30 July 1969 and a dozen mad young men, huddled together like mourners, were outside The Nevill pub in Hove waiting for the minibus that would transport them to distant Chesterfield to watch the semi-final of county cricket's knock-out competition between Derbyshire and Sussex. The nocturnal journey, almost as far as Yorkshire, took about six hours. It would have been better to travel up on the day before the match and book into a hotel. But that would have been too expensive for these spotty-faced enthusiasts. Besides, getting two days off work would have been difficult.

Instead, a cheap-average hotel was sought out in which the night travellers could wash and shave and have breakfast at about 6.30 while reading up on the previews of the great match. Derbyshire were bowled out for 136 in 56.4 overs. It was a slow pitch and the ball stopped frequently, as if to pick up passengers. But it was still a poor score and even those people who subscribe to the notion that bookmakers are pickpockets who allow a chap to use his own hands might have been tempted to have a flutter on a team that included Jim Parks, Tony Greig and John Snow.

Alas, Sussex were bowled out for 49. FORTY-NINE! Alan Ward was a genuinely fast bowler that year, the sort that, from the batsman's point of view, makes the pitch feel too short; he took 2–11 in eight overs and unsettled Sussex. But the real Derbyshire hero was Peter Eyre, bald and furious, who bustled in to take 6–18 in 10.2 overs. The match was all over shortly after lunch. It was a very long minibus ride back to Hove. And your co-author was very distressed.

But Sussex supporters frequently made such journeys throughout the sixties and seventies because their side, no longer amateurs remember, were the original champions of one-day cricket, winning the inaugural Gillette Cup in 1963 and retaining the trophy in 1964. They went on win it again in 1978 and then its successor, the NatWest Trophy, in 1986. Four other finals were reached, in 1968, 1970, 1973 and 1993, in which Sussex were beaten, often in thrilling circumstances. A Sunday League title was also won, in 1982, though Sussex never even reached the final of the Benson and Hedges Cup. These successes helped assuage the frustrations of the Championship-less members at Hove. Some even described the sixties as the third great age of Sussex cricket.

A measure of luck is involved in the winning of one-day competitions. But in the early sixties, at least, Sussex, with a number of suitable players and the most advanced game plan, had proved to be the early masters of limited-overs cricket.

When nostalgic old buffers wax on about how wonderful cricket was in the 1950s, when England, jam-packed with great names, were the best side in the world, it should be remembered that attendance declined steadily in that time following the postwar boom. The introduction of a one-day competition was discussed. An unofficial form of this game, played by Rothmans' International Cavaliers, had already proved immensely popular. But the idea of developing this format met with considerable opposition among the counties, who argued that it would be uneconomical because the revenue from just one day's cricket would quickly be swallowed up if away teams were required to stay for a second or third day in the event of bad weather.

It was then that the idea of involving an interested commercial company was discussed.

Gordon Ross, in that wonderful tome, *Barclays World of Cricket*, tells us:

> That company was the Gillette Safety Razor Company, and it is interesting that in the early correspondence the world of 'sponsorship' was not mentioned. Gillette agreed to underwrite the competition against loss to the tune of £6,500 and this block grant was put into a central pool with all other sources of revenue, and divided up amongst the counties, each getting one slice of the cake for each match in which it played.

The title for the competition in 1963 was 'The First-Class Counties Knock-Out Competition for the Gillette Cup'. Snazzy, hey? Unofficially, it was known as the KO Cup and in 1964 it was renamed the Gillette Cup. Also abandoned in 1964, Mr Ross tells us, was a method of cutting down on overheads. In the first year the visiting teams were often put up in private houses, usually those of home committee members, instead of hotels. It's a wonder that they didn't travel through the night in a minibus.

Matches were played over 65 overs per side, reduced to 60 in 1964 to cut down on the number of dusky finishes, and each bowler was restricted to 15 overs.

Enter Ted Dexter. Here was one of England's greatest attacking batsmen. But his captaincy was sometimes criticised. He appeared aloof – although there was a certain shyness here – and in the field he would often seem bored, practising golf swings and, for all anyone knew, contemplating his investment in the 3.45 at Goodwood, for he was one for the horses. The shorter game, however, appealed to his theoretical mind. He knew that Sussex, as usual, had a number of attacking batsmen, led by himself and Jim Parks. There was also a gifted and experienced seam attack, featuring the gnarled Ian Thomson, the young John Snow, Tony Buss and Don Bates, backed up, if need be, by his own medium-pace and the twirl of Alan Oakman, Ken Suttle and Graham Cooper. Perfect.

Dexter, though, must take the credit for understanding, from the very start, that one-day cricket was, essentially, a defensive game. Fielders should defend the boundary and restrict run-scoring. It seems obvious today, of course, but these were the pioneers of one-day cricket.

In his book, *Ted Dexter Declares*, he says:

> Sussex won two Gillette Cups before the other counties had woken up to the problem. I remember the first game against Kent at Tunbridge Wells. We won the toss and Colin Cowdrey set a very friendly field indeed. We made a big score [Sussex scored 314–7]; it was all very sporting and pleased the big crowd. Kent went in and the picture changed dramatically. There was only one man who looked like doing any good and that was Peter Richardson. It was not my main intention to get him out. I just set the field back, allowed him to take a single, then bowled tight to the other batsman to force him to make the runs and not Richardson.
>
> There were boos and screams and everyone thought that this was a rotten thing to do – there was so much sympathy for Richardson that he received the team [man of the match] award – but there it was, I had shown people what they could be let in for.

Sussex beat Kent by 72 runs in that first-round match at Tunbridge Wells. In the second round they beat Yorkshire at Hove by 22 runs (Parks 90) and in the semi-final they beat Northants at Hove by 105 runs (Dexter 115, Parks 71).

They were in the final, where they played Worcestershire. But, on a saturated wicket, they were bowled out for 168, despite a fine 57 by Parks. Sussex, the ancient masters of being runners-up, would surely come second once again. Dexter said:

> The wicket suited the Worcestershire spinners. Despite a fine fifty from Parks, Sussex made a relatively poor total and looked in real trouble. When Worcestershire batted the Sussex medium-pacers failed in their task to either contain the batsmen or get them out.

My classic formula had encountered the worst possible conditions for its application. What could I do? The answer, just in time, was Alan Oakman. In desperation I threw the ball to him and said, 'It's a spinners' wicket and you are the only man to do the job.' Oakman took it on and turned in a marvellous performance as we put the screws on Worcestershire.

Worcestershire were bowled out for 154 and Sussex won by 14 runs. After 125 years of sometimes tortured history they had finally placed their hands on some silverware. Dexter said that the one-day game did not appeal to him much. But it had presented him with an intriguing problem to solve and he came up with the solution.

Surprisingly, most other counties did not seem to realise what Lord Ted was up to. Well, Mike Smith, the Warwickshire captain did. Sussex and Warwickshire duly reached the second final in 1964. Sussex had beaten

Jim Parks in action during the 1964 Gillette Cup final when Sussex retained their trophy with an eight-wicket win over Warwickshire. His father and uncle both played for the county, but he was the most successful of the family dynasty, with 44 Test appearances for England. *(Sussex CCC)*

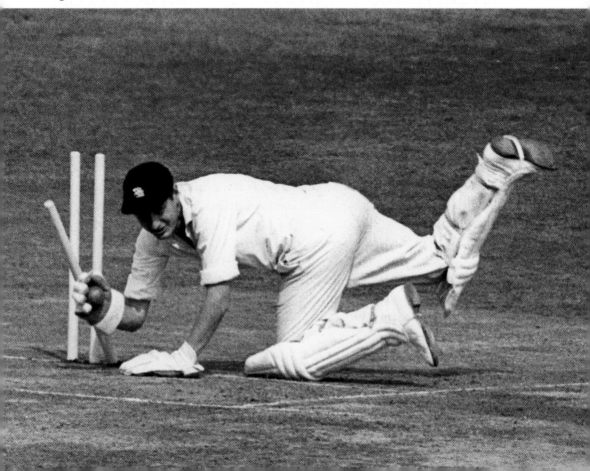

Durham at Hove by 200 runs (Parks 102 not out) and Somerset at Taunton by 16 runs (Cooper 58, Bates 4–28). The semi-final, against Surrey at Hove, was a typical example of what Gillette Cup cricket meant to Sussex in the early sixties. There was a full house and several hundred were locked out. Dexter, at the peak of his powers, took Surrey on and beat them almost single-handedly. He hit a magnificent 84 and Sussex, with cameos from Suttle and Parks, reached 215–8. Surrey were then bowled out for 125, with Dexter and Thomson each returning figures of 3–17.

The final was decided by a wonderful piece of medium-pace bowling by Thomson, who in helpful morning conditions dismissed the first three Warwickshire batsmen cheaply. Warwickshire never recovered, were bowled out for 127 and Sussex got home with eight wickets to spare.

Sussex lost in the Gillette Cup for the first time on 23 June 1965, when Middlesex beat them by 90 runs in a third-round match at Lord's. But three years later they returned to Lord's for their third final, when Warwickshire were again their opponents. They had beaten Derbyshire and then Northants by seven runs in an epic at Hove, followed by Gloucestershire in the semis. They seemed to have beaten Warwickshire in the final, too. They made 214–7 (Greig 41, Parks 57) and Warwickshire appeared out of it at 155–6 before Alan Smith and Dennis Amiss put on 60 to carry their side home.

Sussex seemed to have lost the knack of the shorter game. They were back at Lord's for two more Gillette finals, in 1970 and 1973, only to be beaten both times, first by Lancashire and then by Gloucestershire. In 1978 they returned for an unlikely third triumph. Snow had gone and so, by mid-season, had Greig. Arnold Long was now captain. But there were players here who would take Sussex so close to winning the Championship three years later.

Imran Khan was in his first full season, Paul Parker was a sensation in the covers, Paul Phillipson was a useful all-rounder, while Gehan Mendis and John Barclay batted dependably. They had an easier start than in most years. Or so it seemed on paper. They defeated Suffolk in the first round and were then drawn to play Staffordshire, at Stone, in the second. It was a thriller. Sussex, despite a top four of Kepler Wessels, Mendis, Parker and Imran, were restricted to 221–6. Rain pushed play into a second day when Sussex were surprised by a third-wicket stand of 140, with Nasim-ul-Ghani striking a whirlwind 85. Staffordshire finished on 219–9, losing by just two runs.

They could have gone out in the quarter-final, too, when they edged a ten-over slog against Yorkshire. Then they beat Lancashire in the semis (Parker 69, Javed Miandad 75). They played Somerset in the final, the mighty Somerset of Richards, Botham and Garner.

Long, boldly, put Somerset in to bat and might have immediately regretted his decision when Brian Rose hit 14 off Imran's opening over. But Somerset

Tony Greig in typically swashbuckling pose at Hove in May 1972. *(Sussex CCC)*

faltered and were dependent on Botham's admirably restrained 80 for their total of 207. Barclay and Mendis gave Sussex a good start with a stand of 93, but then Garner and Botham broke through and Sussex, four down for 110, appeared to be heading for their fourth final defeat in a row. They were rescued by Phillipson (32) and man-of-the-match Parker (62 not out), who saw his side home with 6.5 overs to spare.

Sussex were back in 1986. Again, they brushed past Suffolk in the opening round. In the second Allan Green's first century in limited-overs cricket – he was once hailed by John Arlott as a future England player – saw them past Glamorgan. In the quarter-finals against Yorkshire at Leeds they were 86–6 before Ian Gould (88) and Garth le Roux helped them to 213–7. Yorkshire struggled against aggressive fast bowling from le Roux and Adrian Jones, losing four wickets for one run at one point, and were bowled out for 125.

In the semi-final at Worcester, Imran's spell of 3–6 in five overs against his former club proved decisive. Worcestershire were all out for 125 and Sussex got home with five wickets and 11 overs to spare. Lancashire awaited them in their seventh final.

Fowler and Mendis, once of Sussex, placed a question mark against Gould's decision to bowl when they put on 50 for the first wicket in 13 overs. But Dermot Reeve, his medium-paced outswingers assisted by the muggy conditions and the slowness of the pitch, bowled magnificently to take 4–20 from his dozen overs. With the first ball of his third over Reeve had Mendis lbw and with the fifth he dismissed Clive Lloyd, on his final appearance, for a duck, after the great batsman had been given a standing ovation all the way to the wicket. Lancashire, wobbling on 100–5, finally made a most competitive 242–8, with Hayhurst and Fairbrother adding 103 for the sixth wicket.

No team batting second had scored as many as 243 to win a domestic one-day final. Sussex, though, were well placed at 117–1 at tea after 35 overs. Rehan Alikhan had gone cheaply but Green (62) and Parker (85) carried their second-wicket stand to 137 to set up victory. The dismissal of Green brought Imran to the wicket and he scored a fluent and undefeated 50 as Sussex got home with ten balls to spare.

In 1993 there was one more final, although it is painful to recall. It was, arguably, the finest of them all. Sussex scored 321–6, a record for a cup final, with David Smith making 124 and Martin Speight and Neil Lenham securing dazzling half-centuries. If Sussex bowled and fielded properly it would surely be more than enough. The Warwickshire openers fell cheaply and even though Paul Smith and Dominic Ostler added 75 in 16 overs, the task looked beyond them. When Ostler was out, however, Asif Din, his long career unencumbered by outstanding achievement, emerged to play the innings of his life.

Ian Gould receives the NatWest Trophy after Sussex's win over Lancashire at Lord's in 1986. It was the last major honour the county would win for 13 years. *(Sussex CCC)*

He and Dermot Reeve needed to score 158 in 24 overs, more than a run a ball. But Sussex found it difficult to bowl dot balls, and by the time Din's wristy and inventive innings had perished for 104, the match was in the balance, with 20 needed from the final two overs. Ed Giddins then bowled a tight over in the circumstances, conceding just five runs, and with 15 needed for victory from Franklyn Stephenson's last, Sussex were once again favourites. Reeve, though, carved 13 from the first five deliveries and then Roger Twose, facing his only ball of the match, sliced it through the off-side for two. Some Sussex supporters are still recovering.

Sussex, then, have won four of their eight Lord's finals. There was one other trophy, the 1982 John Player League, and it helped make up for their Championship near miss of the year before. Under the zestful captaincy of John Barclay, they won it with some style. They established records for the most wins (14) and the most points (58). In one-day cricket, though, Sussex will always be associated with their Gillette Cup and NatWest Trophy triumphs.

ALL IN THE FAMILIES

As we have said, this is not a history of Sussex County Cricket Club. But any book about the oldest of the counties cannot fail to make reference to the extraordinary family associations, a rich seam that runs through the club in a way that is almost indistinguishable from the club's history. This is merely a glance at a few of those families.

Cricket started here, or at least it started in the Weald of Sussex, Kent and Surrey. The history of cricket is inexplicit. What we do know is that cricket in Sussex was old and gnarled long before the Hambledon club was born. And when Sussex were the best side in the country, which they were before they became formally established in 1839, taking on and beating All-England in 1827, the family names of Broadbridge and Lillywhite were prominent.

More recently, names such as Langridge and Parks have felt more like dynasties. And the tradition goes on and on. When Alan Hill published his engaging volume, *The Family Fortune: A Saga of Sussex Cricket*, in 1978, Tony Greig had played for Sussex but his brother, Ian had not. Nor had the Wells brothers (Colin and Alan), the Newells (Keith and Mark), the Hoadleys (Simon and Stephen), and nor had Neil Lenham, son of Les.

We will pass over the nineteenth century, the Lillywhites, Broadbridges, the Charlwoods and Lucases, and pick up the story in the early years of the twentieth century, the so-called Golden Age of cricket, when Sussex had a particularly strong team.

The Relf brothers, Albert and Robert, were regular members of the side in the first two decades of the century. A third brother, Ernest, played for the county a dozen times. The story of Albert Relf, the best of the three, is one of the saddest in all cricket.

Tall and striking, looking every inch an Edwardian gentleman with his luxuriant moustache, he was an outstanding all-rounder. He bowled accurate medium-pace, often in marathon spells, scored prolifically and was a reliable slip fieldsman. He played 13 Tests and did the double eight times in ten seasons. Like so many, his career was blighted by war, for his best season was 1913 when, in his 40th year, he scored 1,846 runs, took 141 wickets and was one of *Wisden*'s Five Cricketers of the Year. When he retired he became a popular coach at Wellington College. He was well off and had a generally cheerful disposition. He was also devoted to his wife Agnes, and as she lay ill, following a gallstone operation, he became convinced that he would lose her. On Good Friday, 26 March 1937, he shot himself through the heart. The tragedy became all the more poignant when Agnes made a full recovery, inheriting a large estate. In his darkly compelling book, *By His Own Hand, A Study of Cricket Suicides*, David Frith adds:

Sussex cricketers number comparatively highly in the ranks of those who have terminated their own lives . . . retirement from the darkness and claustrophobia of a coalmine is one thing; expulsion from the agreeable 'workplace' of a cricket field is another, especially if it be the handsome expanse of Hove.

In the 1920s, the outstanding Sussex family was called Gilligan. Two of the three brothers, Arthur and Harold, captained Sussex and England. Harold, whose daughter Virginia married Peter May, was a right-hand batsman and change bowler who led England on their first tour of New Zealand in 1929/30. He captained Sussex for one summer, in 1930.

A third brother, Frank, the eldest and a wicketkeeper, captained Oxford University and Essex. He emigrated to New Zealand and was a master at Wanganui Collegiate School for almost 20 years until his death in 1960. Hill tells us that there was one week, in 1929, when all three brothers captained their counties, Harold replacing Arthur, who was busy playing representative cricket.

Arthur was the family's star turn. A fast bowler, an attacking lower-order batsman who scored centuries from six to eleven in the order and a thrilling fielder, usually at mid-off, he was among the most dynamic cricketers of the age. In 1924, at Edgbaston, he took 6–7 as he and Maurice Tate dismissed South Africa for 30, then took 5–83 in the second innings. But some weeks later, while batting, he was struck over the heart and his doctor advised him to stop bowling fast. He was never the same cricketer again. He became president of the MCC and continued to ski and play golf into old age. He was also a popular radio commentator and on his many trips to Australia he would team up with Victor Richardson, whose 'What do you think, Arthur?' became a catchphrase. He was a familiar face at Hove until his death in 1976.

By the time Arthur Gilligan last played, in 1932, the Langridge brothers, John and James, were well established. Jim, who suffered tuberculosis when a boy, became one of the best Sussex all-rounders, a slow left-arm bowler whose misfortune it was to be a contemporary of the great Hedley Verity, though he did play eight Tests. He was also a dependable if slow-scoring batsman and a fine fielder.

He joined the county in 1924 and did not retire until 1953. Twenty times he passed 1,000 runs in a season and he did the double six times. In 1932, the year he took seven Gloucestershire wickets for eight runs at Cheltenham, he was one of *Wisden*'s Five Cricketers of the Year. He played in two Tests against the West Indies the following year and had second-innings figures of 7–56 at Old Trafford, where his victims included the great George Headley. After the Second World War and Verity's death he was called up to play for England again, against India in 1946, but he had figures of 0–64 and did not bat, and the game was rained off – it was not a happy memory.

Jim, or Jas as he was better known, toured Australia under Walter Hammond that winter, 1946/7, though he did not play in a Test. He always regretted that he never played in a Test against Australia. He became Sussex's first professional captain in 1950. He did the job for three years and then had another season as a player before becoming the county coach. According to his son, Richard, who played for Sussex between 1957 and 1971, he was upset by his sacking from that position in 1959 and he died the following year, aged 60.

John Langridge, four years younger than Jim, was thought by many to be the best opening batsman never to have played for England. He played for Sussex for almost 30 years and under 11 different captains, churning out the runs, 34,380 of them in all, including 76 centuries, but the Test appearance never came. He was called up for the 1939/40 tour to India but it was cancelled because of the war.

He scored 1,000 runs in a season 17 times and on 11 occasions topped 2,000. His batting was as well known for its eccentric fidgets and adjustments as it was for its efficiency. He didn't bowl much, but he became a magnificent slip fielder. Only the typesetters objected. The very familiar 'c. Langridge (John) bowled Langridge (James)' was difficult to fit across a single line. His best season was in 1949 when, in his 40th year, he scored 2,914 runs at 60.70, including a dozen hundreds. After retiring in 1955 he became a first-class umpire.

John Marshall, whose *Sussex Cricket*, published in 1959, remains the definitive history of the club, selects the thirties as a particularly rich period for family achievements. There was Maurice Tate, son of Fred, whom we have already discussed, and Duleep, nephew of Ranji. But this was also the decade of Jim Parks senior and his brother Harry, the Langridges, Charlie and Jack Oakes, and George Cox, son of Old George Cox.

In 1937 Jim Parks senior established a record that will surely never be broken. He scored 3,000 runs and took 100 wickets in the season. His son, young Jim, said family bereavement could have been responsible. 'Mother had died the previous year and Dad just threw himself into his cricket to try and forget the loss.' Parks scored 11 centuries that year, with a best of 168 against Hampshire at Portsmouth, and just missed 1,000 runs in May, finishing with an average of 50.54. It was also the year of his solitary Test appearance, when he opened the batting with Len Hutton against New Zealand, scoring 27 and seven.

When Sussex did not re-engage him after the war he played league cricket, umpired and coached Nottinghamshire. It was as coach that he returned to Sussex after an absence of 24 years, to work alongside his son.

Harry Parks was a middle-order batsman and notable outfielder. In 1937 he and his brother added 297 against Hampshire. Three years younger than Jim, he did play after the war, when he opened the batting with John Langridge. He became an umpire for two years and then coached Somerset. In the fifties young Jim Parks emerged as the family's champion player, a gifted strokemaker who complemented the power of Dexter. He had a son, Bobby, who played for Hampshire.

Old George Cox was 52 when he took 17 Warwickshire wickets for 106 at Horsham, his home town, in 1926. Twenty years earlier he had scored 167 not out against Hampshire at Chichester. He was an aggressive, if limited, batsman and a medium-pace bowler who later bowled slow left-arm, sometimes very slow. When he became county coach he was able to keep an eye on his son, who first played for the county just three years after his father's retirement.

The younger George, like John Langridge, might have become an England player but for the war. He sometimes found his father difficult to please. In 1939 he scored 58 and 232 against Northants at Kettering. He did not go home that night ('Don't ask me what I did') but went straight to Hove, where he scored 182 against Lancashire: 'That night I did go home. As I drove up to the house I wondered what the old boy would say.' Cox senior, sitting by the fireside, turned his head slowly as his son came in and said, 'What's up with you then? So you went mad did you?'

George junior would continue going mad for some time. He retired in 1955 and became coach at Winchester College, but he missed the game so much that he returned in 1957, at the age of 46, to score his 50th century and continued playing until 1960. Then he became a popular, witty after-dinner speaker.

Charlie and Jack Oakes, like the Coxes, came from Horsham. We met Charlie in an earlier chapter. Jack's career ended sadly. Suspended for indiscipline – he was accused of not trying in a second XI match against Hampshire – he then resigned from the club. The season before he had scored 1,157 and taken 53 wickets. Alan Hill chronicled his response to the charge. A very aggressive batsman, he said:

> I am an attacking batsman and sometimes, when I'm beaten by a good ball I smile. It doesn't mean that I'm not trying. I tried to hit the opposing spinner off his length and missed by a mile. I laughed and told the umpire I was lucky to still be there.

In the sixties the big family affair was the Buss brothers, Tony and Michael, or 'Omni' and 'Mini' as they were known. Tony arrived at Hove as an off-spinner, then when he found that the job had already been filled, he reinvented himself as an opening bowler, an inspired career move. Though overshadowed first by Ian Thomson and then by John Snow, he was good enough to take 938 wickets at 24.99 and was an important member of the Gillette Cup-winning teams in 1963 and 1964. He took a hundred wickets in a season three times in the middle sixties, and until Mushtaq Ahmed did it in 2003, he was the last Sussex bowler to reach three figures, with 113 in 1967. He went on to become county coach. Younger brother Michael, an all-rounder, was a left-arm medium-pace bowler and a left-handed batsman who turned himself into a dangerous opener in the one-day game.

Ian Greig may not have had the extravagant ability or overpowering personality of his elder brother, Tony, but he was a dependable all-rounder with a strong character of his own. He was captain of Cambridge University before he came to Sussex in 1980, by which time Tony had already been gone for two years. He won his cap the following year, when he was a member of the side that thrillingly finished runner-up to Nottinghamshire. He took 76 wickets at 19.32 with his nippy medium-fast, finishing second in the bowling averages, as well as scoring 911 runs. With his cap pulled down over his eyes, he was also a useful decoy fielder when he swapped positions with the similarly built Paul Parker. It was his best season and, as is so often the case, England waited until the following year before giving him a Test cap, by which time he had lost some of his sharpness. He played twice against Pakistan in 1982 and in his first match returned the same figures, 4–53, that Tony had produced ten years earlier.

In the eighties Sussex had a habit of letting go of players who still had a lot of good cricket left in them, such as Gehan Mendis and Dermot Reeve. Greig junior was another. He was released by Sussex at the end of the 1985 season and had a second successful career at Surrey, whom he captained between 1987 and 1991, before moving to Australia. In 1990 he scored 1,259 runs at 54.73.

The Wells brothers both played for England. Colin never did so at Test level but appeared in two one-day internationals. He was an old fashioned all-rounder, a clean-hitting batsman in the middle order and a medium-pace bowler who 'hit the pitch' and was sometimes quicker than he appeared. With Alan, he put on an unbroken 303 against Kent at Tunbridge Wells in 1987, breaking the 50-year-old record partnership for Sussex brothers, which had been held by Jim and Harry Parks. He moved to Derbyshire in 1992.

Alan, 18 months younger than Colin, was a more classical batsman who did play Test cricket, though only once, against the West Indies in 1995. It was the final Test at The Oval. He got a first-baller, made three not out and was not invited back. He probably deserved a better chance. He was among England's best middle-order batsmen in the nineties, scoring 1,777 championship runs at 61.27 in 1991. He was appointed Sussex captain the following year but his tactical shortcomings were exposed in the 1993 NatWest Trophy final, when he was unable to defend a total of 321. After that there were rumours of a disunited dressing room and Wells was sacked as captain in 1997. He joined Kent on a five-year contract, but with little success.

Of course, in the thirties, there were Jim and 'Tich' Cornford. But they weren't related, silly.

10

THE NEXT STEP

Was any Championship success as widely acclaimed as Sussex's triumph in 2003? Everyone loves an underdog and cricket followers are no different. The fact that Sussex had triumphed over arguably the two biggest names in the domestic game, Lancashire and Surrey, to land the first title in their 165-year history seemed to lend even more romance to the victory. But, having taken up squatters' rights on the big boys' stage, how long will it be before the county are celebrating again? As the players did their lap of honour on that unforgettable afternoon in September 2003, at least the greybeards in the deckchairs at Hove wiped away their tears knowing they would die happy. 'We never thought we would see it, so if it doesn't happen again we won't mind,' was a typical reaction. 'Once is enough for a lot of us, we've waited an awful long time for this.'

Fortunately, once is not enough for the people who run Sussex cricket. The ambition of director of cricket Peter Moores and captain Chris Adams burns bright and, since the revolution of 1997, seems to be matched in the committee room as well. Now, thanks to the generous legacy of a former president, the county's future looks assured.

The man they have to thank is Spen Cama, who, it appears, loved Sussex cricket and accumulating wealth with equal passion. When he died in June 2001, the club knew the will contained a substantial bequest in their favour. His was (and still is) a complicated estate because of the substantial property interests he had in Brighton and Hove. Initially, Sussex thought they might end up with £4.3m. Within a year that figure had risen to £7.4m. Now, with the property market still buoyant, chairman David Green expects Sussex could be better off by at least £10m. The first payment was due to be made in 2004. About the same time the club were declaring a loss of around £370,000 on the previous financial year. Around £125,000 of that is depreciation on the new indoor school, which has been named after Spen Cama.

David Green is a self-made man with interests in aviation, property, construction and soft drinks distribution. He proudly boasts that none of his businesses has ever traded at a loss and almost considers it a personal affront that, in the second year of his chairmanship, Sussex were heavily in the red. Even the prospect of soon having £10m in the bank doesn't necessarily sweeten the pill. 'If we continued to lose £300,000 every year, I don't think anyone would thank us in ten years' time when the Spen Cama money had gone and we were still struggling financially,' he said.

Even with Spen Cama's millions, Sussex will never be able to compete, in financial terms at least, with the likes of Lancashire, whose last accounts showed a turnover of £8.5m compared to Sussex's £2.5m. Lancashire covet their status as a Test match venue, while Green happily admits that Hove, its eight acres hemmed in on all sides by flats and houses, will never stage international cricket. It also benefits Lancashire that the other Old Trafford is just six minutes' walk away. The spillover of corporate hospitality from Manchester United's football matches helped the county generate £437,000 in 2002 through car parking and catering revenue alone. They pulled in another £200,000 by staging pop concerts by the likes of Robbie Williams and Oasis. It means that the annual subsidy from the ECB, which is paid to all the counties, accounts for just 15 per cent of Lancashire's revenue. In Sussex's case the figure is 55 per cent.

Green's mission statement for his chairmanship is simple enough: 'I want us to be competitive on the pitch with good facilities and money in the bank.' Spen Cama's legacy will undoubtedly make that target easier to reach, while if there was ever a substantial cut in the central subsidy from the ECB – because of a shortfall in revenue from the next television contract, for instance – it would not be as devastating for Sussex as it would for some counties.

What made Sussex's triumph in 2003 especially remarkable was that it was achieved with probably the smallest professional squad in the long history of the county game – just 18 players. At £1.2m, their wage bill was among the lowest of the 18 first-class counties, yet on average their players are among the highest paid in the country. Being competitive on the pitch costs money. Ten years ago, when Sussex's cricket wage bill was £422,000, the county carried 24 professionals. Their policy of having a smaller staff, but paying them well with better basic salaries and imaginative incentive schemes for improved performances, was first formulated by former chief executive Dave Gilbert and Peter Moores just before Gilbert's departure in 2001. As Green explained, there is no better example of the policy's success than Mushtaq Ahmed, whose phenomenal displays propelled Sussex to glory.

Mushtaq came to us with a point to prove. He hadn't played county cricket since 1998 and hardly any international cricket for three years. His basic wage was much lower than any international player of his calibre, but we worked out an incentive scheme that gave him an opportunity to boost his earnings on a sliding scale which increased by between £50 and £100 with every wicket above 50 he took. By the end of the season he'd taken 103 and was earning as much as any international player.

The last of the celebratory champagne had just been sipped when Sussex laid down an important marker for the defence of their title by announcing the signing of Ian Ward on a four-year contract in October 2003. Ward, who played Test cricket for England as recently as 2001, believes he can revive his international career at Hove rather than The Oval, where he was a prolific performer at the top of Surrey's batting order for seven years. Two other counties offered him more money, and one of them offered him the captaincy as well, but he chose to move to the south coast.

Not so long ago players were falling over themselves in their rush to leave Sussex. Several factors are behind the renaissance, not the least of which is the reputation of Peter Moores as the most enlightened English-born coach currently working in domestic cricket. There were positive results in eight of the nine home games Sussex played in their Championship triumph, a statistic that reflects well on the work Derek Traill and his groundstaff have done to breathe new life into the hitherto moribund Hove wickets. And now, thanks to the Spen Cama legacy, the transformation of the County Ground into a home fit for the champions is starting to take shape. 'Sussex is now seen as a desirable place to play if you are a top player and knowing that gives me and the management of the club a lot of pleasure,' said chairman Green.

Cricket has been played at Hove 'between Mr Rigden's farm and the railway station at Cliftonville' since 1872, and David Green was appalled, at one of the first meetings he attended after his election to the committee in 1997 when the curtains were drawn, vows of secrecy sworn and members began discussing the possibility of leaving their home of more than 130 years. Two possible areas for relocation, one near Crawley and later the site of a disused cement works at Upper Beeding, were actively discussed. Green was horrified at the prospect of leaving Hove.

A lot of people, and not just Sussex supporters, could never associate Sussex cricket with any other place. I'm no Luddite, but I couldn't see the economic sense in moving. We would have ended up with a white elephant stadium, a massive debt and no one in the ground because our core support base, which is in Brighton and Hove, would have disappeared.

Because of his background in property and construction, Green was asked to look at ways of developing the existing site. David Gilbert, chief executive at the time and someone keen to bring international cricket to Sussex on a regular basis, thought it impossible, but Green disagreed: 'I thought it was rubbish that you couldn't do anything with the land we had, which is about eight acres, and I set about trying to prove it.'

Stage one was completed with the opening of the new indoor school in November 2002. The project cost £860,000, while smaller improvement work in 2003 took overall spending beyond £1m. The money was borrowed against the Spen Cama legacy. But that was only the start. In the summer of 2004 a £400,000 refurbishment of the main pavilion is due to begin. A substantial chunk of that money will be spent to ensure the building, whose flint walls are still as structurally sound now as they were 130 years ago, meets the requirements of the Safety of Sports Grounds Act. Green believes the cost of extending and refurbishing the long room will have paid for itself by the end of the calendar year. If he has his way, it won't be long before you can be joined in holy matrimony on the outfield and carry the bride back up the pavilion steps to a reception in the long room.

> There is a desperate shortage of venues in the area for parties catering for 100 people or so. We must get ten enquiries a week from people who want to hire the pavilion out for wedding receptions and the like which we've had to turn down. Once this work is done we won't need to do that.

The next phase of redevelopment will see the Gilligan Stand at the sea end of the ground, one of the ugliest structures on the county circuit, demolished to make way for a two-storey building. Construction of a new public pavilion on the bottom floor will satisfy a desperate need for facilities for non-members, while new corporate hospitality and media areas are planned for upstairs. Aficionados worried that the best view of the cricket in the ground will disappear along with 'The Gilly' need not fret. There will be a new viewing area on the top deck as well. A proper home for one of the country's finest collections of cricketana will doubtless be included in any development, under the affectionate supervision of the club's librarian, Rob Boddie.

The smaller counties like Somerset and Worcestershire, whose facilities guarantee an all-year income rather than just in the 60-odd summer days when cricket is played, are Green's role models in his dream of making Sussex financially self-sufficient.

> A bit like us, Somerset are out of the mainstream population-wise with a restricted number of members. But they make a profit because they have facilities which are open all year round. It's the same at Worcester. They made something like £300,000 out of catering alone last year, which would easily have covered our loss.

Work on developing the sea end will start in the winter of 2004, all being well. But that won't be the end of it. The county plan to take advantage of a break clause in the lease for the Sussex Cricketer pub at the main entrance to the ground, which earns them over £100,000 a year in rent, to discuss actively the option of developing the site into a hotel, perhaps with a fitness centre and penthouse flats at the top with enviable views of the sea on one side and the cricket ground on the other. 'There is a surprising amount of room on the current site with the option of building back into the ground,' said Green.

The entrance to the ground would change but whatever we do will not spoil the character of Hove. Schemes like this have been talked about for years, but because of the Spen Cama legacy we now have the opportunity to pursue them with real vigour rather than as some pipe-dream. Any scheme which brings forward income into the club for the next 20 years and beyond excites me.

So what sort of cricket could the lucky owners of those penthouses at 'Champions Gate' be watching in a few year's time? If David Green, Peter Moores and the rest have anything to do with it, Sussex will have built on their success of 2003. But will there still be a County Championship and, if so, will there still be 18 first-class counties playing in it and will Sussex still be a members' club?

English cricket is undergoing another period of soul-searching. The loudest voice advocating change belongs to the Cricket Reform Group, a high-profile collection of former players, among them Michael Atherton and Bob Willis, and administrators including Lord MacLaurin, the former chairman of the England and Wales Cricket Board (ECB). They do not believe the game's finances can sustain 18 counties and feel the England team would be better served by a smaller domestic competition where the better England-qualified players competed against each other. Yet Sussex are already pointing the way for their rivals. If the other counties adopted their approach and trimmed their staffs down to 18, around 100 professionals would lose their jobs without the need for a reduction in the number of teams.

A root-and-branch audit of the domestic game seems certain to happen in the next few years, but Sussex would fight tooth and nail to preserve the Championship as it stands. 'I wasn't a supporter of two divisions when it started but I am now,' said Green.

The intensity is there all season, whereas in the past, by August a lot of teams had nothing to play for, were demotivated and the cricket they played was soft. I think the number of counties who are promoted and relegated each season should be reduced from three to two and it is wrong that the team which finishes second in Division Two gets prize money while the side that comes third in Division One does not.

He has little time for the Cricket Reform Group and is happy to set out a vigorous defence of the domestic game in its current form.

Cricket is an industry in this country, albeit a small one. The turnover is over £100m and the ECB is run efficently. The counties are the shareholders, if you like, and the money they get from the central pot goes towards finding and nurturing the international players of the future. James Kirtley, who came through our youth system and eventually played for England, is a good example of how it works.

Green does support an ECB idea that payments to counties are made on a pro-rata basis – dependent on several factors, such as the number of international players they produce and the success of their academies – and he is keen that the number of 'passport of convenience' cricketers earning their living in England should be reduced.

Ward is the latest high-profile recruit to the county since the 'revolution', but a relatively small club like Sussex still need to produce players from within their own boundaries, and Green remains an active and passionate supporter of youth cricket in the county, having first got involved when his own son Jeremy played for the Under-11s.

The game is changing, but it seems Sussex are changing with it. Maybe there will be more Championship triumphs, but none will be celebrated with as much unabashed delight as the first. In 2003 the longest journey was finally over.

Averages and Scorecards

Batting and Fielding

	Mat	I	NO	Runs	HS	Ave	SR	100	50	Ct	St
M.W. Goodwin	16	28	3	1,496	335*	59.84	63.68	4	5	10	–
M.J. Prior	16	24	3	1,006	153*	47.90	74.96	4	3	28	–
P.A. Cottey	15	25	0	1,149	188	45.96	52.06	3	7	8	–
T.R. Ambrose	15	26	3	931	93*	40.47	48.38	–	9	29	7
M.H. Yardy	2	3	0	116	69	38.66	32.31	–	1	3	–
R.S.C. Martin-Jenkins	16	25	3	811	121*	36.86	66.20	1	5	7	–
C.J. Adams	16	27	0	966	190	35.77	63.51	4	2	18	–
R.J. Kirtley	11	13	7	207	40*	34.50	37.70	–	–	3	–
R.R. Montgomerie	16	28	2	884	105	34.00	46.97	1	7	22	–
Mushtaq Ahmed	16	19	2	456	60	26.82	81.42	–	3	3	–
M.J.G. Davis	10	12	2	259	168	25.90	41.24	1	–	4	–
K.J. Innes	7	11	3	182	103*	22.75	45.61	1	–	1	–
B.V. Taylor	7	7	4	55	35*	18.33	23.60	–	–	–	–
J.D. Lewry	11	15	3	215	70	17.91	87.04	–	1	4	–
P.M. Hutchison	4	3	0	23	18	7.66	26.13	–	–	–	–

Bowling

	Mat	O	M	R	W	Ave	Best	5	10	SR	Econ
R.R. Montgomerie	16	3	0	9	1	9.00	1–9	–	–	18.0	3.00
Mushtaq Ahmed	16	836.3	163	2,539	103	24.65	7–85	10	5	48.7	3.03
J.D. Lewry	11	315.2	71	1,020	41	24.87	8–106	3	1	46.1	3.23
R.J. Kirtley	11	430.2	95	1,403	49	28.63	6–26	2	–	52.6	3.26
B.V. Taylor	7	214.1	60	617	21	29.38	4–42	–	–	61.1	2.88
R.S.C. Martin-Jenkins	16	364	82	1,258	31	40.58	3–9	–	–	70.4	3.45
K.J. Innes	7	74	11	297	7	42.42	2–18	–	–	63.4	4.01
M.J.G. Davis	10	220	42	703	14	50.21	3–44	–	–	94.2	3.19
P.M. Hutchison	4	77	12	311	3	103.66	1–58	–	–	154.0	4.03
C.J. Adams	16	1	0	1	0	–	–	–	–	–	1.00
M.W. Goodwin	16	3	0	17	0	–	–	–	–	–	5.66
P.A. Cottey	15	13	1	59	0	–	–	–	–	–	4.53
M.H. Yardy	2	27	3	89	0	–	–	–	–	–	3.29

MIDDLESEX v SUSSEX

at Lord's on 23rd - 26th April - Frizzell County Championship Division 1

UMPIRES :   B. Dudleston   V.A. Holder

Middlesex won the toss and elected to bat

* Captain, + Wicket-Keeper

MIDDLESEX

#	Batsman	1st Innings		2nd Innings	
1	A.J. Strauss *	c. Prior b. Kirtley	10	lbw b. Kirtley	83
2	S.G. Koenig	lbw b. Kirtley	43	c. Prior b. Lewry	7
3	O.A. Shah	b. Lewry	1	lbw b. Innes	61
4	D.C. Nash +	b. Martin-Jenkins	17	b. Mushtaq	29
5	S.J. Cook	b. Mushtaq	5	(9) not out	22
6	E.C. Joyce	lbw b. Kirtley	8	(5) lbw b. Kirtley	49
7	Abdur Razzaq	lbw b. Lewry	3	(6) lbw b. Kirtley	11
8	P.N. Weekes	run out	0	(7) lbw b. Kirtley	33
9	B.L. Hutton	lbw b. Mushtaq	2	(8) not out	11
10	C.B. Keegan	c. Prior b. Mushtaq	8		
11	J.H. Dawes	not out	3		
12					

Target 32

					Extras						Extras	
b 1	lb 4	wd 1	nb 10		16	b 8	lb 11	wd 1	nb 4		24
Overs	48.3		Provisional Total		116	Overs	106.4		Provisional Total		330
Pens	0	Wkts	Total		116	Pens	0	Wkts	7	Total	330

Fall of wickets

1st Inns: 1-24 2-29 3-69 4-74 5-92 6-97 7-97 8-98 9-109 10-116

2nd Inns: 1-19 2-136 3-165 4-200 5-225 6-287 7-288

Bonus Points -   Sussex 3

Bowling

	Ovs	Md	R	Wk	wd	nb	Ovs	Md	R	Wk	wd	nb
Lewry	17	8	34	2	0	1	25	4	50	1	1	0
Kirtley	16	3	51	3	1	4	33	10	87	4	0	1
Mushtaq Ahmed	10.3	4	16	3	0	0	28.4	6	97	1	0	1
Martin-Jenkins	5	2	10	1	0	0	10	2	42	0	0	0
Innes	-	-	-	-	-	-	10	2	35	1	0	0

SUSSEX

#	Batsman	1st Innings		2nd Innings	
1	R.R. Montgomerie	c. Nash b. Keegan	20	b. Keegan	2
2	M.W. Goodwin	c. Shah b. Dawes	16	lbw b. Dawes	23
3	P.A. Cottey	Lbw b. Dawes	0	b. Cook	38
4	C.J. Adams *	c. & b. Weekes	26	lbw b. Razzaq	12
5	T.R. Ambrose	b. Cook	51	lbw b. Dawes	35
6	R.S.C. Martin-Jenkins	c. Hutton b. Dawes	13	lbw b. Weekes	50
7	M.J. Prior +	c. Razzaq b. Weekes	11	lbw b. Keegan	4
8	K.J. Innes	st. Nash b. Weekes	15	c. Hutton b. Keegan	1
9	Mushtaq Ahmed	c. Nash b. Keegan	9	c. Nash b. Keegan	2
10	R.J. Kirtley	not out	20	not out	25
11	J.D. Lewry	c. Hutton b. Razzaq	45	c. Nash b. Dawes	8
12					

				Extras						Extras	
b	lb	wd	nb	13	b 0	lb 4	wd 0	nb 0		4
Overs	73.1		Provisional Total	239	Overs	62.1		Provisional Total		204
Pens	0	Wkts	Total	239	Pens	0	Wkts	10	Total	204

Fall of wickets

1st Inns: 1-37 2-41 3-41 4-92 5-132 6-138 7-154 8-168 9-172 10-239

2nd Inns: 1-24 2-28 3-63 4-79 5-123 6-132 7-136 8-146 9-186 10-204

Bonus Points -   Sussex 1, Middx 3

Bowling

	Ovs	Md	R	Wk	wd	nb	Ovs	Md	R	Wk	wd	nb
Dawes	22	4	58	3	0	0	15.1	3	47	3	0	0
Keegan	19	4	49	2	0	0	21	8	36	4	0	0
Cook	13	2	42	1	0	0	10	0	45	1	0	0
Abdur Razzaq	9.1	0	43	1	0	1	11	0	55	1	0	0
Weekes	10	1	36	3	0	0	3	1	7	1	0	0
Hutton	-	-	-	-	-	-	2	0	10	0	0	0

MIDDLESEX WON BY 3 WICKETS

Scorecards reproduced courtesy of Sussex CCC.

SUSSEX v KENT

at Hove on 30th April - 3rd May - Frizzell County Championship Division 1

UMPIRES : J.H. Hampshire   P.J. Hartley

Kent won the toss and elected to bowl

* Captain, + Wicket-Keeper

SUSSEX

#	Batsman	1st Innings	R	2nd Innings	R
1	R.R. Montgomerie [7]	b. Sheriyar	22	b. Sheriyar	12
2	M.W. Goodwin [3]	b. Saggers	9	lbw b. Tredwell	96
3	P.A. Cottey [2]	c. Ealham b. Sheriyar	19	lbw b. Sheriyar	2
4	C.J. Adams * [1]	c. Blewett b. Sheriyar	54	st. Jones b. Tredwell	11
5	T.R. Ambrose [11]	c. Jones b. Saggers	41	c. Blewett b. Saggers	10
6	R.S.C. Martin-Jenkins [12]	c. Jones b. Sheriyar	16	b. Ealham	34
7	M.J. Prior + [13]	c. Jones b. Ealham	40	st. Jones b. Tredwell	4
8	K.J. Innes [15]	c. Walker b. Ealham	9	lbw b. Ealham	1
9	Mushtaq Ahmed [9]	c. Jones b. Saggers	37	c. Blewett b. Ealham	0
10	R.J. Kirtley [6]	not out	7	not out	14
11	J.D. Lewry [5]	b. Sheriyar	22	c. Jones b. Tredwell	10
12	M.J.G. Davis [8]				

					Extras	3					Extras	4
b 1	lb 0	wd 0	nb 2				b 0	lb 4	wd 0	nb 0		
Overs	72.2			Provisional Total	279		Overs	64.1		Provisional Total		198
Pens	0	Wkts	10	Total	279		Pens	0	Wkts	10	Total	198

Fall of 1st Inns: 1-25 2-42 3-83 4-134 5-158 6-166 7-193 8-242 9-256 10-279

Wickets 2nd Inns: 1-28 2-35 3-55 4-84 5-166 6-171 7-174 8-174 9-174 10-198

Bonus Points - Sussex 2, Kent 3

Bowling	Ovs	Md	R	Wk	wd	nb	Ovs	Md	R	Wk	wd	nb
Saggers	20	3	77	3	0	1	13	4	49	1	0	0
Trott	9	0	53	0	0	0	8	2	29	0	0	0
Sheriyar	20.2	5	65	5	0	0	14	3	34	2	0	0
Ealham	14	4	45	2	0	0	10	3	34	3	0	0
Tredwell	9	2	38	0	0	0	19.1	4	48	4	0	0

KENT

Target 293

#	Batsman	1st Innings	R	2nd Innings	R
1	M.A. Carberry	c. Prior b. Lewry	3	c. Prior b. Kirtley	3
2	R.W.T. Key	b. Kirtley	0	b. Lewry	28
3	E.T. Smith	c. Adams b. Innes	23	c. Ambrose b. Kirtley	33
4	G.S. Blewett	c. Prior b. Lewry	41	c. Montgomerie b. Mushtaq	37
5	M.J. Walker	c. Adams b. Kirtley	40	b. Walker	11
6	M.A. Ealham *	lbw b. Mushtaq	24	lbw b. Mushtaq	15
7	G.O. Jones +	b. Lewry	2	c. Lewry b. Kirtley	0
8	J.C. Tredwell	not out	32	lbw b. Kirtley	10
9	B.J. Trott (10)	b. Innes	0	(10) b. Kirtley	0
10	M.J. Saggers (9)	lbw b. Mushtaq	9	(9) c. Prior b. Kirtley	1
11	A. Sheriyar	lbw b. Mushtaq	2	not out	7
12	A. Khan				

					Extras	9					Extras	14
b 0	lb 7	wd 0	nb 2				b 9	lb 4	wd 1	nb 0		
Overs	67.5			Provisional Total	185		Overs	49.5		Provisional Total		159
Pens	0	Wkts	10	Total	185		Pens	0	Wkts	10	Total	159

Fall of 1st Inns: 1-2 2-10 3-29 4-105 5-114 6-119 7-163 8-181 9-182 10-185

Wickets 2nd Inns: 1-31 2-35 3-97 4-111 5-123 6-124 7-145 8-147 9-147 10-159

Bonus Points - Sussex 3

Bowling	Ovs	Md	R	Wk	wd	nb	Ovs	Md	R	Wk	wd	nb
Lewry	13	2	44	2	0	0	14	1	59	1	0	0
Kirtley	17	6	41	3	0	1	15	4	26	6	1	0
Innes	7	1	18	2	0	0	3	0	14	0	0	0
Martin-Jenkins	12	2	31	0	0	0	4	2	5	0	0	0
Mushtaq	18.5	3	44	3	0	0	13.5	2	42	3	0	0

SUSSEX WON BY 133 RUNS

WARWICKSHIRE v SUSSEX

at Edgbaston on 9th - 12th May - Frizzell County Championship Division 1

UMPIRES : G.I. Burgess   I.J. Gould

* Captain, + Wicket-Keeper

Warwickshire won the toss and elected to bat

WARWKS

#	Batsman	1st Innings		2nd Innings	
1	T. Frost +	b. Kirtley	37	c. Prior b. Lewry	0
2	I.J.L. Trott	c. Montgomerie b. Mushtaq	134	lbw b. Lewry	5
3	M.A. Wagh	b. Mushtaq	43	lbw b. Martin-Jenkins	38
4	I.R. Bell	c. Prior b. Mushtaq	3	lbw b. Davis	107
5	J.O. Troughton	c. Prior b. Kirtley	41	c. sub b. Davis	105
6	D.P. Ostler	lbw b. Mushtaq	1	b. Martin-Jenkins	7
7	D.R. Brown	c. Ambrose b. Mushtaq	0	c. Montgomerie b. Martin-Jenkins	0
8	A.F. Giles *	lbw b. Mushtaq	22	not out	13
9	M.A. Shiekh	not out	57		
10	M.M. Betts	c. Cottey b. Kirtley	20		
11	A. Richardson	b. Martin-Jenkins	47		
12					

					1st Innings						2nd Innings			
b 6	lb 7	wd 0	nb 4	Extras	17	b 8	lb 2	wd 0	nb 0	Extras	10			
Overs	117.3			Provisional Total	422	Overs	58			Provisional Total	285			
Pens	0	Wkts	10	Total	422	Pens	0	Wkts	3 dec	Total	285			

Fall of wickets

1st Inns: 1-86 2-194 3-198 4-233 5-239 6-239 7-269 8-307 9-348 10-422

2nd Inns: 1-5 2-18 3-64 4-246 5-271 6-271 7-285

Bonus Points - Warwks 5, Sussex 3

Bowling

Bowling	Ovs	Md	R	Wk	wd	nb	Ovs	Md	R	Wk	wd	nb
Lewry	11	2	41	0	0	0	9	1	51	2	0	0
Kirtley	30	4	107	3	0	2	14	2	48	0	0	0
Martin-Jenkins	6.3	1	46	1	0	0	13	3	57	3	0	0
Mushtaq Ahmed	48	7	157	6	0	0	13	0	69	0	0	0
Davis	22	7	58	0	0	0	9	0	50	2	0	0

SUSSEX

Target 341

#	Batsman	1st Innings			2nd Innings	
1	R.R. Montgomerie	lbw b. Sheikh	41		lbw b. Betts	0
2	M.W. Goodwin	c. Troughton b. Sheikh	28		lbw b. Betts	10
3	P.A. Cottey	c. Frost b. Richardson	41		lbw b. Brown	55
4	C.J. Adams *	b. Sheikh	22		b. Betts	0
5	R.J. Kirtley	c. Brown b. Giles	31	(9)	c. Frost b. Richardson	6
6	T.R. Ambrose	lbw b. Sheikh	85	(5)	lbw b. Betts	0
7	R.S.C. Martin-Jenkins	c. Frost b. Brown	7	(6)	b. Betts	11
8	M.J. Prior +	c. Ostler b. Betts	84	(7)	b. Brown	5
9	M.J.G. Davis	c. Frost b. Betts	1	(8)	lbw b. Brown	0
10	Mushtaq Ahmed	not out	2		not out	7
11	J.D. Lewry	b. Betts	1		b. Brown	0
12						

					1st Innings						2nd Innings			
b 4	lb 17	wd 1	nb 2	Extras	24	b 5	lb 7	wd 0	nb 0	Extras	12			
Overs	128.4			Provisional Total	367	Overs	43			Provisional Total	106			
Pens	0	Wkts	10	Total	367	Pens	0	Wkts	10	Total	106			

Fall of wickets

1st Inns: 1-67 2-74 3-116 4-165 5-216 6-235 7-360 8-364 9-364 10-367

2nd Inns: 1-12 2-17 3-21 4-21 5-37 6-43 7-43 8-82 9-106 10-106

Bonus Points - Sussex 4, Warwks 3

Bowling

Bowling	Ovs	Md	R	Wk	wd	nb	Ovs	Md	R	Wk	wd	nb
Betts	23.4	2	83	3	0	0	13	2	43	5	0	0
Richardson	29	12	65	1	1	1	13	6	19	1	0	0
Brown	23	7	76	1	0	0	9	4	17	4	0	0
Sheikh	28	11	60	4	0	0	6	2	15	0	0	0
Giles	23	5	60	1	0	0	2	2	0	0	0	0
Wagh	2	1	2	0	0	0	-	-	-	-	-	-

WARWICKSHIRE WON BY 234 RUNS

SUSSEX v NOTTINGHAMSHIRE

at Horsham on 21st - 24th May - Frizzell County Championship Division 1

UMPIRES : M.J. Kitchen   V. Holder

Sussex won the toss and elected to bat

* Captain, + Wicket-Keeper

SUSSEX

		1st Innings			Target 50
1	R.R. Montgomerie [7]	c. Gallian b. MacGill	105	not out	25
2	M.W. Goodwin [3]	c. Pietersen b. Elworthy	38	not out	23
3	P.A. Cottey [2]	lbw b. MacGill	58		
4	C.J. Adams * [1]	c. Gallian b. MacGill	9		
5	T.R. Ambrose [11]	c. Read b. Elworthy	55		
6	R.S.C. Martin-Jenkins [12]	c. Welton b. Harris	49		
7	M.J. Prior + [13]	c. sub b. Elworthy	133		
8	K.J. Innes [15]	not out	103		
9	M.J.G. Davis [8]	not out	32		
10	Mushtaq Ahmed [9]				
11	B.V. Taylor [22]				
12	R.J. Kirtley [6]				

b 2	lb 20	wd 1	nb 14	Extras	37	b 0	lb 2	wd 0	nb 2	Extras	4
Overs	147		Provisional Total		619	Overs	10.2		Provisional Total		52
Pens	0	Wkts	7-Dec	Total	619	Pens	0	Wkts	0	Total	52

Fall of wickets	1st Inns:	1-87	2-210	3-227	4-232	5-312	6-378	7-535
	2nd Inns:							

Bonus Points - Sussex 5, Notts 2

Bowling	Ovs	Md	R	Wk	wd	nb	Ovs	Md	R	Wk	wd	nb
Smith	24	2	97	0	0	2	-	-	-	-	-	-
Harris	20	2	102	1	0	5	0.2	0	6	0	0	0
Gallian	12	2	45	0	0	0	-	-	-	-	-	-
Elworthy	30	3	107	3	1	0	5	1	22	0	0	0
MacGill	50	12	172	3	0	0	4	1	13	0	0	0
Shafayat	4	0	39	0	0	0	-	-	-	-	-	-
Pietersen	7	0	35	0	0	0	1	0	9	0	0	1

NOTTS

		1st Innings			2nd Innings (Following-On)	
1	G.E. Welton	lbw b. Mushtaq	50	(3)	st. Ambrose b. Mushtaq	12
2	J.E.R. Gallian *	c. Prior b. Taylor	36		c. Montgomerie b. Mushtaq	44
3	U. Afzaal	c. Ambrose b. Kirtley	35	(4)	c. Ambrose b. Kirtley	18
4	D.J. Bicknell	lbw b. Kirtley	9	(1)	c. & b. Kirtley	61
5	K.P. Pietersen	st. Ambrose b. Mushtaq	166		c. Cottey b. Mushtaq	1
6	B.M. Shafayat	lbw b. Mushtaq	71		b. Mushtaq	0
7	C.M.W. Read +	lbw b. Mushtaq	0		lbw b. Kirtley	42
8	S. Elworthy	c. Ambrose b. Martin-Jenkins	28		c. Ambrose b. Mushtaq	45
9	G.J. Smith	b. Mushtaq	9		not out	5
10	A.J. Harris	b. Mushtaq	5		st. Ambrose b. Mushtaq	1
11	S.C.G. MacGill	not out	4		c. sub b. Kirtley	2
12						

b 1	lb 1	wd 0	nb 6	Extras	8	b 0	lb 5	wd 0	nb 10	Extras	16
Overs	93.1		Provisional Total		421	Overs	82.2		Provisional Total		247
Pens	0	Wkts	10	Total	421	Pens	0	Wkts	10	Total	247

Fall of wickets	1st Inns:	1-71	2-109	3-126	4-139	5-332	6-332	7-369	8-390	9-398	10-421
	2nd Inns:	1-103	2-111	3-132	4-133	5-142	6-143	7-237	8-239	9-242	10-247

Bonus Points - Notts 5, Sussex 3

Bowling	Ovs	Md	R	Wk	wd	nb	Ovs	Md	R	Wk	wd	nb
Kirtley	21	7	85	2	0	1	24.2	4	74	4	1	3
Martin-Jenkins	17	0	87	1	0	0	6	1	25	0	0	0
Mushtaq Ahmed	37.1	3	163	6	0	2	30	9	81	6	0	0
Taylor	11	3	32	1	0	0	13	3	36	0	0	2
Davis	7	0	52	0	0	0	9	1	26	0	0	0

SUSSEX WON BY 10 WICKETS

SURREY v SUSSEX

at The AMP Oval on 30th May - 2nd June - Frizzell County Championship Division 1

UMPIRES :   A.A. Jones   R. Palmer

Surrey won the toss and elected to bat

* Captain, + Wicket-Keeper

SURREY

		1st Innings		2nd Innings	
1	I.J. Ward	c. Ambrose b. Kirtley	9	c. Goodwin b. Innes	135
2	J.N. Batty +	c. Adams b. Taylor	12	b. Mushtaq	56
3	M.R. Ramprakash	c. Yardy b. Mushtaq	37	c. Prior b. Innes	23
4	G.P. Thorpe	c. Adams b. Mushtaq	156	not out	18
5	A.D. Brown	c. Goodwin b. Kirtley	74	not out	1
6	A.J. Hollioake *	lbw b. Martin-Jenkins	77		
7	Azhar Mahmood	c. Adams b. Kirtley	0		
8	M.P. Bicknell	b. Martin-Jenkins	11		
9	I.D.K. Salisbury	c. Ambrose b. Mushtaq	45		
10	Saqlain Mushtaq	c. Montgomerie b. Martin-Jenkins	32		
11	J. Ormond	not out	1		
12					

b 4	lb 17	wd 1	nb 4	Extras	26	b 0	lb 0	wd 0	nb 0	Extras	0
Overs	119.5			Provisional Total	480	Overs	60			Provisional Total	233
Pens	0	Wkts	10	Total	480	Pens	0	Wkts	3 dec	Total	233

Fall of wickets

1st Inns: 1-22   2-22   3-132   4-263   5-359   6-360   7-379   8-394   9-469   10-480

2nd Inns: 1-137   2-192   3-219

Bonus Points -   Surrey 5, Sussex 3

Bowling

	Ovs	Md	R	Wk	wd	nb	Ovs	Md	R	Wk	wd	nb
Kirtley	33	5	122	3	0	2	14	3	49	0	0	0
Taylor	7.2	2	15	1	0	0	-	-	-	-	-	-
Martin-Jenkins	23.4	8	86	3	1	0	19	3	66	0	0	0
Innes	12	4	59	0	0	0	14	1	64	2	0	0
Mushtaq	36.5	1	159	3	0	0	11	1	47	1	0	0
Yardy	7	1	18	0	0	0	2	0	7	0	0	0

SUSSEX

		1st Innings		2nd Innings	Target 407
1	R.R. Montgomerie	c. Ward b. Ormond	5	b. Mahmood	26
2	M.W. Goodwin	b. Saqlain	60	c. sub b. Saqlain	31
3	M.H. Yardy	c. Thorpe b. Ormond	0	c. Mahmood b. Ormond	69
4	C.J. Adams *	c. Batty b. Mahmood	5	b. Saqlain	0
5	T.R. Ambrose	c. Ramprakash b. Ormond	75	b. Saqlain	1
6	R.S.C. Martin-Jenkins	lbw b. Mahmood	61	b. Mahmood	88
7	M.J. Prior +	b. Saqlain	6	c. Ramprakash b. Mahmood	14
8	K.J. Innes	b. Salisbury	2	c. Mahmood b. Saqlain	1
9	Mushtaq Ahmed	lbw b. Ormond	41	(10) lbw b. Saqlain	36
10	R.J. Kirtley	run out	21	(9) c. sub b. Salisbury	7
11	B.V. Taylor	not out	4	not out	0
12					

b 0	lb 9	wd 2	nb 16	Extras	27	b 9	lb 3	wd 2	nb 6	Extras	20
Overs	73.1			Provisional Total	307	Overs	95.4			Provisional Total	293
Pens	0	Wkts	10	Total	307	Pens	0	Wkts	10	Total	293

Fall of wickets

1st Inns: 1-5   2-13   3-24   4-98   5-189   6-217   7-220   8-279   9-282   10-307

2nd Inns: 1-45   2-83   3-83   4-85   5-198   6-218   7-221   8-242   9-293   10-293

Bonus Points -   Sussex 3, Surrey 3

Bowling

	Ovs	Md	R	Wk	wd	nb	Ovs	Md	R	Wk	wd	nb
Bicknell	3	1	9	0	0	0	-	-	-	-	-	-
Ormond	15.1	2	81	4	1	5	19.4	3	65	1	2	0
Azhar Mahmood	16	1	57	2	0	0	21	4	76	3	0	2
Salisbury	14	1	67	1	0	3	21	5	67	1	0	1
Saqlain Mushtaq	21	4	68	2	0	0	34	15	73	5	0	0
Hollioake	4	0	16	0	1	0	-	-	-	-	-	-

SURREY WON BY 113 RUNS

KENT v SUSSEX

at Tunbridge Wells on 4th - 6th June - Frizzell County Championship Division 1

UMPIRES : D.R. Shepherd   I.J. Gould

Sussex won the toss and elected to bat

* Captain, + Wicket-Keeper

KENT

		1st Innings		2nd Innings	Target 323
1	M.A. Carberry	c. Cottey b. Kirtley	23	b. Mushtaq	40
2	G.S. Blewett	b. Innes	46	c. Prior b. Lewry	0
3	E.T. Smith	lbw b. Kirtley	13	c. Montgomerie b. Lewry	40
4	A. Symonds	c. Innes b. Mushtaq	54	lbw b. Mushtaq	1
5	M.J. Walker	c. Ambrose b. Mushtaq	30	c. Prior b. Lewry	7
6	A.G.R. Loudon	c. Ambrose b. Mushtaq	8	(8) lbw b. Martin-Jenkins	0
7	M.A. Ealham *	c. Martin-Jenkins b. Mushtaq	9	lbw b. Martin-Jenkins	3
8	G.O. Jones +	not out	46	(6) c. Lewry b. Martin-Jenkins	22
9	J.C. Tredwell	lbw b. Kirtley	16	c. Montgomerie b. Mushtaq	11
10	M.J. Saggers	b. Kirtley	2	not out	0
11	A. Sheriyar	lbw b. Mushtaq	7	c. Goodwin b. Mushtaq	4
12					

	b 11	lb 10	wd 0	nb 0	Extras	21	b 0	lb 1	wd 2	nb 0	Extras	3
	Overs	73.2		Provisional Total		275	Overs	47.4		Provisional Total		131
	Pens	0	Wkts	10	Total	275	Pens	0	Wkts	10	Total	131

Fall of wickets 1st Inns: 1-74   2-84   3-90   4-180   5-180   6-198   7-203   8-238   9-250   10-275

2nd Inns: 1-0   2-65   3-66   4-83   5-99   6-110   7-110   8-127   9-127   10-131

Bonus Points - Kent 2, Sussex 3

Bowling	Ovs	Md	R	Wk	wd	nb	Ovs	Md	R	Wk	wd	nb
Lewry	11	4	19	0	0	0	11	2	36	3	2	0
Hutchison	5	0	27	0	0	0						
Martin-Jenkins	10	3	26	0	0	0	7	3	9	3	0	0
Kirtley	21	0	84	4	0	0	9	2	29	0	0	0
Innes	9	1	28	1	0	0	-	-	-	-	-	-
Mushtaq Ahmed	17.2	3	70	5	0	0	20.4	7	56	4	0	0

SUSSEX

		1st Innings		2nd Innings	
1	R.R. Montgomerie	b. Sheriyar	13	lbw b. Saggers	0
2	M.W. Goodwin	Run Out	35	run out	58
3	P.A. Cottey	lbw b. Sheriyar	0	lbw b. Symonds	52
4	C.J. Adams *	c. Ealham b. Sheriyar	62	lbw b. Sheriyar	4
5	T.R. Ambrose	c. Walker b. Blewett	11	lbw b. Symonds	17
6	R.S.C. Martin-Jenkins	c. Tredwell b. Symonds	67	c. Jones b. Sheriyar	84
7	P.M. Hutchison	b. Ealham	18		
8	M.J. Prior +	c. Symonds b. Saggers	23	(7) c. & b. Tredwell	45
9	K.J. Innes	c. & b.. Sheriyar	30	(8) b. Tredwell	0
10	Mushtaq Ahmed	c. Jones b. Saggers	43	(9) c. Loudon b. Sheriyar	9
11	J.D. Lewry	not out	0	not out	1
12	R.J. Kirtley			(10) c. Jones b. Sheriyar	0

	b 2	lb 5	wd 2	nb 0	Extras	9	b 3	lb 12	wd 1	nb 0	Extras	16
	Overs	95.1		Provisional Total		311	Overs	75.5		Provisional Total		286
	Pens	0	Wkts	10	Total	311	Pens	0	Wkts	10	Total	286

Fall of wickets 1st Inns: 1-21   2-25   3-79   4-104   5-136   6-174   7-205   8-249   9-311   10-311

2nd Inns: 1-1   2-112   3-117   4-131   5-184   6-273   7-273   8-284   9-285   10-286

Bonus Points - Sussex 3, Kent 3

Bowling	Ovs	Md	R	Wk	wd	nb	Ovs	Md	R	Wk	wd	nb
Saggers	24.1	6	76	2	0	0	20	4	62	1	0	0
Sheriyar	24	6	49	4	1	0	23.5	1	93	4	1	0
Ealham	20	8	63	1	1	0	10	2	37	0	0	0
Blewett	5	0	21	1	0	0	2	0	17	0	0	0
Tredwell	12	0	65	0	0	0	10	2	37	2	0	0
Symonds	10	2	30	1	0	0	10	1	25	2	0	0

SUSSEX WON BY 191 RUNS

SUSSEX v WARWICKSHIRE

at Hove on 27th - 30th June - Frizzell County Championship Division 1

UMPIRES : M.J. Kitchen V.A. Holder

Sussex won the toss and elected to bat

* Captain, + Wicket-Keeper

SUSSEX — 1st Innings

	Batsman	Dismissal	Runs
1	R.R. Montgomerie [7]	c. Frost b. Brown	66
2	M.W. Goodwin [3]	c. Frost b. Waqar	0
3	P.A. Cottey [2]	c. Frost b. Richardson	188
4	C.J. Adams * [1]	c. Bell b. Waqar	31
5	T.R. Ambrose + [11]	b. Richardson	50
6	R.S.C. Martin-Jenkins [12]	b. Waqar	28
7	M.J. Prior [13]	c. Frost b. Brown	100
8	M.J.G. Davis [8]	b. Waqar	6
9	Mushtaq Ahmed [9]	c. Trott b. Waqar	2
10	R.J. Kirtley [6]	not out	40
11	J.D. Lewry [5]	b. Brown	6
12	K.J. Innes [15]		

b 1	lb 9	wd 0	nb 18	Extras	28
Overs	147.1			Provisional Total	545
Pens	0	Wkts	10	Total	545

Fall of wickets — 1st Inns: 1-3 2-168 3-239 4-342 5-357 6-407 7-431 8-439 9-519 10-545

Bonus Points - Sussex 5, Warwks 3

Bowling

	Ovs	Md	R	Wk	wd	nb
Waqar Younis	24	2	99	5	0	1
Betts	20	1	91	0	0	4
Brown	31.1	8	95	3	0	1
Richardson	34	6	92	2	0	1
Bell	3	0	24	0	0	0
Obuya	19	1	89	0	0	2
Wagh	14	1	40	0	0	0
Trott	2	1	5	0	0	0

WARWKS

	Batsman	1st Innings	Runs	2nd Innings (Following-On)	Runs
1	M.J. Powell *	c. Ambrose b. Martin-Jenkins	60	c. Adams b. Mushtaq	80
2	N.V. Knight	lbw b. Lewry	11	c. Prior b. Mushtaq	64
3	M.A. Wagh	c. Prior b. Mushtaq	39	c. Prior b. Mushtaq	2
4	I.R. Bell	lbw b. Mushtaq	0	c. Martin-Jenkins b. Mushtaq	37
5	I.J.L. Trott	c. Goodwin b. Kirtley	6	lbw b. Davis	31
6	T. Frost +	run out	1	b. Davis	4
7	D.R. Brown	not out	42	c. Adams b. Mushtaq	20
8	C.O. Obuya	lbw b. Kirtley	2	(9) not out	8
9	M.M. Betts	c. Davis b. Mushtaq	21	(8) c. Adams b. Lewry	15
10	Waqar Younis	c. Ambrose b. Kirtley	8	c. Kirtley b. Mushtaq	14
11	A. Richardson	b. Mushtaq	0	c. Ambrose b. Mushtaq	0
12					

b 1	lb 9	wd 1	nb 0	Extras	11	b 2	lb 7	wd 1	nb 0	Extras	10
Overs	59.5			Provisional Total	201	Overs	92.4			Provisional Total	285
Pens	0	Wkts	10	Total	201	Pens	0	Wkts	10	Total	285

Fall of wickets — 1st Inns: 1-22 2-104 3-105 4-122 5-124 6-131 7-140 8-171 9-198 10-201

2nd Inns: 1-135 2-139 3-146 4-185 5-196 6-236 7-249 8-267 9-284 10-285

Bonus Points - Warwks 1, Sussex 3

Bowling

	Ovs	Md	R	Wk	wd	nb	Ovs	Md	R	Wk	wd	nb
Kirtley	15	2	57	3	1	0	16	2	62	0	1	0
Lewry	10	2	35	1	0	0	9	2	41	1	0	0
Mushtaq	22.5	6	55	4	0	0	32.4	9	85	7	0	0
Martin-Jenkins	10	1	40	1	0	0	12	4	38	0	0	0
Davis	2	1	4	0	0	0	23	6	50	2	0	0

SUSSEX WON BY AN INNINGS & 59 RUNS

SUSSEX v ESSEX

at Arundel on 9th - 12th July - Frizzell County Championship Division 1

UMPIRES : B. Leadbeater   D.J. Constant

* Captain, + Wicket-Keeper

Essex won the toss and elected to bat

SUSSEX

		1st Innings		2nd Innings	Target 256
1	R.R. Montgomerie [7]	c. Hussain b. Brant	1	c. Foster b. Dakin	1
2	M.W. Goodwin [3]	b. Brant	11	b. Dakin	18
3	P.A. Cottey [2]	c. Middlebrook b. Dakin	107	c. Foster b. Dakin	98
4	C.J. Adams * [1]	c. Foster b. Napier	20	c. Habib b. Middlebrook	0
5	T.R. Ambrose + [11]	c. Flower b. Grayson	88	not out	93
6	R.S.C. Martin-Jenkins [12]	lbw b. Grayson	6	not out	21
7	M.J. Prior [13]	lbw b. Brant	13		
8	M.J.G. Davis [8]	c. Habib b. Grayson	12		
9	Mushtaq Ahmed [9]	c. Dakin b. Grayson	34		
10	R.J. Kirtley [6]	not out	35		
11	J.D. Lewry [5]	c. Flower b. Middlebrook	22		
12	K.J. Innes [15]				

b 0	lb 3	wd 3	nb 4	Extras	10	b 7	lb 4	wd 15	nb 0	Extras	26
Overs	110.5		Provisional Total		359	Overs	77.1		Provisional Total		257
Pens	0	Wkts	10	Total	359	Pens	0	Wkts	4	Total	257

Fall of	1st Inns:	1-4	2-13	3-53	4-231	5-233	6-250	7-254	8-280	9-323	10-359
wickets	2nd Inns:	1-1	2-31	3-32	4-204						

Bonus Points- Sussex 4, Essex 4

Bowling	Ovs	Md	R	Wk	wd	nb	Ovs	Md	R	Wk	wd	nb
Dakin	25	5	67	1	0	0	16	2	54	3	0	0
Brant	25	4	90	3	0	0	7	0	27	0	1	0
ten Doeschate	10	1	53	0	0	2	-	-	-	-	-	-
Napier	16	2	45	1	0	0	7	0	24	0	0	0
Middlebrook	17.5	1	54	1	0	0	23.1	1	78	1	0	0
Grayson	17	2	47	4	3	0	24	7	63	0	9	0

ESSEX

		1st Innings		2nd Innings	
1	A.P. Grayson	c. Grayson b. Kirtley	0	b. Davis	71
2	N. Hussain	c. Montgomerie b. Mushtaq	95	c. Mushtaq b. Lewry	22
3	J.S. Foster +	c. Montgomerie b. Lewry	12	run out	1
4	A. Flower	lbw b. Kirtley	37	lbw b. Davis	54
5	A. Habib	c. Ambrose b. Lewry	0	c. Ambrose b. Lewry	53
6	R.C. Irani *	c. Adams b. Lewry	15	c. Adams b. Davis	6
7	J.D. Middlebrook	lbw b. Martin-Jenkins	14	c. Adams b. Lewry	23
8	J.M. Dakin	c. Kirtley b. Lewry	35	(9) b. Lewry	0
9	G.R. Napier	not out	89	(10) not out	10
10	R.N. ten Doeschate	b. Lewry	31	(8) lbw b. Mushtaq	6
11	S. Brant	c. Prior b. Mushtaq	3	b. Lewry	2
12					

b 2	lb 7	wd 0	nb 0	Extras	9	b 0	lb 19	wd 5	nb 2	Extras	26
Overs	114.5		Provisional Total		340	Overs	93.4		Provisional Total		274
Pens	0	Wkts	10	Total	340	Pens	0	Wkts	10	Total	274

Fall of	1st Inns:	1-0	2-23	3-95	4-97	5-115	6-149	7-203	8-215	9-331	10-340
wickets	2nd Inns:	1-49	2-50	3-140	4-187	5-193	6-243	7-258	8-262	9-262	10-274

Bonus Points- Essex 4, Sussex 3

Bowling	Ovs	Md	R	Wk	wd	nb	Ovs	Md	R	Wk	wd	nb
Kirtley	24	4	88	2	0	0	17	2	48	0	1	1
Lewry	29	7	72	5	0	0	19.4	6	52	5	0	0
Mushtaq Ahmed	36.5	10	102	2	0	0	30	4	92	1	0	0
Martin-Jenkins	17	3	44	1	0	0	8	3	19	0	0	0
Davis	8	0	25	0	0	0	19	3	44	3	0	0

SUSSEX WON BY 6 WICKETS

LEICESTERSHIRE v SUSSEX

at Leicester on 15th - 18th July - Frizzell County Championship Division 1

UMPIRES :   P.J. Hartley   J.F. Steele

Leics won the toss and elected to bat

* Captain, + Wicket-Keeper

LEICESTERSHIRE

#	Batsman	1st Innings		2nd Innings	
1	J.K. Maunders	lbw b. Kirtley	0	lbw b. Mushtaq	27
2	D.I. Stevens	st. Ambrose b. Mushtaq	51	lbw b. Mushtaq	50
3	D.L. Maddy	lbw b. Mushtaq	30	c. Martin-Jenkins b. Innes	40
4	B.J. Hodge	c. Montgomerie b. Mushtaq	47	lbw b. Kirtley	18
5	T.R. Ward	lbw b. Mushtaq	4	c. Prior b. Mushtaq	50
6	P.A. Nixon +	b. Mushtaq	4	lbw b. Mushtaq	11
7	J.N. Snape	b. Kirtley	36	run out	20
8	P.A.J. DeFreitas *	b. Martin-Jenkins	103	c. Goodwin b. Martin-Jenkins	8
9	D.D. Masters	run out	0	c. Ambrose b. Martin-Jenkins	0
10	C.E. Dagnall	not out	15	c. Cottey b. Mushtaq	15
11	R.M. Amin	b. Martin-Jenkins	0	not out	6
12					

				Extras	30					Extras	13
b 1	lb 22	wd 5	nb 2			b 1	lb 9	wd 3	nb 0		
Overs	85.5			Provisional Total	320	Overs	95.5			Provisional Total	258
Pens	0	Wkts	10	Total	320	Pens	0	Wkts	10	Total	258

Fall of wickets

1st Inns: 1-0   2-60   3-107   4-123   5-127   6-154   7-250   8-251   9-320   10-320

2nd Inns: 1-70   2-93   3-128   4-150   5-162   6-225   7-234   8-234   9-237   10-258

Bowling

	Ovs	Md	R	Wk	wd	nb	Ovs	Md	R	Wk	wd	nb
Kirtley	21	6	68	2	1	0	22	7	72	1	0	0
Lewry	6	1	18	0	0	1	-	-	-	-	-	-
Martin-Jenkins	13.5	1	66	2	0	0	25	9	53	2	1	0
Mushtaq Ahmed	33	4	93	5	0	0	41.5	18	96	5	1	0
Innes	12	1	52	0	0	0	7	1	27	1	0	0

SUSSEX

Target 163

#	Batsman	1st Innings		2nd Innings	
1	M.W. Goodwin	lbw b. DeFreitas	34	b. Masters	11
2	R.R. Montgomerie	b. DeFreitas	52	b. Amin	28
3	P.A. Cottey	c. Nixon b. DeFreitas	147	b. Amin	58
4	C.J. Adams *	lbw b. DeFreitas	0	lbw b. Maddy	16
5	T.R. Ambrose	b. Dagnall	2	b. Snape	25
6	R.S.C. Martin-Jenkins	lbw b. Dagnall	7	not out	6
7	M.J. Prior +	c. Hodge b. Maddy	96	not out	4
8	K.J. Innes	not out	14		
9	Mushtaq Ahmed	st. Nixon b. Amin	21		
10	R.J. Kirtley	c. Maunders b. Amin	0		
11	J.D. Lewry	c. Snape b. DeFreitas	0		
12					

				Extras	43					Extras	18
b 15	lb 16	wd 2	nb 10			b 10	lb 2	wd 2	nb 4		
Overs	137.5			Provisional Total	416	Overs	38.5			Provisional Total	166
Pens	0	Wkts	10	Total	416	Pens	0	Wkts	5	Total	166

Fall of wickets

1st Inns: 1-58   2-161   3-161   4-187   5-215   6-370   7-382   8-415   9-415   10-416

2nd Inns: 1-30   2-48   3-96   4-156   5-158

Bowling

	Ovs	Md	R	Wk	wd	nb	Ovs	Md	R	Wk	wd	nb
Dagnall	30	10	87	2	1	0	2	0	20	0	1	0
Masters	27	5	89	0	0	2	8.2	1	31	1	0	0
Amin	19	5	50	2	0	0	11	1	41	2	1	2
Maddy	17	1	70	1	0	0	7	0	23	1	0	0
Snape	4	0	10	0	0	0	1.5	0	6	1	0	0
DeFreitas	29.5	10	55	5	1	3	2.4	0	5	0	0	0
Maunders	5	0	12	0	0	0	-	-	-	-	-	-
Stevens	5	1	11	0	0	0	-	-	-	-	-	-
Hodge	1	0	1	0	0	0	6	0	28	0	0	0

SUSSEX WON BY 5 WICKETS

NOTTINGHAMSHIRE v SUSSEX

at Trent Bridge on 25th - 28th July - Frizzell County Championship Division 1

UMPIRES : J.H. Hampshire   A.G.T. Whitehead

Sussex won the toss and elected to bat

* Captain, + Wicket-Keeper

NOTTS

		1st Innings		2nd Innings (Following-On)	
1	D.J. Bicknell	c. Prior b. Kirtley	15	c. Montgomerie b. Kirtley	75
2	J.E.R. Gallian *	b. Kirtley	6	lbw b. Kirtley	0
3	G.E. Welton	c. Yardy b. Kirtley	12	c. Cottey b. Hutchison	8
4	R.J. Warren	c. Cottey b. Martin-Jenkins	42	not out	114
5	K.P. Pietersen	c. Adams b. Kirtley	139	c. & b. Montgomerie	81
6	C.L. Cairns	c. Prior b. Martin-Jenkins	1	not out	7
7	C.M.W. Read +	c. Montgomerie b. Mushtaq	0		
8	P.J. Franks	c. Yardy b. Hutchison	43		
9	G.D. Clough	c. Adams b. Mushtaq	16		
10	A.J. Harris	b. Kirtley	1		
11	C.E. Shreck	not out	0		
12					

b 3	lb 12	wd 0	nb 6	Extras	21	b 4	lb 2	wd 0	nb 0	Extras	6
Overs	87.5			Provisional Total	21	Overs	73			Provisional Total	291
Pens	0	Wkts	10	Total	296	Pens	0	Wkts	4-Dec	Total	291

| Fall of | 1st Inns: | 1-16 | 2-35 | 3-46 | 4-127 | 5-139 | 6-140 | 7-254 | 8-290 | 9-296 | 10-296 |
| wickets | 2nd Inns: | 1-1 | 2-34 | 3-144 | 4-275 | | | | | | |

Bonus Points : Notts 2, Sussex 3

Bowling	Ovs	Md	R	Wk	wd	nb	Ovs	Md	R	Wk	wd	nb
Kirtley	23	9	60	5	0	3	11	4	32	2	0	0
Hutchison	17	5	60	1	0	0	16	2	66	1	0	0
Mushtaq Ahmed	28.5	2	87	2	0	0	9	2	41	0	0	0
Yardy	5	0	14	0	0	0	13	2	50	0	0	0
Martin-Jenkins	14	1	60	2	0	0	12	2	43	0	0	0
Cottey	-	-	-	-	-	:	9	1	44	0	0	0
Montgomerie	-	-	-	-	-	-	3	0	9	1	0	0

SUSSEX

		1st Innings	
1	M.W. Goodwin	b. Clough	148
2	R.R. Montgomerie	c. Read b. Cairns	32
3	P.A. Cottey	c. Harris b. Franks	53
4	C.J. Adams *	c. Franks b. Harris	46
5	M.H. Yardy	c. Read b. Harris	47
6	R.S.C. Martin-Jenkins	not out	121
7	M.J. Prior +	c. Clough b. Franks	17
8	K.J. Innes	not out	6
9	Mushtaq Ahmed		
10	R.J. Kirtley		
11	P.M. Hutchison		
12			

b 0	lb 6	wd 5	nb 16	Extras	27
Overs	113			Provisional Total	497
Pens	0	Wkts	6-Dec	Total	497

| Fall of | 1st Inns: | 1-60 | 2-197 | 3-295 | 4-297 | 5-434 | 6-474 |
| wickets | | | | | | | |

Bonus Points: Sussex 5, Notts 2

Bowling	Ovs	Md	R	Wk	wd	nb
Harris	28	5	98	2	1	2
Shreck	28	4	109	0	0	0
Cairns	18	5	63	1	0	5
Franks	19	3	102	2	4	1
Clough	16	0	76	1	0	0
Pietersen	4	0	43	0	0	0

MATCH DRAWN

SUSSEX v SURREY

at Hove on 30th July - 2nd August - Frizzell County Championship Division 1

UMPIRES : M.R. Benson   M.J. Harris

*Captain, + Wicket-Keeper

Sussex won the toss and elected to bat

SUSSEX

#	Batsman	1st Innings	R	2nd Innings	R
1	R.R. Montgomerie [7]	b. Salisbury	90	lbw b. Bicknell	2
2	M.W. Goodwin [3]	b. Ormond	75	c. Ward b. Saqlain	29
3	P.A. Cottey [2]	lbw b. Saqlain	1	c. Ramprakash b. Mahmood	41
4	C.J. Adams * [1]	c. Batty b. Ormond	107	lbw b. Saqlain	23
5	T.R. Ambrose + [11]	c. Mahmood b. Salisbury	43	not out	76
6	R.S.C. Martin-Jenkins [12]	b. Bicknell	40	b. Salisbury	45
7	M.J. Prior [13]	c. Thorpe b. Ormond	0	not out	50
8	M.J.G. Davis [8]	c. Clarke b. Ormond	0		
9	Mushtaq Ahmed [9]	c. Batty b. Mahmood	26		
10	R.J. Kirtley [6]	(11) not out	1		
11	P.M. Hutchison [23]	(10) c. Ward b. Bicknell	5		
12	B.V. Taylor [22]				

				Extras	41					Extras	36
b 6	lb 13	wd 0	nb 22			b 9	lb 8	wd 0	nb 14		
Overs	126		Provisional Total		429	Overs	87.5		Provisional Total		302
Pens	0	Wkts	10	Total	429	Pens	5	Wkts	5 dec	Total	302

Fall of wickets

1st Inns: 1-149 2-150 3-232 4-330 5-363 6-363 7-367 8-415 9-423 10-429

2nd Inns: 1-7 2-67 3-89 4-108 5-228

Bonus Points - Sussex 5, Surrey 3

Bowling

	Ovs	Md	R	Wk	wd	nb	Ovs	Md	R	Wk	wd	nb
Bicknell	26	5	94	2	0	3	16	5	54	1	0	2
Ormond	25	6	106	4	0	0	10	3	17	0	0	0
Hollioake	7	3	23	0	0	0	0.5	0	11	0	0	1
Mahmood	18	5	61	1	0	3	4	1	3	1	0	0
Saqlain	36	5	84	1	0	5	35	7	97	2	0	4
Salisbury	14	0	42	2	0	0	22	0	98	1	0	0

SURREY

#	Batsman	1st Innings	R	2nd Innings	R
1	I.J. Ward	lbw b. Kirtley	20	lbw b. Davis	33
2	J.N. Batty +	c. Ambrose b. Hutchison	12	not out	65
3	M.R. Ramprakash	c. Ambrose b. Kirtley	104	not out	14
4	G.P. Thorpe	c. Davis b. Martin-Jenkins	23		
5	J. Ormond	(11) not out	42		
6	R. Clarke	(5) c. Mushtaq b. Martin-Jenkins	12		
7	A.J. Hollioake *	(6) lbw b. Mushtaq	13		
8	Azhar Mahmood	(7) lbw b. Mushtaq	9		
9	M.P. Bicknell	(8) lbw b. Mushtaq	42		
10	I.D.K. Salisbury	(9) st. Ambrose b. Mushtaq	1		
11	Saqlain Mushtaq	(10) b. Martin-Jenkins	68		
12	A.D. Brown				

Target 377

				Extras	9					Extras	2
b 1	lb 6	wd 0	nb 2			b 0	lb 2	wd 0	nb 0		
Overs	102.3		Provisional Total		355	Overs	26		Provisional Total		114
Pens	0	Wkts	10	Total	355	Pens	0	Wkts	1	Total	114

Fall of wickets

1st Inns: 1-32 2-32 3-75 4-89 5-116 6-126 7-215 8-215 9-301 10-355

2nd Inns: 1-82

Bonus Points - Surrey 4, Sussex 3

Bowling

	Ovs	Md	R	Wk	wd	nb	Ovs	Md	R	Wk	wd	nb
Kirtley	28	4	90	2	0	0	6	1	23	0	0	0
Hutchison	16	2	58	1	0	1	7	1	30	0	0	0
Mushtaq	38	7	123	4	0	0	6	1	26	0	0	0
Martin-Jenkins	17.3	3	67	3	0	0	3	0	17	0	0	0
Davis	3	0	10	0	0	0	4	1	16	1	0	0

MATCH DRAWN

SUSSEX v LANCASHIRE

at Hove on 14th - 17th August - Frizzell County Championship Division 1

UMPIRES : B. Dudleston   A.A. Jones

Sussex won the toss and elected to bat

*Captain, + Wicket-Keeper

SUSSEX

#	Batsman	1st Innings	R	2nd Innings	R
1	R.R. Montgomerie [7]	c. Law b. Martin	72	c. Sutcliffe b. Martin	70
2	M.W. Goodwin [3]	c. Hegg b. Wood	9	c. Sutcliffe b. Martin	1
3	P.A. Cottey [2]	c. Schofield b. Hogg	18	c. Hegg b. Martin	0
4	C.J. Adams * [1]	lbw b. Schofield	140	c. & b. Chapple	190
5	T.R. Ambrose + [11]	c. Sutcliffe b. Wood	18	c. & b. Chapple	44
6	R.S.C. Martin-Jenkins [12]	c. Law b. Wood	18	lbw b. Chapple	13
7	M.J. Prior [13]	c. Hegg b. Keedy	9	not out	35
8	M.J.G. Davis [8]	lbw b. Hooper	3	not out	16
9	Mushtaq Ahmed [9]	lbw b. Schofield	60		
10	P.M. Hutchison [23]	lbw b. Schofield	0		
11	B.V. Taylor [22]	not out	13		
12					

				Extras						Extras	
b 8	lb 6	wd 1	nb 10	Extras	25	b 2	lb 8	wd 0	nb 4	Extras	14
Overs	100.3		Provisional Total		385	Overs	104.4		Provisional Total		383
Pens	0	Wkts	10	Total	385	Pens	0	Wkts	7	Total	383

Fall of wickets

1st Inns: 1-12 2-60 3-132 4-156 5-190 6-252 7-257 8-332 9-332 10-385

2nd Inns: 1-2 2-2 3-155 4-268 5-313 6-348 7-383

Bonus Points - Sussex 4, Lancs 3

Bowling	Ovs	Md	R	Wk	wd	nb	Ovs	Md	R	Wk	wd	nb
Martin	15	2	64	1	0	1	21	5	61	3	0	0
Wood	17	2	64	3	0	3	17.4	2	72	1	0	1
Chilton	12	2	33	0	1	0	-	-	-	-	-	-
Hogg	8	2	24	1	0	1						
Keedy	24	6	76	1	0	0	19	3	61	0	0	0
Hooper	12	2	48	1	0	0	22	4	65	0	0	0
Chapple	7	0	48	0	0	0	21	3	89	3	0	1
Schofield	5.3	2	14	3	0	0	4	0	25	0	0	0

LANCASHIRE

#	Batsman	1st Innings	R	2nd Innings	R
1	M.J. Chilton [21]	c. Montgomerie b. Davis	65	b. Taylor	9
2	I.J. Sutcliffe [5]	c. Prior b. Mushtaq	43	c. Montgomerie b. Taylor	12
3	M.B. Loye [1]	c. Goodwin b. Taylor	2	lbw b. Mushtaq	33
4	S.G. Law [2]	c. Montgomerie b. Mushtaq	96	c. Adams b. Taylor	7
5	C.L. Hooper [17]	c. & b. Mushtaq	23	c. Adams b. Taylor	1
6	C.P. Schofield [15]	b. Mushtaq	3	b. Davis	18
7	W.K. Hegg [10] * +	(8) c. Montgomerie b. Mushtaq	31	(8) c. Montgomerie b. Mushtaq	25
8	P.J. Martin [24]	(9) b. Taylor	9	(9) c. Prior b. Mushtaq	0
9	G. Chapple [3]	(7) c. Goodwin b. Taylor	54	(7) lbw b. Mushtaq	7
10	J. Wood [7]	lbw b. Mushtaq	30	lbw b. Mushtaq	0
11	G. Keedy [23]	not out	0	not out	2
12	K.W. Hogg [22]				

b 10	lb 3	wd 0	nb 8	Extras	21	b 6	lb 7	wd 0	nb 12	Extras	25
Overs	121		Provisional Total		377	Overs	73.2		Provisional Total		139
Pens	0	Wkts	10	Total	377	Pens	0	Wkts	10	Total	139

Fall of wickets

1st Inns: 1-99 2-102 3-150 4-189 5-192 6-289 7-307 8-321 9-358 10-377

2nd Inns: 1-27 2-28 3-56 4-64 5-97 6-109 7-128 8-132 9-132 10-139

Bonus Points - Lancs 4, Sussex 3

Bowling	Ovs	Md	R	Wk	wd	nb	Ovs	Md	R	Wk	wd	nb
Hutchison	14	2	50	0	0	0	2	0	20	0	0	3
Taylor	24	8	56	3	0	4	26	12	42	4	0	3
Mushtaq Ahmed	48	10	124	6	0	0	33.2	14	49	5	0	0
Martin-Jenkins	9	1	48	0	0	0	-	-	-	-	-	-
Davis	26	2	86	1	0	0	12	6	15	1	0	0

SUSSEX WON BY 252 RUNS

ESSEX v SUSSEX

at Colchester on 20th - 23rd August - Frizzell County Championship Division 1

UMPIRES : A. Clarkson   N.J. Llong

Sussex won the toss and elected to bat

* Captain, + Wicket-Keeper

ESSEX

#	Batsman	1st Innings	R	2nd Innings (Following-On)	R
1	D.D.J. Robinson	c. Cottey b. Mushtaq	64	run out	12
2	W.I. Jefferson	c. Goodwin b. Mushtaq	55	c. & b. Martin-Jenkins	59
3	A. Flower	c. Ambrose b. Lewry	50	c. Prior b. Mushtaq	32
4	A. Habib	lbw. Mushtaq	0	b. Mushtaq	11
5	R.C. Irani *	c. Adams b. Taylor	3	c. Ambrose b. Taylor	38
6	J.S. Foster +	c. Montgomerie b. Davis	31	lbw. Mushtaq	3
7	J.M. Dakin	lbw b. Davis	6	c. Goodwin b. Taylor	7
8	J.D. Middlebrook	c. Lewry b. Martin-Jenkins	33	c. Davis b. Taylor	5
9	G.R. Napier	c. Prior b. Mushtaq	34	not out	21
10	Mohammad Akram	not out	0	lbw b. Taylor	10
11	A.P. Palladino	absent hurt	-	absent hurt	-
12					

					1st Extras						2nd Extras	
		b 0	lb 5	wd 0	nb 2	Extras	7	b 2	lb 3	wd 0	nb 6	Extras	11
		Overs	77.5		Provisional Total	283	Overs	68.3		Provisional Total	209
		Pens	0	Wkts	9 (AO)	Total	283	Pens	0	Wkts	9 (AO)	Total	209

Fall of wickets
1st Inns: 1-101 2-144 3-144 4-163 5-208 6-214 7-219 8-281 9-283
2nd Inns: 1-24 2-109 3-123 4-130 5-164 6-164 7-172 8-185 9-209

Bonus Points : Essex 2, Sussex 3

Bowling	Ovs	Md	R	Wk	wd	nb	Ovs	Md	R	Wk	wd	nb
Lewry	12	4	46	1	0	0	8	1	28	0	0	0
Taylor	17	3	52	1	0	0	16.3	6	50	4	0	3
Mushtaq Ahmed	25	2	87	4	0	0	28	7	83	3	0	0
Martin-Jenkins	11.5	2	32	1	0	0	12	4	30	1	0	0
Davis	12	0	61	2	0	1	4	1	13	0	0	0

SUSSEX

#	Batsman	1st Innings	R
1	R.R. Montgomerie	b. Palladino	97
2	M.W. Goodwin	b. Akram	210
3	P.A. Cottey	run out	23
4	C.J. Adams *	b. Akram	0
5	T.R. Ambrose +	c. Flower b. Akram	4
6	R.S.C. Martin-Jenkins	c. Foster b. Middlebrook	10
7	M.J. Prior	not out	153
8	M.J.G. Davis	b. Akram	8
9	Mushtaq Ahmed	b. Akram	0
10	J.D. Lewry	c. sub b. Middlebrook	70
11	B.V. Taylor	b. Dakin	3
12			

					Extras	
	b 0	lb 9	wd 0	nb 20	Extras	34
	Overs	119		Provisional Total	607
	Pens	5	Wkts	10	Total	612

Fall of wickets
1st Inns: 1-202 2-270 3-270 4-303 5-325 6-438 7-452 8-454 9-595 10-612

Bonus Points: Sussex 5, Essex 3

Bowling	Ovs	Md	R	Wk	wd	nb
Mohammad Akram	29	2	130	5	0	5
Dakin	20	1	120	1	0	2
Napier	24	5	149	0	0	2
Palladino	16	6	40	1	0	0
Middlebrook	26	1	126	2	0	0
Robinson	4	0	33	0	0	1

SUSSEX WON BY AN INNS & 120 RUNS

SUSSEX v MIDDLESEX

at Hove on 5th - 8th September - Frizzell County Championship Division 1

UMPIRES: J. Holder   R. Palmer

* Captain, + Wicket-Keeper

Middlesex won the toss and elected to bat

SUSSEX

		1st Innings		2nd Innings	
1	M.W. Goodwin [3]	lbw b. Dawes	14	lbw b. Dawes	4
2	R.R. Montgomerie [7]	c. Nash b. Dawes	21	not out	54
3	P.A. Cottey [2]	c. Hutton b. Keegan	15	lbw b. Dawes	7
4	C.J. Adams * [1]	c. Nash b. Cook	20	c. Hutton b. Weekes	30
5	T.R. Ambrose + [11]	c. Hutton b. Keegan	12	not out	11
6	R.S.C. Martin-Jenkins [12]	c. Hutton b. Dawes	8		
7	M.J. Prior [13]	c. Shah b. Weekes	148		
8	M.J.G. Davis [8]	c. Dawes b. Keegan	168		
9	Mushtaq Ahmed [9]	c. Shah b. Weekes	57		
10	J.D. Lewry [5]	c. Peploe b. Keegan	21		
11	B.V. Taylor [22]	not out	35		
12	C.D. Hopkinson [21]				

				Extras						Extras	
b 5	lb 2	wd 7	nb 4	Extras	18	b 1	lb 1	wd 0	nb 0	Extras	2
Overs	152.2			Provisional Total	537	Overs	27.5			Provisional Total	108
Pens	0	Wkts	10	Total	537	Pens	0	Wkts	3	Total	108

Fall of   1st Inns: 1-26   2-37   3-66   4-70   5-82   6-107   7-302   8-399   9-431   10-537

wickets   2nd Inns: 1-10   2-22   3-92

Bonus Points -   Sussex 5, Middx 3

Bowling	Ovs	Md	R	Wk	wd	nb	Ovs	Md	R	Wk	wd	nb
Dawes	35	2	126	3	3	0	7	3	25	2	0	0
Keegan	32.2	4	120	4	0	0	7	2	29	0	0	0
Cook	30	7	83	1	0	1	2	0	9	0	0	0
Peploe	28	2	100	0	4	1	6	2	20	0	0	0
Weekes	27	3	101	2	0	0	5.5	0	23	1	0	0

MIDDLESEX

		1st Innings		2nd Innings	
1	A.J. Strauss *	c. Prior b. Martin-Jenkins	138	c. Ambrose b. Lewry	4
2	S.G. Koenig	b. Lewry	5	lbw b. Martin-Jenkins	16
3	B.L. Hutton	lbw b. Lewry	1	c. Martin-Jenkins b. Taylor	36
4	O.A. Shah	lbw b. Mushtaq	140	st. Ambrose b. Davis	34
5	E.C. Joyce	lbw b. Mushtaq	22	b. Mushtaq	31
6	P.N. Weekes	c. Ambrose b. Mushtaq	31	c. Prior b. Mushtaq	65
7	D.C. Nash +	c. Adams b. Mushtaq	15	(8) b. Lewry	5
8	S.J. Cook	b. Davis	11	(9) b. Mushtaq	11
9	C.T. Peploe	not out	0	(7) lbw b. Lewry	13
10	C.B. Keegan	c. Adams b. Mushtaq	3	not out	3
11	J.H. Dawes	c. Prior b. Mushtaq	0	lbw b. Mushtaq	2
12					

				Extras						Extras	
b 7	lb 13	wd 0	nb 6	Extras	26	b 11	lb 11	wd 0	nb 8	Extras	30
Overs	100			Provisional Total	392	Overs	96.2			Provisional Total	250
Pens	0	Wkts	10	Total	392	Pens	0	Wkts	10	Total	250

Fall of   1st Inns: 1-17   2-33   3-252   4-309   5-334   6-374   7-387   8-387   9-390   10-392

wickets   2nd Inns: 1-4   2-42   3-79   4-124   5-152   6-201   7-215   8-241   9-244   10-250

Bonus Points -   Middx 4, Sussex 3

Bowling	Ovs	Md	R	Wk	wd	nb	Ovs	Md	R	Wk	wd	nb
Lewry	20	6	53	2	0	0	25	8	73	3	0	0
Taylor	15	2	66	0	0	3	10	1	30	1	0	4
Mushtaq Ahmed	40	4	145	6	0	0	35.2	8	80	4	0	0
Martin-Jenkins	14	2	46	1	0	0	7	3	12	1	0	0
Davis	11	0	62	1	0	0	19	4	33	1	0	0

SUSSEX WON BY 7 WKTS

LANCASHIRE v SUSSEX

at Old Trafford on 10th - 13th September - Frizzell County Championship Division 1

UMPIRES : J.W. Lloyds A.G.T. Whitehead

Lancashire won the toss and elected to bat

* Captain, + Wicket-Keeper

LANCASHIRE — 1st Innings

#	Batsman	Dismissal	Runs
1	M.J. Chilton	c. Ambrose b. Taylor	6
2	I.J. Sutcliffe	c. Davis b. Lewry	38
3	M.B. Loye	c. Montgomerie b. Martin-Jenkins	144
4	S.G. Law	not out	163
5	C.L. Hooper	lbw b. Lewry	33
6	C.P. Schofield	b. Taylor	1
7	G. Chapple	b. Lewry	14
8	W.K. Hegg * +	not out	26
9	P.J. Martin		
10	J. Wood		
11	G. Keedy		
12			

b 4	lb 12	wd 1	nb 8	Extras	25
Overs	77.5			Provisional Total	450
Pens	0	Wkts	6-Dec	Total	450

Fall of wickets — 1st Inns: 1-21 2-66 3-307 4-363 5-368 6-414

Bonus Points : Lancs 5, Sussex 2

Bowling

Bowling	Ovs	Md	R	Wk	wd	nb
Lewry	26.3	3	125	3	1	0
Taylor	35	8	114	2	0	4
Martin-Jenkins	23	7	73	1	0	0
Mushtaq Ahmed	37	6	99	0	0	0
Davis	5	1	23	0	0	0

SUSSEX — 1st Innings / 2nd Innings (Following-On)

#	Batsman	1st Innings Dismissal	Runs		2nd Innings Dismissal	Runs
1	M.W. Goodwin	not out	118	(6)	lbw b. Keedy	57
2	R.R. Montgomerie	lbw b. Keedy	10	(1)	lbw b. Martin	2
3	P.A. Cottey	c. Chapple b. Wood	40	(4)	c. sub b. Keedy	32
4	C.J. Adams *	c. Chapple b. Wood	1	(2)	c. Law b. Wood	35
5	T.R. Ambrose +	b. Wood	0		c. Sutcliffe b. Wood	2
6	R.S.C. Martin-Jenkins	c. Hegg b. Keedy	2	(7)	b. Martin	6
7	M.J. Prior	c. Law b. Keedy	2	(8)	c. Schofield b. Keedy	10
8	M.J.G. Davis	c. Law b. Keedy	2	(9)	c. Sutcliffe b. Keedy	11
9	Mushtaq Ahmed	c. Chilton b. Hooper	54	(10)	c. & b. Schofield	16
10	J.D. Lewry	b. Hooper	2	(11)	not out	7
11	B.V. Taylor	c. Schofield b. Keedy	0	(3)	lbw b. Keedy	0
12						

b 9	lb 3	wd 0	nb 8	Extras	20	b 0	lb 2	wd 0	nb 0	Extras	2
Overs	73			Provisional Total	251	Overs	87			Provisional Total	180
Pens	0	Wkts	10	Total	251	Pens	0	Wkts	10	Total	180

Fall of wickets — 1st Inns: 1-28 2-122 3-126 4-126 5-143 6-147 7-157 8-238 9-240 10-251

2nd Inns: 1-20 2-21 3-61 4-67 5-73 6-96 7-125 8-146 9-164 10-180

Bonus Points: Sussex 2, Lancs 3

Bowling

Bowling	Ovs	Md	R	Wk	wd	nb	Ovs	Md	R	Wk	wd	nb
Martin	15	4	40	0	0	2	20	7	43	2	0	0
Chapple	15	2	54	0	0	0	-	-	-	-	-	-
Keedy	28	5	106	5	0	0	32	6	61	5	0	0
Wood	9	3	17	3	0	2	14	4	27	2	0	0
Hooper	5	0	17	2	0	0	17	3	33	0	0	0
Schofield	1	0	5	0	0	0	4	0	14	1	0	0

LANCS WON BY AN INNS & 19 RUNS

SUSSEX v LEICESTERSHIRE

at Hove on 17th - 20th September - Frizzell County Championship Division 1

UMPIRES : T.E. Jesty   M.J. Kitchen

Leics won the toss and elected to bat

* Captain, + Wicket-Keeper

SUSSEX — 1st Innings

#	Batsman		Dismissal	Runs
1	M.W. Goodwin [3]		not out	335
2	R.R. Montgomerie [7]		c. Nixon b. DeFreitas	10
3	P.A. Cottey [2]		c. Nixon b. DeFreitas	56
4	C.J. Adams * [1]		c. Drakes b. Walker	102
5	T.R. Ambrose + [11]		c. Sadler b. Hodge	82
6	R.S.C. Martin-Jenkins [12]			
7	M.J. Prior [13]			
8	M.J.G. Davis [8]			
9	Mushtaq Ahmed [9]			
10	J.D. Lewry [5]			
11	B.V. Taylor [22]			
12	M.H. Yardy [20]			

b 12	lb 9	wd 0	nb 8	Extras	29
Overs	126			Provisional Total	614
Pens	0		Wkts	4-Dec Total	614

Fall of wickets 1st Inns: 1-24 2-151 3-418 4-614

Bowling	Ovs	Md	R	Wk	wd	nb
DeFreitas	28	4	94	2	0	2
Drakes	19	2	64	0	0	0
Masters	18	0	88	0	0	1
Maddy	4	0	21	0	0	0
Wright	19	0	95	0	0	0
Snape	12	0	72	0	0	1
Walker	19	1	92	1	0	0
Hodge	6	0	51	1	0	0
Maunders	1	0	16	0	0	0

LEICS — 1st Innings / 2nd Innings

#	Batsman		1st Innings Dismissal	Runs		2nd Innings Dismissal	Runs
1	J.K. Maunders		c. Lewry b. Martin-Jenkins	21		c. Martin-Jenkins b. Lewry	15
2	D.L. Maddy		c. Cottey b. Taylor	55	(7)	lbw b. Lewry	29
3	B.J. Hodge		b. Mushtaq	36	(5)	c. Ambrose b. Lewry	1
4	J.L. Sadler		st. Ambrose b. Mushtaq	0	(6)	b. Lewry	145
5	L.J. Wright	(6)	c. Montgomerie b. Mushtaq	0	(9)	not out	11
6	P.A. Nixon +	(5)	c. Ambrose b. Taylor	1	(8)	c. Goodwin b. Lewry	0
7	G.W. Walker	(10)	not out	4	(4)	c. sub (Hopkinson) b. Lewry	21
8	P.A.J. DeFreitas *	(8)	b. Martin-Jenkins	23	(10)	b. Lewry	0
9	J.N. Snape	(7)	c. Ambrose b. Lewry	13	(2)	c. Adams b. Taylor	1
10	V.C. Drakes	(9)	c. Ambrose b. Martin-Jenkins	8	(11)	c. Ambrose b. Lewry	0
11	D.D. Masters		b. Mushtaq	2	(3)	c. Martin-Jenkins b. Taylor	119
12							

b 5	lb 6	wd 1	nb 4	Extras	16	b	lb	wd	nb	Extras	38
Overs	69.5			Provisional Total	179	Overs	88.1			Provisional Total	380
Pens	0		Wkts	10 Total	179	Pens	0		Wkts	10 Total	380

Fall of wickets

1st Inns: 1-42 2-111 3-117 4-117 5-118 6-118 7-142 8-167 9-174 10-179

2nd Inns: 1-16 2-20 3-65 4-69 5-227 6-353 7-353 8-370 9-370 10-380

Bowling	Ovs	Md	R	Wk	wd	nb	Ovs	Md	R	Wk	wd	nb
Lewry	15	4	37	1	0	0	24.1	3	106	8	0	0
Taylor	18	6	40	2	1	2	21.2	6	84	2	0	8
Martin-Jenkins	12	6	20	3	0	0	9.4	0	60	0	0	0
Mushtaq Ahmed	24.5	3	71	4	0	0	-	-	-	-	-	-
Davis	-	-	-	-	-	-	25	9	75	0	0	0
Cottey	-	-	-	-	-	-	4	0	15	0	0	0
Goodwin	-	-	-	-	-	-	3	0	17	0	0	0
Adams	-	-	-	-	-	-	1	0	1	0	0	0

SUSSEX WON BY AN INNINGS & 55 RUNS

INDEX

Main sections are indicated by **bold** type